GREAT NORTHERN RAILWAY ENGINE SHEDS

ISBN 1 899624 26 0

FOR CHRISTINE & JANE

First published in the UK by
BOOK LAW/RAILBUS in association with CHALLENGER
309 Mapperley Plains, Nottingham, NG3 5RG
Printed and bound by The Amadeus Press, Cleckheaton, West Yorkshire

GREAT NORTHERN RAILWAY
ENGINE SHEDS

by
Roger Griffiths & John Hooper

Volume 3
Yorkshire & Lancashire

BOOK LAW/RAILBUS in association with CHALLENGER

INTRODUCTION (or perhaps, "Authors' Comment"?)

Initially, it was intended that the history of the engine sheds of the Great Northern Railway would be produced in two volumes, but the sheer amount of material finally amassed dictated that either a lot would have to immediately be discarded, or the work be expanded to three volumes. The choice was not at all difficult to make!

Three volumes it would be then, but no less than eleven years would elapse to actually publish the whole work. The delay was initially exacerbated by a change of publisher between the production of Volumes 1 and 2. The first book, of 1989, was Irwell Press' very first work in print and that company's rapidly expanding, and changing fortunes thereafter resulted in a delay in getting out Volume 2. This delay reached such an extent that it would be seven years before the second book appeared, but this time coming from a new stable - that of Challenger Publications. At that time, the sleeve note to Volume 2 predicted that the third book would soon follow and be published at the end of the same year - 1996 - but this too was not to be. The fledgling Challenger's equally rapid growth saw to it that Volume 3 would have to wait a further three years and more, before it came to be. So, it is with considerably more than a large sigh of your authors' joint relief that the third and final volume of this work has at last come to print - we thank our readers and correspondents for the extreme patience they have shown!

Overall, it has been more than 18 years since detailed research began, and almost double that time since some of the more basic material was brought to hand. Needless to say, many people have been contacted and most contributed something or other - from the smallest tit-bit to reams of material containing locomotive rosters and shed workings. Others supplied photographs or lay open their personal collections for our use, whilst a select few gave us the benefit of their personal knowledge and experiences after life long careers working at former GNR engine sheds. We made many friends over the years, and some of those people come readily to mind - the late Kenneth Leech, a gentlemen of the first order - Sid Checkley who was fortunate enough to work at Colwick, King's Cross and Lincoln when those erstwhile sheds were hives of seemingly unending activity; consequently our chapters covering those sheds were all the richer from his input - Syd Outram, contacted after a chance meeting in Bradford, and who in retirement was able to impart much about the Bradford District's various sheds; besides the loan of a few choice photgraphs. We have been fortunate indeed.

During a four year stint of visits to the Public Record Office at Kew, virtually every Great Northern Railway file, map, minute book, plan and report were scrutinised in an effort to piece together the history of that company's engine sheds. Many LNER and BR archives were also consulted - the Railway Archive at Kew is still growing as further records 'come to light'.

A labour of love it has very much been then and without the steadfast support of two very special people, it is unlikely that labour could eventually have borne fruit. This tribute to Christine and Jane cannot be more sincerely made and it is to those two ladies that we gratefully dedicate this work.

Roger Griffiths, Cotham, Bristol.
John Hooper, Manche, Normandy.

CONTENTS

THE SHEDS

APPENDICES

Cover Illustration: **GNR 4-4-2 No.250 and 4-4-0 No.1368 stand outside the GNR's shed at York, 17th June 1922. In the foreground the remains of York South roundhouse Number 1, of 1850, are being cleared away following the disastrous fire of the year before.** *Authors' collection.*

A group of Ardsley shed's workers pose for the camera around the turn of the century. Note that only one of these hardy artisans - engine cleaners perhaps? - is not wearing a flat cap and that the depot's original northlight roof was, at that time, still in good repair. *Authors' collection.*

ARDSLEY

The mining area of Ardsley, between Wakefield and Leeds, was destined to become one of the Great Northern Railway's largest centres for goods traffic. Basically, it developed into the clearing house for West Riding produce - coal and woollen goods mainly - on its journey to markets at home and abroad. But, Ardsley had a small beginning, being for its first week simply a station on the Bradford, Wakefield & Leeds Railway. That small company had been incorporated by an Act of 10th July 1854 and completed its line between Leeds and Wakefield on 3rd October 1857. Services were worked from the start by the GNR and L&YR jointly, or more accurately, the latter had running powers over the route.

Regarding the "Bradford" portion of the BW&L's title, access to that city was achieved by running powers over the GN-worked Leeds Bradford & Halifax Junction Railway, the company which turned Ardsley into a junction station on 10th October 1857, one week after the BW&L's inception. The LB&HJ had obtained powers for its line from Gildersome to Ardsley on 10th July 1854 - the same day on which the BW&L was incorporated and reflecting the close association between the two companies. Alas, their triangular relationship with the GNR was initially not a smooth one, with the LB&HJ having been dissatisfied with the GN's handling of its coal traffic since 1856. Finally, the dispute flared into a partial estrangement of the two small companies from the GNR, commencing 1st January 1859.

From that date, the BW&L had decided to appoint its own goods and traffic staff, to which the GN reacted by withdrawing its engines and wagons from goods work over the Gildersome and Ardsley branches. Both minor railways had therefore to quickly find alternative motive power and as far as the BW&L was concerned, it purchased its first locomotive on 28th February 1859. By 1860, three other engines were operating in the BW&L fleet, being joined by two more in 1863, but hiring of locomotives was also being resorted to. Details of the hiring come from the BW&L's Journal and Accounts books, the only artefacts which appear to have survived to reach the Public Record Office. The following extracts cover the period 1857-1862 and despite their brevity, they make illuminating reading:

31-12-1857: There is reference to the BW&L and LB&HJ having an 'Ardsley Joint Account.'

March 1858: Situated at Ardsley was something known as "Slips," because the BW&L paid £115-1-3d to the GNR, for hire of an engine at 'Ardsley Slips.'

31-8-1859: The BW&L received payment of £25-11-9d from the LB&HJ for the latter's proportion of the cost of ballasting some sidings at Ardsley.

July 1861 - Construction Account:
£100 paid to W. Barratt for works at Ardsley.
£200 paid to I. Thornton for works at Ardsley.

August 1861 - Construction Account:
£50 paid to W. Barratt for works at Ardsley.

September 1861 - Construction Account:
£250 paid to I. Thornton for works at Ardsley.
£65 paid to W. Barratt for works at Ardsley.
£36-16-10d paid to F.W. Firth for iron for the engine shed at Ardsley.
£73-14-0d paid to Illingworth Ingham for timber for the engine shed at Ardsley.

December 1861: £119-7-0d paid to George Boulton for hire of engines, at the rate of 7/- per hour (i.e. 341 hours).

£154-14-0d paid to an unnamed hirer for hire of engines.

May 1862 - Construction Account:
£150 paid to Nelson & Sons for water tank and pipes at Ardsley.
£248 paid to F. Wild for plumbing water and gas at Ardsley.
£4-10-0d paid to Singleton & Co. for stores at Ardsley cottages.

From the above it can be seen that the BW&L and LB&HJ were running a very much joint operation at Ardsley, with the former hiring engines for special purposes (Ardsley Slips) in 1858 and still hiring motive power 2½ years later, after two years of semi-independent operation. The reference to hiring engines from George Boulton, a contractor, shows that severance from the GN was quite complete. But it is the Construction Account payments that give the most vital information because here is chronicled the progress of erection of the somewhat obscure first engine shed at Ardsley.

While BW&L/LB&HJ traffic was being totally worked by the GNR, based on engine shed facilities at Leeds, Bradford and Wakefield/Knottingley, there was no need for more than a water tank at Ardsley - that paid for in August 1858 probably. However, when the two small companies broke away and had to provide their own engines, there arose a need for an engine shed, for which Ardsley was the logical location. From the figures above it can be surmised that the contracting firms of W. Barratt and I. Thornton were preparing the site, laying foundations and building walls, from about July 1861. By September that year the builders were ready to put the roof on the building, hence the supplies of iron and wood during that month. Came the winter and construction assumedly proceeded very slowly - or even halted for a while possibly - as it is not until the following May that payment is made for the "finishing touches" of water and gas plumbing etc.

The engine shed that finally opened around mid-1862, was sited in the fork of the lines to Leeds and Bradford, approximately ¼ mile north of Ardsley station. Not too far away, on the line to Bradford, was Tingley station and on more than one occasion the authors heard the engine shed referred to by the name of "Tingley;" whether this was ever an official designation is not known, but unlikely. Measuring 115ft x 40ft, the two road, dead-end depot was brick-built, with a single-pitch slated gable roof and arched openings; inside the shed each road was equipped with a 95ft pit. A 55ft x 8ft timber-built coke stage stood just outside the northern shed entrance, with a 35ft pit alongside; at the stage's western end was a water tank, supported by a timber trestle; the tank measured 8ft x 8ft and was 4ft high, holding just over 2,500 gallons therefore. No turntable was installed to complete the shed's facilities, but the cottages referred to in the Construction Account - six of them - were built on the south side of the Bradford line, between the shed and station; presumably some of them at least were for use by locomotive shed staff. During all this, the GNR had not been totally out of the picture and on 20th October 1862, even went so far as to accept a recommendation from the engineer to its Yorkshire Committee, to lay a water main from Morley to Ardsley, at a cost of £1,100. This provision does not seem to have benefited the engine shed, however, which continued to obtain its water from a nearby spring.

Just before completing its shed, the BW&L opened another section of railway, on 7th April 1862, from Wrenthorpe to Flushdyke. Then, on 21st July 1863, the company obtained an

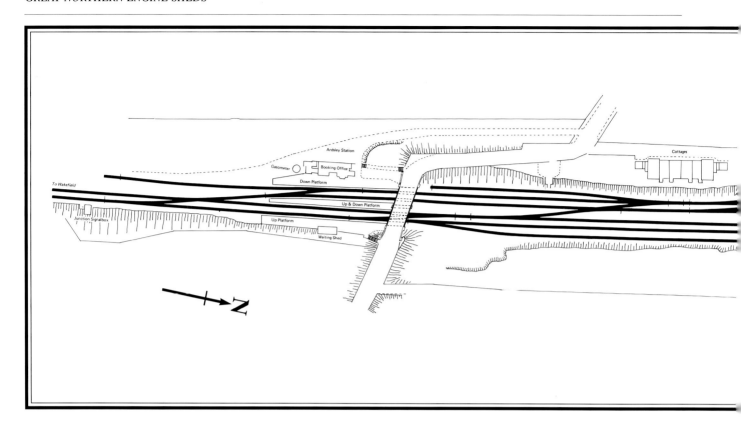

Amongst the many various types of motive power absorbed by the LNER through the 1923 Grouping was this former East & West Yorkshire Union Railway 0-6-2ST. It became LNER Class N19, No.3115, and is seen at Ardsley shed prior to its 1928 withdrawal. *Authors' collection.*

ARDSLEY 1863

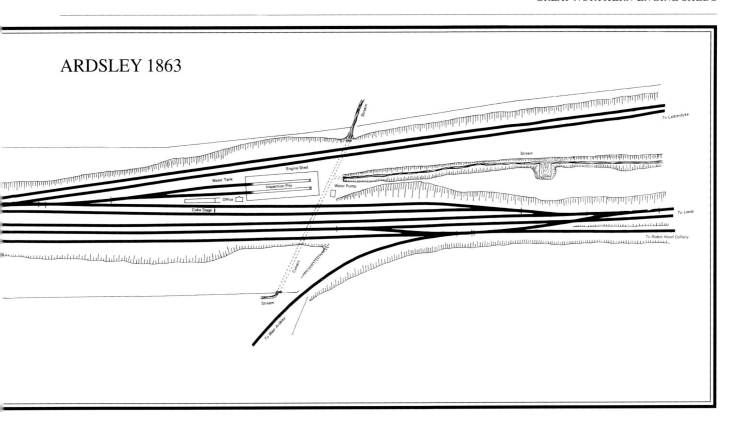

The previous illustration reminds us that for a few short years following the Grouping, Ardsley had a sub-depot in the guise of the former E&WYR shed at Robin Hood. The only known photograph of that obscure, but fascinating building is presented here, its slightly dubious quality being heavily outweighed by its rarity value. The date is around 1902. *Authors' collection.*

Act empowering itself to change its name to the West Yorkshire Railway. Just after that, on 19th August 1863, the LB&HJ completed its last section of line, from Adwalton to Batley, where it linked up with the WYR after that company had extended its line from Flushdyke to Ossett on 7th April 1864 and from Ossett to Batley, on 15th December in the same year.

Opening of the WYR's last piece of railway was succeeded on 1st January 1865, when the GNR reappeared on the scene, to again take over working of all WYR and LB&HJ traffic. Process of absorption was also started and the GN assumed full control of the WYR on 5th September 1865 (the LB&HJ had gone before, on 5th July). Before that though, the GN had to deal with an emergency at Ardsley shed. On 7th April 1865, Wilson 0-6-0 No.147 (built November 1850) was standing in the depot yard when its boiler exploded. By great good fortune nobody was injured and apparently there was little material damage. At the subsequent enquiry no reason could be put forward for the mishap - the engine had been shopped only a few months previously and passed the statutory boiler tests at that time.

Number 147's shedmates at Ardsley would have included the five engines taken over by the GN from the WYR. These were WYR No.1, a Todd 2-2-2, given GN No.261 and withdrawn 1871; Nos.2 and 3, Wilson 2-4-0's, becoming GN 262 and 263 and surviving until 1872 and 1875 respectively. WYR Nos.5 and 6 were Manning Wardle 0-6-0T, which became GN 470 and 471, to both be withdrawn 1872. Regarding missing WYR No.4 - another 2-2-2 - that engine had been taken out of service before the GN takeover.

There matters rested until 13th February 1869, when Stirling reported on water supplies at Ardsley shed. It seems that the summer of 1868 had been very dry and the spring supplying the depot had "dried up." Stirling arranged for an alternative supply from the West Yorkshire Iron Company and had been running an engine on it, with satisfactory results. Also he had the Iron Cos. water analysed by one Edward Riley of Leeds, who declared it to be all right for use in locomotive boilers. What Stirling did not state was how all the other engines at Ardsley had fared for water in the meantime. Probably he did not literally mean "dried up" when referring to the spring, which during the winter months had fully reactivated itself and supplies to the shed were once again sufficient. To conclude his report, the Locomotive Engineer asked that the engine shed's tank be enlarged, to insure against further spells of dry weather. It may be assumed this was done, as the subject does not reappear in the Minutes. It also seems unlikely that the GN availed itself of the Iron Company's water, as at a date unknown, supplies to the shed were undertaken by Wakefield Rural Sanitary Authority.

By 1873, Ardsley's original station was either no longer up to the demands of traffic, or it was in the way of planned development, as on 17th October of that year, the Engineer was asked to prepare "...further plans and estimates for a new station and also cottage accommodation for the men employed at Ardsley..." The housing referred to was probably meant for the use of Traffic and/or Goods Department staff, as an 1886 plan showed that the houses near the engine shed had not been expanded upon.

Despite the ever increasing traffic passing through Ardsley, it is obvious the shed was operating at a low key, at least in 1876, as evidenced by some figures for coal consumption. On 10th September that year Stirling advised that the average of the previous ten weeks' coal use at Ardsley had been 32 tons - in other words, between 4¼ to 5 tons per day, allowing for no

Sunday duties. Those figures indicate the shed was supporting but a handful of locomotives, almost certainly shunting tanks, while 'main line' power would have been supplied by Leeds and Bradford depots. Activities must have gradually increased though, because on 5th February 1884 came the opening of four tenders for construction of a new tank house at Ardsley shed; Messrs. W. Nicholson's price of £154 was accepted. The 1886 plan referred to above shows that the coke stage and water tank outside the shed entrance had been taken away, and a new water tank (on a tankhouse), coal stage and water crane had been installed at the rear of the shed, alongside the Leeds line. In addition, two 220ft stabling roads had been laid alongside the coal stage.

It would seem the shed continued to supply shunting engines only though, as on 5th June 1890, Stirling opened the door for major change at Ardsley, by declaring that mileage incurred in light engine movements to and from Leeds and Bradford had reached the high annual figure of 80,000. To save all that wasted effort, plus it seems, a not inconsiderable bill for enginemens' overtime, the Locomotive Engineer recommended a new engine shed be built at Ardsley, large enough to accommodate 60 engines. Stirling delivered this report to the Way & Works Committee, which immediately advised the GN's Yorkshire Committee that the new depot should be built on the Up side and would cost an estimated £80,235 in total. The Surveyor was duly instructed to report on purchase of the necessary land from Cardigan & Trustees, while the Engineer was given the go ahead to prepare plans.

Buying of the land went through, at a price unknown, and on 2nd April 1891, nine tenders for construction of the shed were opened. Messrs. Thorp & Son's figure of £91,487 was the highest, while at the other end of the scale, the firm of Walter Binns & Co., which had recently completed another GN shed, at Holmfield, won the contract with a price offer of £55,550-11-9d. Once Binns & Co. started work though, it was found that due to the nature of the ground, much deeper foundations would be required for the shed. In addition it would be necessary to lengthen Fall Lane bridge, to allow building of a new station there, all of which would require extra earthworks, the cost of which had risen considerably. All this was calculated by Stirling to bring total costs up by £8,600 and he delivered his doubtless unwelcome news to the Board, on 5th May 1892. Binns & Co's contract was duly amended to cover the additional expense.

Exactly three weeks later, the Locomotive Engineer gave the following progress report and request for more expenditure: "...the contractors are well in hand with the new engine shed at Ardsley and I now wish to make provision for the (workshop) tools. An overhead travelling crane from Messrs. Craven (hand-operated and of 35 tons capacity), for £800; a stationary engine and boiler will also be necessary and with new shafting etc., will cost £1,000. I propose to put in a few machines - lathes, shaping machines, drills etc. At present I do not propose an expenditure of more than £1,500 as it is not necessary to put wheel lathes and other expensive machinery in, as such work can be done here (Doncaster) or Bradford..." The Locomotive committee recommended this expenditure to the Board on 3rd June 1892, but further costs were incurred from 19th November 1892, when Stirling asked if an Engine Balancing Machine (weighing table) could be provided at Ardsley. He said that the existing table at Doncaster (built by Dennison of Leeds), was about to be replaced and recommended it be re-installed at Ardsley, at an estimated cost of £440; this was sanctioned on the following 2nd December.

4

An example of stopgap GNR motive power, employed at a time of dense traffic and full order books among the UK's locomotive builders. Baldwin 2-6-0 No.1182 is posed in the yard at Ardsley, having just been erected from a kit of parts imported from the USA. *Authors' collection.*

Few classes of locomotive saw a length of service in one area that gained them a local appellation. Such, however, were the Class J50 0-6-0T whose long association with the GNR's lines in West Yorkshire caused them to be nicknamed "Ardsley Tanks". Class members 3161 and 3217 stand at Ardsley in September 1934 - note the modifications that had been made to the shed's roof. *Authors' collection.*

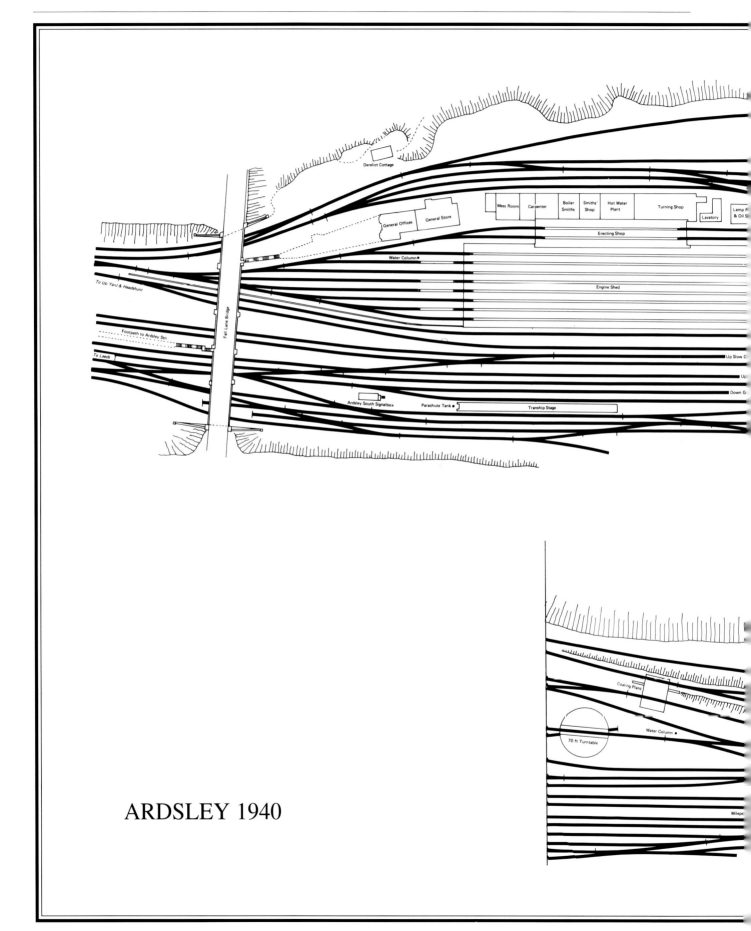

ARDSLEY 1940

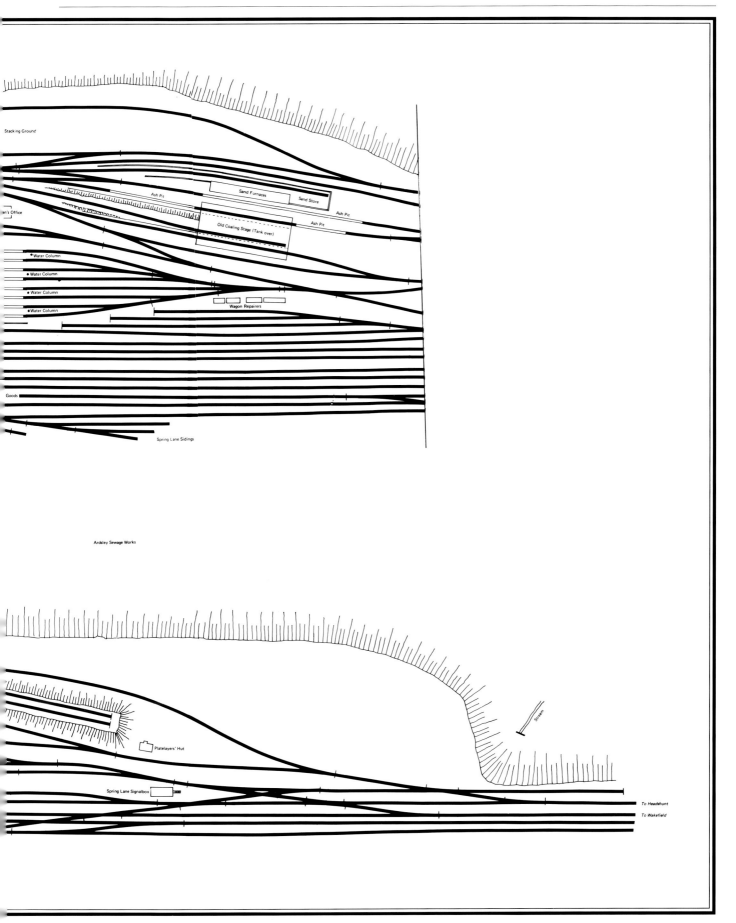

Stacking Ground

Sand Furnaces

Sand Store

Ash Pit

Ash Pit

Ash Pit

...an's Office

Old Coaling Stage (Tank over)

● Water Column

● Water Column

● Water Column

Wagon Repairers

● Water Column

Goods

Spring Lane Sidings

Ardsley Sewage Works

Stream

Platelayers' Hut

Spring Lane Signalbox

To Headshunt

To Wakefield

A precise opening date for Ardsley's new shed has not been discovered. It is very likely the depot was brought into use in stages, starting around the autumn of 1892, as on 4th October the Board heard about a memorial sent on 22nd September, by the drivers and other staff at Ardsley. In it, the men stated they had been instructed by the Locomotive Department to remove their families to Ardsley, yet there was insufficient suitable accommodation. The memorial further noted that property speculators were building houses in the area, but they were not suitable as their prices ranged upwards from £200, so would the company consider provision of its own staff accommodation? The outcome of the housing matter is not entirely certain, but it seems the GN did take on some of the houses in the district. Whatever, this incident would indicate the large shed had commenced operation, but, as Walter Binns & Co. did not have their final account settled until the first half of 1893, it is reasonable to assume the contractors had been working at the shed until the early part of that year, at least. Final cost of the new shed was £65,025-19-8d, which represents a further increase of £875-7-11d over tendered price plus the other earlier authorised surcharge of £8,600. This last extra amount was due to more foundation works, building a new signal box and closets for the workmen and provision of a temporary footbridge, while Ardsley Fall Lane bridge was being lengthened.

As completed then, Ardsley new engine shed was a large, 8-road 455ft x 120ft building, capable of holding 88 engines - an increase over the Locomotive Engineer's originally planned capacity. Built in brick, with a period northlight roof, the shed was of the through type, with a 45ft turntable sited at the far end of both east and west locomotive yards. Even for a depot the size of Ardsley, provision of two turntables was lavish - the reason why duplicate facilities were installed is not known. In addition to pits along the internal length of each shed road, there were external pits on every road, just outside the depot's eastern entrance and pits on four roads at the western end. Along the shed's north side was the 2-road repair shop which measured 230ft x 40ft and was, like the engine shed, a through structure, but having a lofty gabled roof to accommodate the overhead crane within. Offices, stores and some workshops were ranged in a block along the north side of the repair shop. This block also contained the stationary engine plant with its tall chimney that was for years a local landmark. Other buildings at each end of the main block housed further offices, shops, messing facilities etc. In the eastern yard stood Ardsley's massively proportioned coaling stage, which was equipped with a wagon ramp, instead of the previous norm of fitting a coaling platform with steam or hand powered bucket cranes. Adoption of the wagon ramp introduced a concept that with the glaring exception of Kings Cross Top Shed, would quite quickly be extended to virtually all major GN engine sheds. The coal stage scaled 140ft x 65ft and was topped by a 200,000 gallon water tank which had the novel device of two smoke vents, 3ft - 6in. wide by 48ft long, taken up through the water space over the coaling road.

Mention of the shed's water tank brings us to a matter that takes us back to 1892. On 20th July that year, Stirling started on the problem of water supplies to Ardsley engine shed, a subject that reached epic proportions and would more or less continually occupy the GN's attention of the next four years or so. The Locomotive Engineer commented that present water supplies for Ardsley came from Wakefield Rural Sanitary Authority, at a cost of 1/- (5p) per 1000 gallons. At the current consumption rate of 60,000 gallons per day, the GN were, therefore, paying about £1,000 a year. Stirling expected this demand would double with the opening of the new locoshed, so a search had been made for an alternative water supply. Unfortunately, such supplies as were found, when analysed, proved unsuitable for locomotive use, so Stirling had hammered out a new deal with the Wakefield authority. At first, WRSA had said 11d. (4½p) per 1,000 gallons, later modifying this to the following sliding scale: 11d. per 1,000 for the first 75,000 gallons per day, 10d for the next 75,000 and 9d. thereafter: the GN were to guarantee to take a minimum of 100,000 gallons a day for ten years. Understandably, Stirling had refused this and finally reached a compromise which he offered to the Board: 10d per 1,000 gallons, for the first 100,000 a day, 9½d. for the next 50,000 and 9d. for each 1,000 above 150,000: the guarantee of 100,000 per day remained, but over the reduced period of five years. Stirling calculated that the company would end up paying about £1,650 per annum, at those rates, for the new shed. He added that the WRSA would have to spend £1,500-2,000 to secure a supply for the GN and felt, in the circumstances, the 5 year guarantee, in order to recoup costs, was reasonable. The Board sanctioned the arrangement next day, but subsequent events indicate that no long-term agreement was actually made with the Wakefield Authority.

Because of the water costs it was having to pay, the GN started boring for water in the vicinity of Ardsley shed in 1893. The job had been tendered about May of that year, being awarded on 1st June, to a Mr. J. Simpson, at a cost of £152, for a 100 yard bore. Costs of £1,000 to provide a 1 million gallon reservoir, as suggested by the Loco Engineer, were not given the go-ahead at that time (or ever). By the latter half of 1893, the Way & Works Committee heard that the Ardsley bore, which was on the west side of the line, had struck at a depth of 60 yards, with the water rising to within 69 feet of the surface: on analysis it had been found to be of 'fair' quality. Unfortunately the 7in. pump was not powerful enough, so a second well was bored, this time of 12in. diameter, coming into use on 19th December 1893. By the next month, Stirling was able to report that the new pump was forcing water into the large tank (200,000 gallons) at the engine shed, and the small tank (30,000 gallons) at West Yard. At the same time, the original small well was still in use, but its 7in. pump was being lowered and adjusted, to increase its efficiency.

Despite this arrangement, which probably ended the Wakefield Authority's supply, the Locomotive Engineer recommended a further bore be made on the east side of the line. This was approved and by 31st May 1894, Stirling was able to report that the drilling contractor, Messrs. Legrand & Sutcliffe, had made good progress, with a 7 inch bore down to a depth of 123 feet. A steam winch had been fixed for dealing with the boring and Stirling hoped that a good supply of water would be struck 'within a week.' Alas for hopes! Late in 1894, after an expenditure of £2,000, (double the budgeted costs), Legrand & Sutcliffe eventually found water, but at a flow of 12,000 gallons per day, it was insufficient for use.

At the original boreholes all was not satisfactory either. On 20th March 1895, Stirling commented that the well pumping engine received insufficient steam from the central boiler (doubtless because it had not been set up to feed a 12 inch pump in addition to the first 7 inch one!). A separate boiler was recommended, provision of which would cost £218 - this was agreed. But, on 30th October 1895, Stirling had to report: "...the water at Ardsley is 'bad' and the condition of the engines is

Pre-war modifications (i) Ardsley's new mechanical coaling plant nears completion in 1937; note the Southern Railway wagon in the foreground, adorning an LNER publicity picture. In October 1941 it was discovered that a subterranean fire was burning in the tip that had been formed in 1892, to provide the required level for the shed's yard, at its eastern end. The fire was found to be advancing towards, and threatening the foundations and structure of, the mechanical coaler and tracks in its vicinity. This was a serious situation to which the LNER quickly reponded by making numerous boreholes in the path of the fire and injecting cement slurry. That treatment effectively halted the problem and in January 1945 the area was officially declared 'safe'. *British Railways.*

becoming 'dangerous.' I recommend immediate arrangements to be made to take water from Morley Corporation, or other good source..." The Engineer's advice was rapidly acted upon and the GN and its successors then embarked upon a period of over 70 years of having to take good, but expensive water from the local water authorities.

That was not the end of the story though, as the well water continued to be used for washing out, but the earlier problems over pumping capacity soon re-occurred, this time from the opposite aspect. On 1st October 1896, the Way & Works Committee received the following brief historical report from Ivatt: "... the original artesian well had not been sufficient. A second well, with 12in. pipe and direct-acting steam pump had been sunk, and been all right for a while, but then there was insufficient water for the pumps to lift..." The Committee resolved that the best solution would be to disconnect the 12in pipe and 7in. pump and attach the 7in. pipe to the 12in. pump, which would be operated at slow speed. It was further resolved to contract this work to specialists, so Legrand & Sutcliff were awarded the £250 job.

Even then, the tale is not quite told, because in 1902 came the Ardsley experiment with the Desrumaux Patent Water Softener apparatus, the inconclusive story of which is more fully covered in the chapter on water in Volume 2. From all available evidence, that event *did* close the book on the subject of water at Ardsley engine shed!

Returning to 1894, the 2nd of May saw approval for £60 to be spent on purchase of a cottage standing in the shed yard, for use rent free, by the depot watchman. The fact the watchman did not have to pay rent is probably owing to his accommodation's less that salubrious situation, but other shed staff did not fare so well at the hands of the parsimonious GN Board! As alluded to above, the company were obliged to provide housing for at least some of the shed staff, apparently by purchase of privately constructed residences of better than average quality. Sure enough, by 23rd March 1896, the GN's surveyor reported that he considered the locomotive foremens' houses contained "superior accommodation" and the company must therefore ask for an increase in rent from 5/6d. (27½p), to 8/- (40p) per week. When this had been put to the men they had understandably objected - the 2/6d probably represented nearly 10% of their weekly earnings in those days - and the kindly Ivatt had supported them. Unfortunately the GN's Directors did not agree, so the men's objection was overruled and their rent increased.

With Doncaster, Kings Cross and Peterborough workshops so busy during the latter part of the 1890's, Ardsley's repair shop was a boon to the GN and a programme of heavy repairs and even some rebuilding was carried out within the confines of its relatively limited space. Indeed, the whole British locomotive industry was in a period of boom, with full order books and lists of waiting customers. So, when the GN had to urgently seek additional engine power to meet traffic requirements, the company turned to an American locomotive builder, Burnham Williams & Co. of the Baldwin Locomotive Works, Philadelphia. The deal reached involved the shipping from the USA of twenty bar-framed 2-6-0's in kit form, for final erection by the GNR. As the GN's main works were fully employed it was decided that all twenty Baldwin Moguls would be put together, up to steaming condition, at Ardsley. The engines duly arrived during 1899 and 1900 (Baldwin Works Nos:16927-36 and 17321-5/55-9 of those years, respectively), to receive GN numbers 1181-1200 and

Classification H; all were initially stationed in the GN's West Riding District. If the Baldwins had arrived one or two years later, it is fairly certain they would not have been erected at Ardsley as, by 1902, Doncaster's large new Crimpsall shop had been commissioned and heavy repairs/rebuildings at Ardsley ceased.

A Way & Works Committee meeting of 4th November 1902 saw Ivatt commenting upon the enginemens' Mutual Improvement Class at Ardsley. The engineer said that the classes were held in a room in one of the tankhouses, which he considered was "not suitable." Rather than encourage the men's tendency to repair to local hostelries for their classes, with undoubtedly much less attention to detail being shown, Ivatt said that for £100 a purpose-built brick classroom could be put up, complete with fireplaces, etc. The Committee wholeheartedly supported the engineer's suggestion, so the expenditure was authorised on 7th November. Just over three years later, on 25th November 1905, another minor improvement was made when £50 was sanctioned to extend and connect up a turntable road. Whether the east or west table was involved is unknown, but it was noted that the work was to be put in hand at once, so it would seem there may have been some pressing problems over engine movements to and from the turntable.

1906 saw Ardsley start to participate in the GNR's steam railmotor era, when on 19th February, railcars No.7 and 8 commenced operation between Ossett, Dewsbury and Batley. On 4th April 1906, Ivatt gave the following report on the steam cars' performance thus far: "...between Ossett and Batley, the railcars have effectively taken the place of the train service and additional trips are being run, with 21 trips per day. Car mileage for the month of March was 1,750, with 13,886 passengers being carried and earnings per car per mile have worked out at 7d...On the Ossett-Batley line the Avonside cars were unsatisfactory and concern has been raised about their oscillation..." Presumably the Avonside problem was overcome, but steam railmotors were taken out of use around the start of World War One, a conflict which eventually saw the necessary employment of females in such jobs as engine cleaning. Some were working at Ardsley by 1917, and on 1st May that year, Gresley asked for provision of temporary accommodation (changing rooms and toilets etc.), for the ladies "as recently carried out at King's Cross." The engineer's estimate of £153 was approved.

It seems the GNR did little else to improve Ardsley shed before the company became part of the LNER, to be joined in the new amalgamation on 1st July 1923, by the formerly independent East & West Yorkshire Union Railway. The E&WYU was a coal carrying railway, running from an end-on connection at Colliery Junction, with the GN's branch from Lofthouse North Junction. Proceeding north, the E&WYU passed through Robin Hood and Rothwell, to its northern outlet, on the Midland Railway's Normanton-Leeds line at Stourton Junction; there were a number of colliery spurs and a longish branch line, to Newmarket Colliery. The only depot for the E&WYU's handful of engines was at Robin Hood, a two road structure of fairly basic construction, unpretentious, with coal, water and repair facilities. Robin Hood became sub-depot of Ardsley for three years, until it was closed by the LNER in July 1926, to subsequently be demolished; the men, machines and duties transferred to the main shed. Incidentally, the E&WYU's last Locomotive Superintendent, one Dick Mitchenson, continued in the LNER's employ, to finish his career as Shedmaster at Copley Hill.

Ardsley had one other sub-shed for a number of years, or rather, had engines outstationed at Wakefield, at a number of different buildings belonging to other railway companies. These were a couple of Lancashire & Yorkshire Railway sheds near Kirkgate station and a MSLR/MR joint shed at Balne Lane, near Wakefield Westgate station. The latter was closed in 1923 and the one-time GCR firemen and machines moved to Ardsley, while the drivers continued to book on and off at Westgate. It is interesting to recall that MSLR/GCR men had previously been stationed at Ardsley, for workings to Manchester via Wath and southwards, to Mexborough; the tenancy ended in 1907, with opening of the GCR's yard at Wath. With regard to L&YR Wakefield sheds, GN association appears to have ended sometime around the end of the 1890's. For fuller details, the reader should refer to the section on 'Other Companies' Sheds' (Vol.2) that housed GN motive power. Ardsley also provided shunting pilots for Hunslet Goods Station from its opening in 1899; engine sidings and a turntable were installed there. For more details *see* "Stabling Points" (page XX).

The first BW&L shed at Ardsley was part of the GN's West Riding or Yorkshire District, together with Leeds and Bradford depots. At an uncertain date the District was subdivided into Leeds and Bradford Locomotive Districts, but after subdivision the West Riding's former flexible allocation of engines was largely maintained and locomotives continued to be freely moved around between the three sheds. In Leeds District, Ardsley was grouped with Leeds (Wortley) then (Copley Hill) sheds, having a common locomotive allocation, which makes somewhat difficult the determining of which engines were where. Put simply though, after Ardsley's 8-road depot opened, it was considered the main shed and was predominately a goods engine depot, with some local passenger workings and having certain 'summer only' excursion duties; the smaller Leeds shed provided power for main line passenger and the majority of local workings. It would seem, however, that Leeds District Locomotive Superintendent had his 'seat' at Leeds rather than Ardsley, because when on 1st May 1902, a direct telephone line was authorised, between the Leeds and Bradford Districts, it connected Bradford shed with Copley Hill.

The West Riding's continuing homogeneity of locomotive movement was maintained until LNER days when the new company had more rigid principles of operation put into practice. That caused some ill feelings at times, usually at Ardsley, which lost to Bradford and Copley Hill depots, such duties as summer excursion traffic and Whitemoor goods duties. Nevertheless, Ardsley invariably gained, during the late August-early September "Bowlingtide" holiday, when many heavy excursion trains, often double-headed, took the hard-working citizens of the West Riding to such places as the East Coast resorts. That traffic required the temporary transfer of a considerable number of engines to the area - usually to Ardsley shed. As an illustration, 1935's Bowlingtide saw twenty-two 0-6-0's - eight J6, ten J11 and four J39, moved to Ardsley from ex-GC and GN depots at Annesley, Boston, Colwick, Doncaster, Immingham, Kings Cross, Langwith, Lincoln and Retford.

As noted earlier, Ardsley's allocation up to the 1890's was likely limited to a few shunting tanks and perhaps a few 0-4-2 or 0-6-0 for local trips, etc. However, Stirling planned for 60 engines to be accommodated and on 1st June 1896, Ivatt reported that 70 were allocated (at the same time, 49 were working from Wortley). There would have been numbers of 0-4-2 at Ardsley no doubt, but 0-6-0's predominated, with Stirling's J9 a major

force - as they should have been, being known as they were "West Riding Goods". The class' association with the depot was long, for the last survivor, by then LNER Class J7 No.4027, was not withdrawn from Ardsley until September 1936. Ivatt's J5 and J6 were also numerous by the early 1900's, to remain as LNER Classes J3 and J4, until BR times, although J4 tended to "come and go" a bit - for example, none were present during most of the Second World War, but a couple had returned by 1947.

Stirling saddle tanks of Class J14 (J53) provided shunting power for Ardsley's various yards, first arriving in 1892. After a few years they were joined by Ivatt's very similar J13 (J52) and those classic GN 0-6-0ST designs set a longevity record of 69 years at Ardsley, before the last two (J52) were taken out of service in March 1961. In 1898/9, C2 tanks came to West Riding District, but whether any were initially allocated to Ardsley is not clear - probably one or two were stationed there, along with the odd Stirling 0-4-4T; certainly four of the 4-4-2T were at Ardsley by Grouping, but all had moved on by 1933; then, during the war, No.4536 was resident for some time.

Came the turn of the century and appearance on the scene of the Baldwin Moguls. Most stayed at Ardsley all their lives, but some went to Nottingham District for a time and one was even tried out - unsuccessfully - on certain London commuter workings. Generally though, the 2-6-0 were structurally not up to the demands made of them and all the 'Americans' had returned to Ardsley by July 1912, when the first - No.1185 - was withdrawn, with the remainder soon following.

Around 1908, L1 0-8-2T were introduced into the West Riding, most going to Ardsley no doubt, a presence maintained until January 1914, when all went back to Colwick; during their time in Yorkshire, the 0-8-2T were used mainly on trips between Wakefield, Ardsley and Bradford. The engines from which the L1 were derived, Ivatt's K1 and K2 "Long Tom" 0-8-0, did not appear at Ardsley until after World War One. The solitary K3 also came to the shed, and by the late 1900's most of the surviving 0-8-0 were operating in the West Riding, from where they worked to Doncaster, March, and Hull, as well as within their home district. As LNER Class Q2 they were progressively replaced by ex-GC O4 2-8-0 from the mid-1920's, but the singleton K3 (Q3) was another of Ardsley's "last survivors," No.3420 becoming the final GN 0-8-0 in service, used on Bradford (City Road) trips until withdrawal in 1937.

A tank engine class which had a long stay at Ardsley was the N1 0-6-2T, which arrived from 1907 to start a 52 year association with the West Riding. The class, in condensing and non-condensing form, became familiar sights throughout the region, on the many local passenger services. It should be noted though, that condenser-equipped examples usually had the condensing pipes blanked off, to maintain blastpipe pressure at a maximum, a very necessary requirement for working in West Riding District! On average, only about three N1 were stationed at Ardsley, but it was there that a further last survivor, No.69462, was condemned in April 1959. Logical development of the N1, Gresley's N2, also came to West Yorkshire, at first around 1926, with a brief appearance. Then in 1928/9, twenty of the class built by the Newcastle-on-Tyne firm of Hawthorn, Leslie & Co., were sent to Ardsley for running-in, before being allocated to other sheds. A firm allocation occurred from 1931, when five came to Ardsley for mixed duties; all had gone again though, by around the end of World War Two. R. H. N. (Dick) Hardy, who worked as a fireman at Ardsley, remembers the N2 as "very unsteady engines and shy steaming...the N1's were far better in

(*above*) Pre-war modifications (ii) The new coaler was accompanied by a new 70ft diameter, vacuum operated turntable, also seen here nearing completion in 1937. Note this time that GWR and LMS wagons featured in an LNER photo! *British Railways.*

(*below*) Post-war modifications (i) This May 1952 view of the east end of Ardsley shows the neatly bricked-in end screen to the roof, which in 1946, had received a new covering in steel, concrete and asbestos. This was however, a partial job which completely belied the decrepit situation at the depot's west end and which would have to be dealt with, starting the following year! *N.E.Preedy.*

the West Riding." Mr. Hardy adds the comment that N2 were removed from Ardsley (and Copley Hill) after a number of failures "had gone down the bank at Bramley!"

While discussing 0-6-2T, it is worth noting that Ardsley was used for other 'running-in' duties in the late 1920's, this time concerning Messrs. Robert Stephenson and Doncaster-built examples of GE pattern N7, before they too went to depots elsewhere. Ex-GC N5 made their debut too, in the Thirties, and worked on various duties for some years (Nos.5518 and 5530 were still present during the war period), before moving on to Bradford and Copley Hill sheds.

Ivatt's 4-4-0 do not seem to have been on Ardsley's roster very often - D3 No.1302 was based at the depot around Grouping, and No.4075 (at least) saw use by Ardsley in the 1930's, but apart from some special passenger workings, the 4-4-0's duties are a mystery. The same cannot be said though, about Gresley's J23 (LNER J50/1) 0-6-0T. They were specifically designed for, and arrived in the West Riding District in 1913 and thereafter dominated the local railway scene to such an extent that they became known as the "Ardsley Tanks." Their main use was on local goods and coal trains, shunting and banking over the many hilly sections of line. In the mid-1920's some of Ardsley's J50/1 were exchanged for ex-GC J57, ex-NBR J83 and ex-NER J77, for comparison of performances on shunting duties: the results seem to have been inconclusive and all engines returned to their normal haunts after about 3 months. Ardsley's complement of J50 totalled 32 at Grouping, rising to 34 by 1933, and falling to around 25 by Nationalisation. From the early 1950's the J50 began to move away, mostly to London, to replace such types as N1 and J52. In 1959 there was still a dozen on Ardsley's strength, but by the early 1960's one of the most common sights and sounds of the West Yorkshire railway scene was no more.

Gresley's H1 and H2 Moguls operated from Ardsley from 1914, mostly on lodging turns to such places as Liverpool, March and Grimsby. Around 1928, B8 and K3 from other sheds took over, but the latter class did come onto Ardsley's roster from late in 1937. One of the K3's main duties was night goods work to Immingham, until the class left around the start of the Second World War. BR re-introduced the 2-6-0's in 1959, from which time they stayed until final withdrawal of the last examples - in true Ardsley tradition, yet another "last survivor," only this time there were three of them!

On the heavy freight side, as remarked above, Ivatt 0-8-0 were superseded by O4 from the mid-1920's. The O4 had a disadvantage though, inasmuch they were too long for Ardsley's two 45' turntables and had to be turned on the triangular junction at Lofthouse. Accordingly, by 1928 all O4 had been replaced by ex-GC Q4 0-8-0. There were eleven at Ardsley by 1933 and twenty in 1936, around the time a larger turntable was provided at the shed. That didn't cause the Q4 to be moved away though and they continued to serve until just around the dawn of BR, when O4 appeared once again to replace them. Needless to say, Ardsley had the last surviving Q4 - No.63243 - which was taken out of service in October 1951. Extraordinarily, GN 2-8-0 classes appear never to have worked at Ardsley, so the O4's second coming lasted until the type was finally moved away on 8th August 1962. For a brief interlude though, LNER Class O6 (Stanier 8F 2-8-0) Nos.3154-3158 were stationed at the depot from August 1946 to March 1947, while the Woodhead tunnels were under repair and some LNER trans-Pennine services were routed over the LMS' Standedge line.

Of the other goods engine classes, J39 were a dominant

feature of Ardsley, with the first four arriving in 1927. By 1930, seven of the 0-6-0 were at the depot, and nineteen at the start of World War Two, but the maximum number seems to have been twenty-five, in 1953. Of the class, which was employed on all manner of goods duties and summer/Bowlingtide extras, No.2701 was at Ardsley for all its existence - August 1928 to November 1962.

It will be recalled that the GN used steam railmotors in the West Riding - and elsewhere - in the early part of the 20th century, a move that was only partially successful. Nevertheless, the LNER re-introduced the species, this time utilising Sentinel-pattern steam engines, and they served in West Yorkshire, based at Copley Hill shed, until the latter part of the war, when an increasingly poor reliability record led to their withdrawal. After removal from service, however, not all the railmotors were immediately broken up and two could still be seen at Ardsley late in 1946. On 13th December that year, Nos.51909 and 51913 were noted lying dead, alongside the depot, together with a sorry looking A4, No.13 DOMINION OF NEW ZEALAND, which had failed some time previously.

Grouping brought ex-GCR classes to Ardsley other than those already mentioned. B4 and B6's both made double appearances - coming first in the early '20's, to leave again about 1935. B4 re-appeared at the beginning of the war and by 1940, Nos.6098, 6099 and 6101 were at the shed. The allocation reached five in 1943 (6098 to 6102) being used mainly on the Bradford-London services as far as Doncaster, the Thorpe Arch munitions workers trains, and a variety of local passenger jobs to Doncaster, as well as the very heavy Colchester-Leeds turn. The B4 lasted until November 1950, when only a single example remained, the one named engine and in apple green livery to boot: 1482 IMMINGHAM added to Ardsley's folklore of last survivors. So did the B6 which, during their first foray, were used on long distance goods and excursion passenger trains. Returning to Ardsley in mid-1946, the class saw out its last eighteen months or so on goods work. The C14's were another wartime import, when 6123, 6126 and 6129 arrived in 1941, being joined soon after by 6120, 6121, 6124, 6125, and 6131. In 1947, all nine were still working from Ardsley on Bradford-Wakefield-Leeds services, which continued until the class left in 1955. Another 'foreign' class was J27, of which six were assigned to Ardsley in 1935. Nos.2350, 2354, 2357, 2358, 2359, and 2388 were present a year later and the class remained until 1942.

Six months after Grouping, E&WYUR engines came onto Ardsley's roster - three 0-6-0T and two 0-6-2T. Of the former, two were classified J84 and the other, J85, while one 0-6-2T was immediately withdrawn, leaving its sister engine to become LNER Class N19. All came to Ardsley shed itself, together with their men, when the E&WYU's Robin Hood depot closed in July 1926. Gradually the former E&WY engines were taken out of service - the N19 and one J84 in 1928, the other 0-6-0T in 1930, and the J85 in 1933. Their replacements on the still busy E&WYU network were varied and the following saw use for differing periods of time: J52, J53, J54 - the last surviving J52, Nos.68869 and 68875, were employed in their final days, until withdrawn in March 1961; ex-GC J62 No.5888, from September 1930, being condemned in July 1937; ex-GER J67 and J69, from the mid-1930's to the mid-1940's (J69 7370 allocated in March 1936); an ex-NER J77 for a time in the early '30s' and an ex-H&BR 0-6-2T of Class N12, that saw use during 1936-38 almost exclusively on the Newmarket Colliery branch. From 1942 to 1946, various Y3 Sentinels were stationed at Ardsley for duties at Wrenthorpe Yard

Post-war modifications (ii) An interior picture from September 1953 clearly shows how badly the roof and its supports at Ardsley's west end had deteriorated. *British Railways.*

Post-war modifications (iii) September 1953 saw work commence on the removal of the old roof. Note that despite their external condition, the wooden cross beams seem internally to have still been very sound. *British Railways.*

Post-war modifications (iv) By November 1953 the old roof has been completely removed and work is in hand providing the foundations for the new covering's supports. This picture also gives a glimpse of the shed's eastern end roof style. *British Railways.*

Post-war modifications (v) March 1954 saw the concrete support columns, transverse beams and hangers for the smoke ducts in place. Meanwhile, the day-to-day duties of a busy engine shed carry on around all the civil engineering work. *British Railways.*

and one at least was tried on E&WYU workings - unsuccessfully as it turned out. To see out the days of steam on the E&WYU, J94 Nos.68008, 68011, 68015, 68045 arrived in 1961, to replace the J52. The 'Austerities' may possibly have been preceded by ex-LMS 0-6-0T, of which Nos.47443, 47589, 47632 and 47640 were allocated to Ardsley early in 1959. What the 'Jinties' did is not known, but they probably worked the local yards, in between spending long periods out of use! As a sidenote, LMS Ivatt 2-6-0 Nos.43075 and 43101 were also at Ardsley in early 1959, the class' presence increasing to 43070, 43096, 43101, 43132, 43137, 43141 six years later. Again the LMS Moguls' duties are a complete unknown to the authors, but presumably they were of a general nature. Then, around 1960, LMS 2-6-2T Nos.41250, 41253, 41263, 41274 were stored at Ardsley, even though they were nominally allocated to Low Moor shed.

The post-Gresley era saw Thompson's B1 arrive at Ardsley, just as the LNER's days were coming to an end. By 1952, nine of the 4-6-0 were stationed there, being used on many duties, with one daily express turn, from Leeds to Cleethorpes and back. Numerous B1 'passed through' Ardsley between September 1956 and January 1957, after the ex-GN sheds in the West Riding were transferred to BR's North Eastern Region. The 4-6-0 came from other NE Region depots, on their way to ex-Midland Railway sheds that had also been transferred from the Midland Region. (Incidentally, that transfer to NE Region resulted in Ardsley's three V2 being moved away - they had arrived about 1954 and were the only members of the class ever to be allocated). Ardsley's alocation of B1 increased and by May 1965, seventeen were operating from the shed. Of these it is interesting to note that no fewer than eight bore names, these were:

61013 TOPI
61014 ORIBI
61016 INYALA
61017 BUSHBUCK
61030 NYALA
61237 GEOFFREY H. KITSON
61238 LESLIE RUNCIMAN
61240 HARRY HINCHCLIFFE

(As an aside, 61016 and 61030 were named after the same species of antelope, but in different African dialects.)

Even 'grander' named engines were stationed at the shed by BR, when ten Peppercorn A1 and six Gresley A3 Pacifics passed through the depot between September 1951 and October 1965. The engines involved, and their sojourns at Ardsley were:

60123	9/51 from Copley Hill	9/57 to Copley Hill	
60123	4/62 from Copley Hill	10/62 withdrawn.	
60144	9/51 from Copley Hill	2/53 to Grantham	
60130	2/53 from Grantham	9/57 to Copley Hill	
60130	9/64 from Copley Hill	10/65 withdrawn.	
60080	6/61 from Holbeck	6/63 to Neville Hill	
60092	6/61 from Holbeck	6/63 to Gateshead	
60036	9/61 from Copley Hill	6/63 to Gateshead	
60069	9/61 from Copley Hill	10/62 withdrawn.	
60070	9/61 from Copley Hill	6/63 to Neville Hill	
60077	9/61 from Copley Hill	6/63 to St Margarets	
60131	4/62 from Copley Hill	7/63 to Neville Hill	
60134	4/62 from Copley Hill	7/63 to Neville Hill	
60135	4/62 from Copley Hill	11/62 withdrawn.	
60118	11/62 from Copley Hill	7/63 to Neville Hill	
60117	9/64 from Copley Hill	12/64 to Gateshead	
60117	1/65 from Gateshead	6/65 withdrawn.	
60148	9/64 from Copley Hill	12/64 to Gateshead	
60148	1/65 from Gateshead	6/65 withdrawn.	

It is not clear what duties were covered by the A3's but the A1 were normally employed on an overnight parcels train to London, returning on an early afternoon Leeds express.

Thompson L1's were late performers on Ardsley diagrams. They appeared first in 1961 and worked out their remaining months on local trips and goods to Bradford, via the Morley line. Their size was against the L1 though - in the confines of some of the district's goods yards - and all the big tanks had gone to the scrapyard by December 1962. Lastly, of the BR Standard locomotive classes, they were common enough sights in West Yorkshire but surprisingly none seem ever to have been stationed at Ardsley. That did not apply to the WD 2-8-0 however, with a singleton being allocated in 1956, three in November 1960 and thirteen by mid-1962.

Determining actual locomotive allocations in pre-Grouping days is made difficult by Ardsley's combining with Leeds shed. Leeds Locomotive District supported a total of 145 engines in 1905 and 137 in 1912. At Grouping Ardsley had an allocation of 95, while Copley Hill had 45; subsequent figures were: October 1931 - 101 and 38, and here we can detail the engines seen on a visit to Ardsley in September 1931:

D3	4076
G3	6404
J3	3331, 3336, 3343, 3378, 3388, 3398, 4082, 4086, 4097, 4102, 4104, 4122, 4126, 4144, 4152, 4159
J6	3606
J7	4027
J39	1286, 2698
J50	586, 601, 603, 610, 3157, 3167, 3169, 3172, 3213, 3215, 3216, 3217, 3219, 3220, 3226, 3234, 3235, 3239, 3240
J51	3158, 3160, 3161, 3162, 3163, 3168, 3171, 3178, 3218
J54	3858
J55	3913, 3915, 3928
J62	5888
J68	7036
J77	614, 1349
J85	3114
N1	390, 4593
N2	2688
O4	6301, 6628
Q1	3446
Q2	3405, 3452, 3453, 3455
Q3	3420
Q4	5144, 5159, 6135, 6143
Q5	771, 773
	Total: 77.

To continue - September 1933 saw 90 locomotives at Ardsley and 45 at Copley Hill; March/April 1936 - 105 and 46; January 1947 - 93 and 32. Sufficient to illustrate perhaps, that in 1905 and 1912, Ardsley would have had an allocation of about 95 engines. Following on from that then, it is reasonable to assume that in 1945, the shed would still have been populated by some 90 locomotives. Yet a Sunday visit, on 11th November that year, found only 55 engines in residence which surely was a distorted picture, given the hectic times. The engines seen were:

B16	2379
C14	6120, 6121, 6122, 6123, 6129, 6131*
J3	4129, 4146, 4153
J6	3521, 3525, 3569, 3629*, 3636
J39	2775

J50	601, 603, 610, 1041, 1070, 3168, 3169, 3172, 3178, 3186, 3212*, 3215, 3216, 3217, 3218, 3220, 3226, 3231, 3232, 3239, 3240
J52	3963, 4053, 4249, 4272, 4273
K2	4651, 4678
K3	2765
N1	4572, 4581, 4593
O4	6554, 6633
Q4	5146, 5159, 5163, 6177
V2	4816

Those engines marked * were in repair shop. Q4 No.5163 had a Lincoln shed allocation plate in the cab, N. ENG painted on the front buffer beam, and LANG chalked on the same buffer beam! (Doubtless it was an engine that Ardsley staff would regret receiving!).

After Nationalisation, August 1950 saw 88 locos on Ardsley's strength, falling to 63 early in 1959 and only 45 in May 1965, five months before closure.

Such allocations of motive power were necessary to meet the depot's various assigned duties. By kind permission of Dr. John Sykes, the authors are able to present a typical breakdown of all Ardsley's 'Links', as in force during the 1930's, but it may be assumed the pattern had been little changed since Ardsley's second shed opened:

No.1 Link - Passenger Link *(Monday to Saturday)*
No.1 Passenger working 0300 0946 1719
No.2 Passenger working 0405 1515 2024
No.3 Passenger working 0441 1515 2311
No.7 Passenger working 0441 1909 1208
Other passenger working 1828 2212
(It may be assumed No.1 Link's duties were all local trains. The link comprised 20 turns in the early 1940's, reducing to 18 by the end of the war. Entry was voluntary, men could opt to join when a vacancy arose).

No.2 Link - Lodge Link *(Monday to Saturday)* *(L = lodging turn)*
Annesley	L2035		
Deansgate	L2225		
Doncaster	0305	0925	
Frodingham	L1825	L1402	L0800
Gorton		L0500	L0750
Grimsby		L0025	L0230
Hull	0115		
Liverpool	L2255		
Milford		0635	1635
Notton Pilot	1159		
Sheffield	L2353		
Wath	0435	0950	

No.3 Link - No.1 Train Link *(Mon-Sat., unless otherwise stated)*
Batley	0240 0824 0420
Bradford	0910
Bradford City Rd	1935(M-F) 1030 1700(SO)
Bullcroft	1210
Doncaster	0435(Pu) 0110 1755 2150(M-F) 2212(SO)
Drighlington	0720
Featherstone	1355
Glasshoughton	0740
Halifax	0433
Hemsworth Jct.	1905(M-F) 1640 (SO)
Hunslet	0625
Kirkgate	1705 0305 1830

Milford	1145 2350
Prince of Wales	0815
Pudsey	1520(M-F) 1310(SO) 0635
Sharlston West	1225(M-F) 1200(SO)
Shipley	1325(M-F) 1210(SO)

No.4 Link - No.2 Train Link *(Monday to Saturday)*
Batley	0320 1730
Bradford	0905 0005
Bradford City Rd	1140
Bullcroft	0125
Doncaster	0040 1600 2005
Halifax	0705
Hemsworth Jct.	1610
Hunslet (Leeds)	1510 0210
Kirkgate	0435
Laisterdyke	0945 1410
Lofthouse	1245
Milford	2300
Prince of Wales	1430
Roundwood	0625
Shaw Cross	1005
South Kirkby	0925
Stanley	0605
Wrenthorpe	1655

No.5 Link - Relief Link *(Monday to Saturday)*
Banker	0750 2350 1613
Bradford City Rd	2030
Leeds	0005
Morley & Gil/sto	1125
Robin Hood	0530 1810 1150 0605 1150
	1810 1210
	0530 1810

No.6 Link - Pilot Link *(Mon - Sat unless otherwise stated)*
North End Pilot	0110 1750 0700
Shed	0800 2400 1600 0800 2400 1600
Spring Lane Pilot	0120(T-S) 0320(MO) 1805 0825

No.7 Link - Pilot Link *(Monday to Saturday)*
Batley	1135
Batley Pilot	0620 1330
Dewsbury	1240
Dewsbury Pilot	0824
Hunslet Pilot	0445 1153
Transfer Pilot	1240
Wrenthorpe Pilot	0110 1909 0657

No.8 Link - Eye-sight Link *(Monday to Saturday)*
Ash-pit Relief	0600 2200 1400
Ash-pit Relief	0700
Shed Shunting	0600
Shop Pilot	0700
Yard Pilot	0730

It goes without saying that Ardsley's yards were the destination of many incoming workings involving Lodging Turns from other depots. Details of such duties lodging at Ardsley in the 1930's are set out in the table on page 21.

Post-war modifications (vi) After a year's work, and expenditure amounting to £40,000, the re-roofing is virtually completed, as seen in this October 1954 picture. The brick end screen and partially rebuilt side walls are clearly visible, as are the galvanised metal inverted v-shaped smoke uptakes. This re-roofing did not follow the BR standard of lightweight steel frames and asbestos coverings; further proof perhaps of the former GNR Yorkshire District's independence, carried through the LNER era, into BR times? Resident B1 No.61110, credited with being the last engine to be dispatched by Ardsley before closure, can be seen inside the shed. *British Railways.*

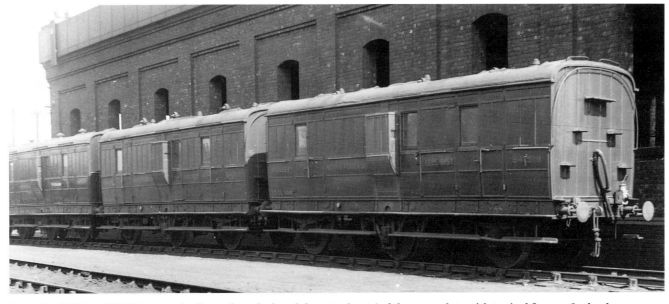

Both the GNR and LNER strategically stationed a breakdown train at Ardsley, complete with typical former 6-wheel passenger brake coaches such as these relegated to the duties of tool vans, etc. Ardsley's large double-sided coaling stage is seen in the background; for a better view the reader should consult Volume One of this trilogy. *Authors' collection.*

A mid-1960s south western aspect of Ardsley shed with a (very) Black 5 No.45454 passing Ardsley South signalbox on a local passenger train. When seen from this angle it is clear that the shed's roof is "stepped" upwards in three sections, from east to west. Was this a legacy of the split re-roofing work, or could it be that the shed was built on a slight up-slope? If the albeit unlikely latter case prevailed, this would give Ardsley an attribute unique among Britain's engine sheds. *P.Sunderland.*

Originating Depot	Loco Cl.	Arrival Yard	Time	Departure Yard	Time
Annesley	J11	Spring Lane	0715	Old Coal Yard or Up Yard	2150
Boston*	J6	Spring Lane	0620	Up Yard	2010
Brunswick (Liverpool)	J39	Spring Lane or	0410	Leeds Low Yard	2330
		Leeds Low Yard	0600	or Old Coal Yard	2330
Frodingham	O4, Q4	Spring Lane	0345	Relieve at Nostell	1402
Frodingham	O4, Q4	Nostell	1500	Up Yard	0925
Gorton	O4	Spring Lane	0645	Old Coal Yard	0015
Gorton	O4	Spring Lane	1630	Up Yard	0615
Immingham	O4	Spring Lane	1145	Up Yard	0150
Immingham	O4	Skellow or S. Kirkby	1500	Monkton	1030
Sheffield	J11, O4	Spring Lane	0720	Up Yard	0033
Trafford Park	B9	Spring Lane	0405	Old Coal Yard	2340

Runs during the potato season only.

Naturally, Ardsley's importance ensured it was included in the LNER's 1930's programme of engine shed improvement and modernisation. On the 24th October 1935, the Board heard the following report: "...There are 100 engines employed mainly on goods and coal traffic, with covered accomodation for 60. About 50,000 tons of coal is dealt annually at the single-ended coal stage. The 45ft turntable, which was put down in 1892, is insufficient for, and too small for modern engines. Some of the clerks have to be accommodated in an old building which is situated a short distance from the depot and which has been condemned by the local health authorities as 'unfit for habitation'..." The recommended improvements, that were estimated to cost £28,808, were; provision of a 70ft articulated turntable, 300 ton mechanical coaling plant, office accomodation in lieu of that horrible hut (the former depot watchman's abode), and other items. To back up the case for modernisation the Directors heard that eighteen men of various grades could be dispensed with and three engines withdrawn, resulting in an estimated net saving of £5,399 per annum.

The above report reveals two additional items of information; namely the apparent pre-1935 removal of one 45ft turntable (from the west end of the yard), and the fact that the coal stage, designed for double-sided working, was actually used on one side only. Assuming the report to be accurate, then quite what caused these changes has not been revealed in the papers studied by the authors so far.

The suggested improvements were authorised and Gresley subsequently made these recommendations:

20th February 1936 - That a quote of £3,795 for a Hot Water Washing-Out Plant, from the Economical Boiler Washing Company be accepted. Approved.

26th March 1936 - That the tender offer of £7,437 - 18 - 8d. by Henry Lees & Co. for a 300 ton mechanical coaling plant be accepted. Approved.

26th March 1936 - That Cowan Sheldon & Co. Ltd's quotation of £1,563, for a 70ft articulated turntable be accepted. *Gresley added that Cowans Sheldon could only hold that price if they also got the job of providing a similar turntable at Colwick engine shed!*

Cowans Sheldon's mild attempt at blackmail worked and Ardsley got its 70ft turntable - installed in the eastern shed yard, which had its track layout necessarily remodelled. Because of the 'made-up' nature of the ground, the turntable foundations were supported by reinforced concrete piles that went no less

than 25ft into the earth. All the works were completed by the latter part of 1937, but although the depot then had a mechanical coaler, the old coal stage was not removed - could not be in fact, as it supported the 200,000 gallon water tank, still very much in use of course. In fact, while the mechanical coaler was receiving a general repair around mid-1948, the original coal stage was once again pressed into service.

1946 and over five decades of use saw the east end of the shed's northlight roof require replacement. The LNER achieved this by use of a light steel frame, supporting corrugated asbestos covering with a brick end screen. Only the nine easternmost bays or 'saw teeth' of the northlight were so treated - not surprising really as this was where locomotives had generally always been prepared, so smoke etc., had therefore been heavier than at the west end of the shed. Nevertheless, within seven years, BR had to reroof the remainder of the depot, which was done using precast concrete beams and asbestos covering, and smaller end screen. So, the result was a hybrid roof which would require little further attention and be retained for the remainder of the shed's service life.

Transfer in June 1956, from the Eastern to North Eastern Region of BR, had little effect upon Ardsley. Neither did the preceding year's Modernisation Plan, as only a few shunting diesels seem to have been stationed at the shed (specifically, Nos.D2591 to D2601, which replaced J50's on shunting duties in the local yards). However, as a follow-up to the Modernisation Plan, the 1963 Beeching Report did affect the depot, in that it axed virtually all the remaining ex-GNR lines in West Yorkshire. Related closure of many small yards in favour of installations like Healey Mills Yard further reduced Ardsley's usefulness so the shed inevitably closed - on 30th October 1965. It is recorded that the very last engine to be despatched from the depot was B1 No.61110, to bring down the curtain on Ardsley's 103 years of engine shed history.

Demolition followed at a date yet unknown, and today, from the nearby M62 motorway, the overgrown site of the shed and yards may be viewed, with only a double track electrified main line passing through on its way to Leeds.

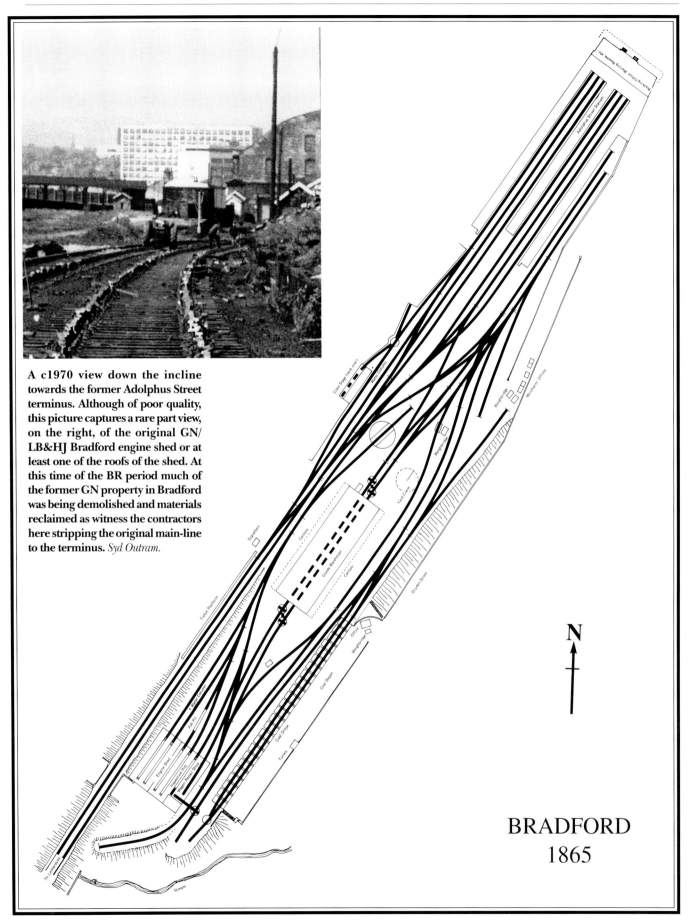

A c1970 view down the incline towards the former Adolphus Street terminus. Although of poor quality, this picture captures a rare part view, on the right, of the original GN/LB&HJ Bradford engine shed or at least one of the roofs of the shed. At this time of the BR period much of the former GN property in Bradford was being demolished and materials reclaimed as witness the contractors here stripping the original main-line to the terminus. *Syd Outram.*

N

**BRADFORD
1865**

BRADFORD

The city of Bradford was for many years the centre of Britain's one-time booming woollen industry. By the early 1890's a large percentage of the quarter million population was employed in some 300 mills, turning out woollen and worsted goods, while most of the remainder of the workforce was occupied in Bradford's considerable coal mining and ironfounding concerns. All of this conjures up visions of something that epitomizes "dark Satanic mills" - the very thing that most attracted Victorian railway builders.

First rails into the city were those of the Leeds & Bradford Railway (later, Midland Railway), whose line via Shipley was opened to the public on 1st July 1846. That was exactly six years and one day before passing of the Act of Incorporation of the Leeds, Bradford & Halifax Junction Railway, which company concluded an agreement with the GNR, on 14th July 1854, for the latter to run its services and provide all stock, plant and staff.

LB&HJ operations started 1st August 1854, with trains running over a connection to the L&Y's line, with running powers to gain access to Halifax. The L&Y, incidentally, had opened its route from Low Moor on 9th May 1850. At Bradford, the LB&HJ had planned its own terminal station at Adolphus Street, complete with goods warehouse and, an engine shed. However, for the first ten months the LB&HJ had to use temporary buildings as its station's roof threatened to collapse and had therefore, to be strengthened. This fact is perhaps revealed by the Minutes of an LB&HJ Board meeting of 23rd May 1854, at which the directors were asked: "....that the amended estimate for the intended station at Bradford, as shown on the plans drawn up by Mr. Hawkshaw, for the sum of £10,500 be accepted. The work is to be of similar construction to the Lancashire & Yorkshire Company's station and the whole to be completed within six months...." It was resolved to proceed and Mr. Hawkshaw was authorised to order the following articles from Messrs. Dunne & Hattersley, of Windsor Bridge Ironworks, Pendleton, near Manchester:

One 40ft turntable for Bradford, @ £300
Two 18ft traversers, @ £170 each
One water crane for Bradford, @ £44
(Plus various warehouse turntables and cranes)

From the Minutes of the next Board meeting, on 10th June 1854, comes the first real mention of Bradford's engine shed, when it was resolved that: "....Mr. Hawkshaw be authorised to take necessary steps for providing the water tank, erecting the engine house and a place for coke and water and the requisite conveniences, the estimate to be sent to the Secretary...." On the same day it was also resolved: "....that notice be given by the Secretary to the Great Northern Company, that the line will be ready for public traffic on the last day of August next...." That projected opening date of 31st August is interesting. Presumably once the GNR 'took over,' following the 14th July agreement, things were speeded up somewhat!

The above would indicate that Adolphus Street station and engine shed were brought into use towards the end of 1854, but in reality this did not take place until 1st June 1855. Certainly, the shed was not in operation at the beginning of that year, as the GN's Rule Book, issued at the time, shows no engine turns under operation from Bradford, all duties being centred upon Leeds. As eventually opened though, the engine shed was almost

square in planform, measuring 94ft wide, by 95ft 8in. long. Constructed in stone, the dead-end building was sub-divided by an internal wall into two sections, 38ft and 56ft wide, with the larger on the north side. Each section had its own single-pitch slated roof, with Queen Post trussing and raised central smoke vent. The roof over the 56ft portion of the depot covered four roads, while the 36ft section contained two roads. All six tracks had arched entrances into the shed and met, to pass a single line of rail between the goods warehouse and main lines. Beyond the warehouse, some 185 yards away, was the 40ft turntable, while the stone-built coke stage, complete with a 30,000 gallon water tank above, stood on the opposite side of the main lines to the turntable; water supplies came from Bradford Corporation. Altogether a cramped and very inconvenient layout, dictated by the amount of land available and the fact that the whole Adolphus Street complex was built on the side of a hill, sloping down to the terminus; the gradient on the main line past the shed was of the order of 1in 46! In fact, the locomotive shed site had to be 'dug in' to the hillside to such an extent that behind the depot a bank reached almost to the full height of the roof!

Apart from its line to Leeds, the LB&HJ opened a branch to Gildersome on 1st August 1854 and this provided the company's first main source of goods traffic, in the form of coal. By 1856 the LB&HJ was beginning to express dissatisfaction with the GN's handling of those coal trains, a most apposite point, with the Gildersome line being extended to link up with the Bradford Wakefield & Leeds Railway, at Ardsley. That particular extension had received Assent to its Act on 10th July 1854, but because of the difficult terrain was not completed until 10th October 1857. The new section of line opened a through route between Wakefield and Bradford, allowing a more direct outlet for LB&HJ mineral and goods traffic. Nonetheless, the dispute between the LBHJ and GNR smouldered on, exacerbated by a further argument about payment by the GN, for running powers over LB&HJ tracks at Leeds (*see* section on Leeds (Wortley) shed). The latter disagreement was not settled until 1861, but two years before that, on 1st January 1859, the GNR withdrew its engines and men from coal workings over the Gildersome and Ardsley branches. That meant the LB&HJ had to quickly find its own motive power, which it eventually did - six 0-6-0's, and on 8th May 1860, the small company had the temerity to ask if the GN would undertake to repair LB&HJ engines at Doncaster! Despite the fact that the GN was still working LB&HJ services elsewhere, it cannot be surprising to learn that the LB&HJ request was denied.

To look after its stud of engines, the railway appointed, in 1859, one F.Rouse to the post of Locomotive Foreman at Bradford whilst at the same time, the GNR appointed their own locomotive foreman at Bradford - a Mr. Judd. This would appear to indicate that both companies had their own locomotive sheds, but from all available evidence it seems that the 4-road and 2-road shed was in joint use. This probably, was not a comfortable arrangement, leading to an LB&HJ Minute of 8th August 1860, which records that the Board thought it necessary to provide new sheds for its engines and carriages. The suggestion at the time was that land should be bought at Bradford, for the erection of a new goods warehouse, with subsequent conversion of the existing warehouse (i.e. in front of the locoshed), into an engine shed and workshops.

The next relevant Minute dated from 8th May 1861, when the LB&HJ Board resolved to provide an ashpit on each road of the engine shed, under the instruction of a Mr. Brayshaw.

BRADFORD
ADOLPHUS STREET

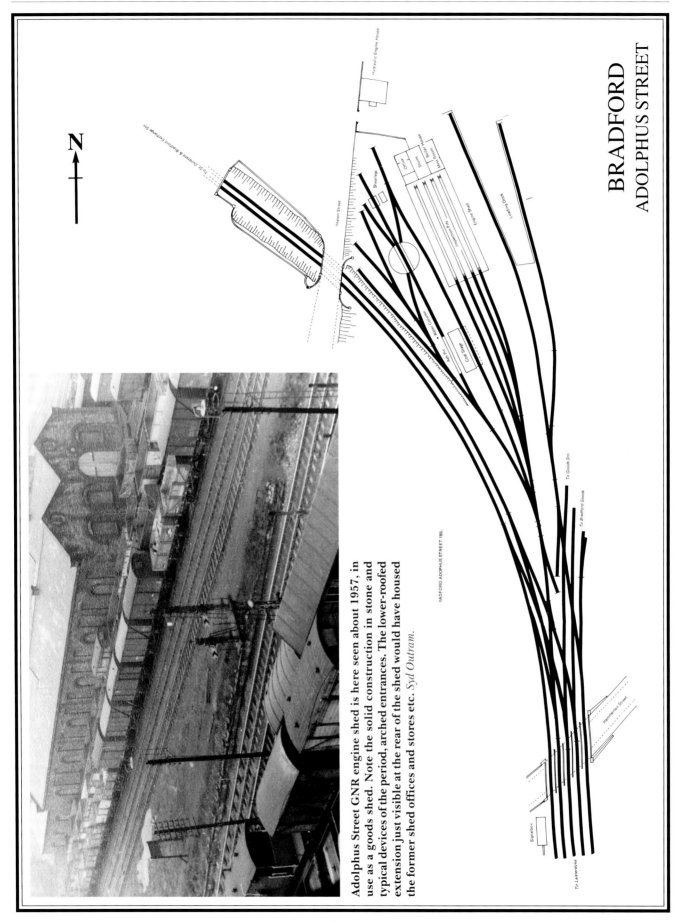

N

To St. Dunstans & Bradford Exchange Stn.

Hydraulic Engine House

Heaton Street

Shearlegs

Office

Stores

Boiler House

Mess Room

Inspection Pit

Engine Shed

Loading Dock

Water Column

Ash Pit

Coal Stage

To Goods Stn.

To Bradford Goods

BRADFORD ADOLPHUS STREET 18b.

Hammerton Street

Signalbox

To Laisterdyke

Adolphus Street GNR engine shed is here seen about 1957, in use as a goods shed. Note the solid construction in stone and typical devices of the period, arched entrances. The lower-roofed extension just visible at the rear of the shed would have housed the former shed offices and stores etc. *Syd Outram.*

Following that, comes an 1864 plan of Bradford, which shows a proposed new goods warehouse on an area of land on the opposite (south) side of the main lines to the engine shed - so the LB&HJ had gone ahead with the suggestion made in August 1860. The same plan reveals that the original engine shed still functioned and internal ashpits were indeed present on the five southernmost roads. The sixth road did not have a pit, but immediately to its rear, a spur entered the shed at a right-angle, accessed by way of a wagon turntable. The author's conjecture is that this was where the LB&HJ was carrying out its repairs to wagons as well as engines, occupying the four road part of the shed, while the GN had use of the two road section. This is confirmed because no other engine shed or workshop is revealed on the plan, or the several other plans in the authors' possession which date from the same period.

Although the new goods shed did get built, it transpired there was no need to convert the old warehouse to an engine shed. That was because the GN and LB&HJ patched up their quarrels, leading to a return to all-GN working on 1st July 1863. Two years after, on 5th July 1865, came the total absorption of the LB&HJ by the GN, with the smaller company's stock of locomotives becoming GNR Nos.162 and 395-399. It was not long before further developments were put in train. On 25th July 1865, with the near prospect of North Eastern and Manchester Sheffield & Lincolnshire Railways' trains entering Bradford, over former LB&HJ tracks, the GN's General Manager said that additional engine shed accommodation would be required. He recommended that a new shed be built and the existing premises be converted into a wool warehouse. Total estimated costs were put at £8,785, with the whole project being referred to the Yorkshire Committee for action.

Action was duly forthcoming , but not quite in the suggested manner it seems. Early in 1866 Sturrock was making strong representations about the company obtaining extra locomotives for the Leeds and Doncaster districts. On 10th March that year Mr. Clark commented to the Yorkshire Committee that while the new engine shed in course of erection at Bradford had foundations for a building to cover twelve engines, the upperworks would provide cover for only eight. Mr. Clark strongly urged that full use should be made of the new building's potential, which was approved, and Bradford's second GN locomotive depot opened 11th February 1867. The first shed was not, in fact, adapted for use as a wool warehouse, because on 10th March 1868, the General Manager, in a report to the Board, recommended that the "small" engine shed at Bradford should be converted into a stables, "with a lean-to added." Nothing seems to have happened though, until 1st July 1875, when tenders were issued for alterations of the building into stables. The job involved creation of 105 stalls for use by the GN's own cartage animals, and the successful tender price was £1,738-18-3d - the contractor was not identified in the Minutes. The company did get its wool warehouse, however, as an 1895 plan shows that appellation for the building on the opposite side of the main line, while the goods shed immediately in front of the first engine shed was by then a grain shed.

Quite how many years the locomotive shed survived as stables is not known, or what, if any, other uses it was put to. Certainly, that same 1895 plan shows the building was still serving GN horses, with the lean-to mentioned in the General Manager's report of 1868 having been added across the width of the building at the rear. Then, early in 1895, £450 was expended in: "....repairing gale damage to the stables at Bradford..." and on

6th June that same year, the GN Board spent £175 in additionally taking over the nearby stables of the well known firm of Pickfords, the move being necessary because of booming traffic. Whatever use was made of it, Adolphus Street engine shed had a long life, as it was not demolished until 1970. Incidentally, the depot's coke stage also saw further use for many years, first as a blacksmith's shop - an annexe to the stables not doubt - and later as a workshop and stores, when a blacksmith's shop 'proper' was built in front of the stables; the stage too was not removed until 1970.

BRADFORD (ADOLPHUS STREET) NO.2 SHED

Note: The "Adolphus Street No.2" appellation is the authors' own, as no identifying name for the GN's second shed has been discovered. Perhaps "Hammerton Street Junction" could be considered more appropriate, as the shed stood in the 'V' of that junction, which had been opened on 7th January 1867; tracks led from it, downgrade to Mill Lane Junction, St. Dunstans, where the L&YR was joined to allow the GN access to Market Street terminus.

As stated above, the GN's second Bradford engine shed opened 11th February 1867. The contractor involved in construction appears to have been Messrs. Bray, Waddington & Co., as the Minutes note that the company was completing the shed's water tank on the day after the depot's official opening. That tank's capacity was 38,000 gallons, with supplies continuing to come from the City Council's waterworks. The tank was sited atop the 65ft x 20ft coke stage, which stood near to the south-east corner of the shed, had a 12ft wide canopy over the wagon road and was constructed in stone. The same building material was used for the shed itself, which was dead-end in pattern and scaled 215ft x 65ft. Internally, each of the four roads was 170ft in length, with the remainder of the space at the rear being utilised for offices, stores, workshops etc. That area was single storey in height and possessed its own twin slated, hipped roofs. Two longitudinal single pitch slated roofs provided cover for the recommended twelve engines, that gained access via the four arched entrances. Smoke vents were placed atop the roof ridges and a circular vent was let into each gable end, just below the roof apices; arch-topped side windows completed a rather attractive building.

Originally, it had been planned to provide a turntable at the new shed, but because of the limited space available on the falling ground, it was decided to use the relatively close-by St. Dunstans triangular junction for turning - not only for engines, but coaching stock too. This was a decision which the GN would come to regret in time, but not until after it had earned the company a little money. On 11th July 1870 the L&YR approached the GN to ask if 'Lanky' engines could use St. Dunstans triangle for turning, while the turntable at Low Moor engine shed was under repair. The GN Board approved the measure "....subject to charges being agreed...."

Apart from seeing the inception of a new engine shed, the years 1866/7 had witnessed plans laid for new GN lines in the Bradford area. On 28th June 1866 an Act was passed for the Bradford Eccleshill & Idle Railway, followed on 12th August 1867 by an Act for the Idle & Shipley Railway. A Deviation Act was necessary for the BE&I, being granted the Royal Assent on 18th July 1872, so that the first section, from Bradford to Idle, could open for mineral traffic only, in February 1873. Extension to

Only an aerial view could give a true idea of how Bradford's three GNR engine sheds were sited in relation to each other. In a picture dated June 1962, we can see, in the foreground, the single arched roof of the former Adolphus Street passenger terminus. To the upper left of this, beyond the triple-roofed goods shed, stands the original 6-road GNR/LB&HJ shed, with its twin gabled roofs and just discerned, one open arched entrance door. Just up and to the right, is a side/rear view of the 1867 4-road GNR-built shed known as "Adolphus Street". Above and beyond that, again in side view can be seen the 1883 10-road Bowling Junction (Hammerton Street) depot, accomodating some diesel multiple units. *Aerofilms.*

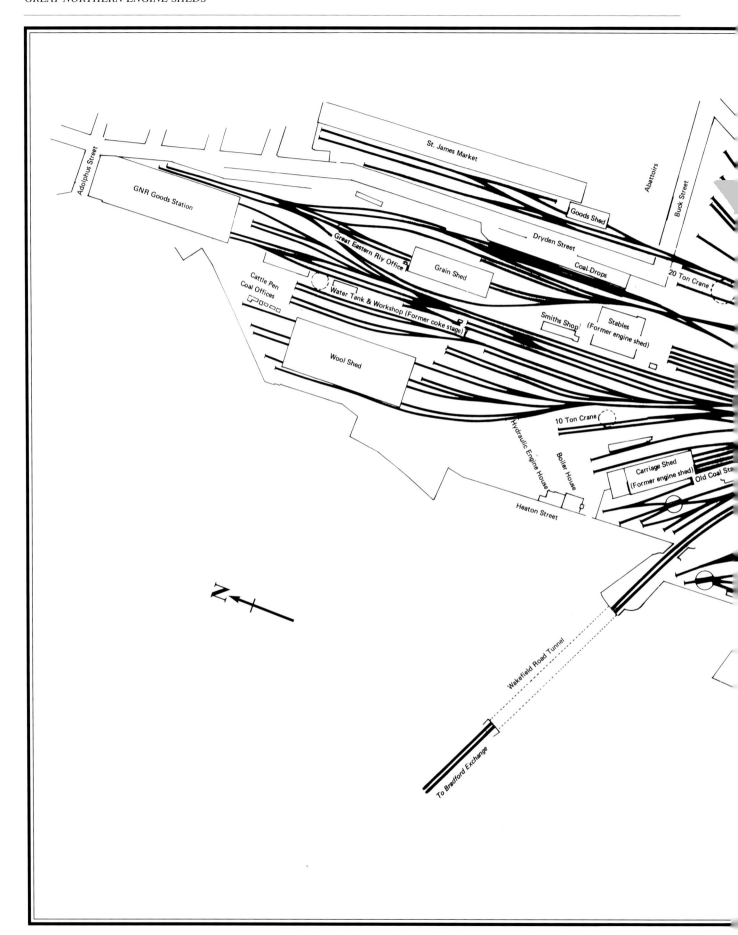

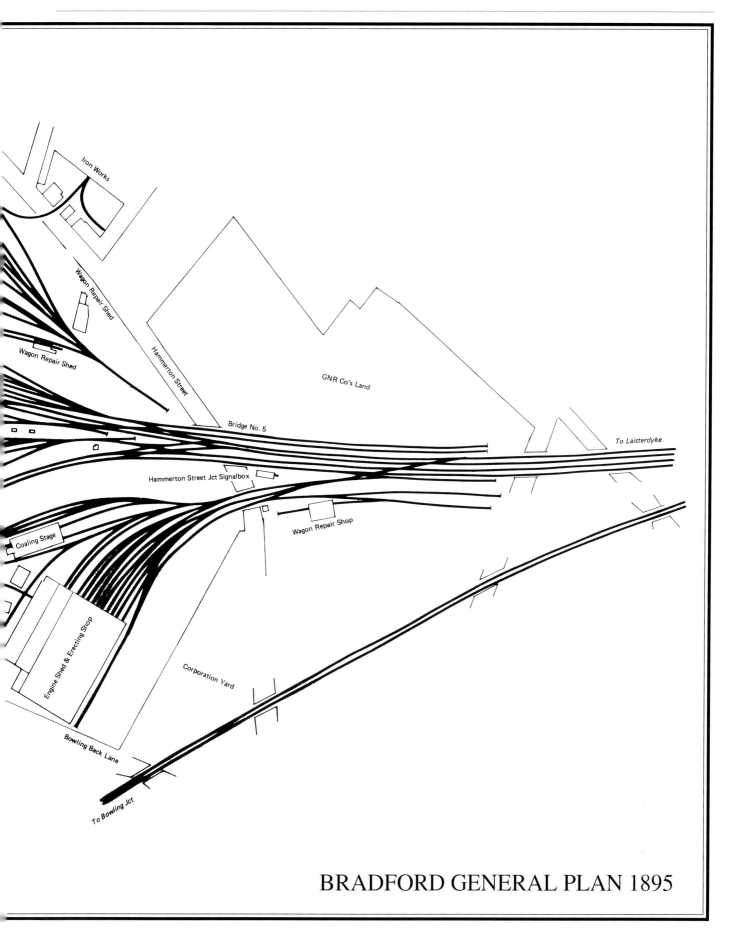

Iron Works

Wagon Repair Shed

Wagon Repair Shed

Hammerton Street

GNR Co's Land

Bridge No. 5

To Laisterdyke

Hammerton Street Jct Signalbox

Wagon Repair Shop

Coaling Stage

Engine Shed & Erecting Shop

Corporation Yard

Bowling Back Lane

To Bowling Jct

BRADFORD GENERAL PLAN 1895

Shipley, for goods traffic, came on 4th May 1874, with passenger trains not commencing until 18th January 1875. Meantime, further Acts had been passed. For example, on 24th July 1871, the Bradford & Thornton Railway, promoted by a separate company, and taken over by the GN under yet another Act, passed on 18th July 1872. That acquisition led to the Halifax Thornton & Keighley Railway Act of 5th August 1873, thereby setting the stage for what was arguably, the most costly venture in the GN's history.

Five months after inception of the branch from Bradford to Idle, on 3rd July 1873, Stirling obtained approval for expenditure of £258, for provision of an additional siding at Bradford shed. Whether the siding was intended for use by locomotives or coal wagons was not recorded, but possibly the latter, as by 10th September 1876, Stirling recorded that the average of the previous ten weeks' coal consumption at Bradford had been 346 tons. Allowing for a fairly 'dead' Sunday, that represents a usage of over 50 tons a day - about five or six loads from the wagons of the day. So, assuming it would be normal practice to keep several days supply of coal on hand, it is probable that storage space was required for a minimum of some twenty wagons, plus more for empties.

Certainly, traffic was increasing, and with new lines opening and more in prospect, it had become clear by 1876 that Adolphus Street terminus would not be able to cope much longer. Accordingly, agreement was reached with the L&YR for the GN's Bradford passenger services to jointly use Bradford Market Street station, later renamed 'Exchange', with subsequent conversion of Adolphus Street station into a goods depot. Part of the alterations at Adolphus Street included removal of a considerable amount of earth from the basement areas, and a Minute of 24th October 1876 notes that the spoil was: "...being used for filling, on land recently purchased from Horfalls Trustees, at Hammerton Street Junction..." That reference was to 32,770 square yards (6¾ acres) of land on the opposite (east) side of Hammerton street Junction to the engine shed, for which the GN paid £12,171 and had exchanged contracts on 3rd June 1875; it was an area that will soon interest us closely.

April 1878 saw commencement of goods services on the Bradford-Queensbury-Thornton line, to be followed by passenger trains on 14th October the same year. The latter date also saw the start of goods workings over the Queeensbury-Holmfield railway, completing at last the GN's own route throughout, from Bradford to Halifax; the Halifax-Holmfield section (incorporated by an Act of 30th June 1864, as the Halifax & Ovenden Railway), had been open for goods traffic since 1st September 1874. But, conditional to his approval for opening of the Queensbury-Holmfield line, with passenger trains in prospect, the Board of Trade inspector insisted that turntables be installed at Bradford and Halifax. This apparently was done at Bradford Exchange station, 'on the cheap' as it were, by use of a small turntable, and passenger workings commenced on 1st December 1879. The result was that officialdom quickly caught up with the GN's parsimony and on 24th March 1880, Stirling had to "urge" replacement of the turntable at Bradford "... as required by the Board of Trade, to alleviate all-tank engine working of some lines..." Even greater urgency was added to this request in May 1880, when the Locomotive Engineer reported that use of triangular junctions at St Dunstans *and* Laisterdyke, for turning engines and coaches was adding to the already 'chronic' congestion - 55 trains a day were using the section between Laisterdyke and Bradford. The upshot was

provision of a 50ft turntable at the south side of Bradford engine shed and enlargement of that at Exchange station, also to 50ft.

The shed's belated turntable was destined to be short-lived though. On the 6th August 1879, Stirling had written to the Way & Works Committee about the need for additional engine shed accommodation at Bradford and Leeds. As noted in the chapter devoted to Leeds (Wortley) engine shed, Stirling seems to have overstated his case with regard to available shed space at each place, saying there was room for only 8 engines. Yet, both Bradford and Leeds sheds could hold 12 engines - Bradford easily so, with 4 internal tracks of 170ft length. Nevertheless, the Committee thought the matter should be dealt with by a Special Committee, consisting of Lord Colville and Messrs. R.Tennant and J.Shuttleworth, reporting directly to the GN Board. In the meantime, the company's Engineer was to draw up plans for cheap, temporary sheds using brick bases and wooden walls. The special committee's findings are lost in history and the temporary sheds were never proceeded with it seems, so on 23rd June 1880, the Locomotive Engineer wrote again, this time to the GN Board, advising of: "...the great need for more engine shed accommodation in the (Yorkshire) District..." His letter was read out on 2nd July and the Board asked the Engineer to prepare plans and estimates for presentation to the Locomotive Committee 26 days later.

It was agreed that provision of a new engine shed would proceed and after first suggestions that it should be sited at Laisterdyke it was, after investigation, decided to build it on the east side of Hammerton Street Junction, on the land bought by the company in 1875. Plans were produced by the Engineer on 31st March 1881, but it was evident that the parcel of land was not of sufficient size. So, a further land purchase was quickly concluded - preliminary negotiations had already taken place it seems, during the latter part of 1880 and early 1881. This time though, developed land was involved and all in all, the GNR bought over 200 cottages from a Mr W.Cole, for £3,000, in an area flanked by Bowling Back Lane. The company tried to obtain an adjoining plot of land, but the owner, a Mr W.Schofield, refused to sell, so the GN's projected development plan had to be amended to skirt his property. What happened to the hapless tenants of Mr Cole's 200 cottages was not recorded, but it seems they could hardly have been more hapless, when the average value of their homes was less than £15 each!

With the necessary land secured, tenders for construction of the engine shed were issued, and subsequently opened on 10th August 1881. Prices ranged from a high of £33,246-7-1d, to the lowest, at £29,570-11-4d. After "due consideration" by the GN Board the lowest tender, from Messrs. Armitage & Hodgson was accepted, with the price split - £21,510 for the shed and associated structures, and the remainder being expended on site preparation. The latter operation took some time as the old problem of falling ground pertained. The 1876 tipping of earth had helped, but Armitage & Hodgson still had to build up the land level by an average of 13ft and provide massive foundations averaging 20ft in depth, with the greatest piling being driven to 24ft 6in. This meant that construction was a more protracted business than normal, with the consequences that the GNR's third engine shed at Bradford did not open until March 1883.

With commissioning of the new shed, Adolphus Street No.2 depot closed for locomotive purposes and immediately turned over for use as a carriage shed. The turntable and coal stage were removed around 1900, but essentially, the building remained unaltered, even when usage passed from carriage shed

A close-up of an abandoned Adolphus Street shed in 1970; the building is 103 years old and the demolition men are just about to move in. *Syd Outram.*

GNR 0-4-2 No.35 and its crew pose in front of Bowling Junction shed sometime in the 1890s, offering a rare glimpse of the depot's original northlight roof. *K.Leech collection.*

Bowling Junction's turntable was sited, as may be seen, at the shed's eastern extremity. Note the elevated line with single wagon - the original coaling stage's storage line - with behind, loaded wagons waiting to feed the mechanical coaling plant. April 1957. *Syd Outram.*

Green liveried, ex-Great Central 4-6-0, LNER B4 No.6099, is seen at Bradford in the early 1930s. All ten of the B4's were resident in the West Riding by 1926 allocated between Ardsley and Copley Hill sheds. 6099 was an Ardsley engine from 2nd January 1926 to 21st November 1942 except for a three month spell in early 1940 when it resided at Gorton. After going to Doncaster in 1942, it then went to Copley Hill in June 1945 and then later in the year began a near six month allocation to Bradford from 2nd December finally returning to Ardsley in May 1946 from where it was withdrawn in November 1947. Another B4, No.6101, had several spells at Bradford from 1941 to 1946. This picture is also valuable in that in the background it offers a very rare glimpse of Bowling Junction shed's original coaling stage. *Authors' collection.*

to goods shed sometime around 1919. After only a short time as a goods shed, three of the four entrances were bricked up. As such, it continued to serve well into British Railways' times, to be demolished in August 1970, during the general clearance of the Adolphus Street complex. Thus, for 87 years it was possible to view three generations of GN engine shed at Bradford, as superbly depicted by the aerial photograph on page 26, dating from June 1962.

BRADFORD (BOWLING JUNCTION)

Note: The GNR of course normally referred to this shed - and its two antecedents - merely as Bradford. Nevertheless, over the years, it was also variously alluded to in GNR and LNER official documents as "Bowling," "Bowling Back," "Bowling Junction" and "Hammerton Street." Bowling Junction is adopted here as that was the most common usage, until formally being used by the LNER in its latter period. Hammerton Street *was* also used by the LNER, but less frequently so - this being the name by which the shed became most widely known to generations of "spotters," in the BR era.

Bradford's third and last Great Northern engine shed comprised a 10-road dead-end building constructed in stone and having a period northlight roof, with slates on the unglazed faces. The depot's capacity was variously quoted as 50 or 60 engines, which at 250ft in length (by 145ft in width), would both be correct, if referring to tender engines only, or a mixture of tender and tank types. Adjoining the shed on the western side was a stone built repair shop, scaling 220ft by 40ft, with a slated hipped roof carried high enough to permit installation of an overhead travelling crane. The repair shop was dead-end in pattern and situated along the outside of its western wall were an office, boiler house and various workshops, all single storey structures in stone, each featuring slated gabled roofs; at the rear of the repair shop were a fitting shop and cleaners' mess room. West of all these came an access road, then a stores block and a 57ft by 30ft office building. North of the stores block came the 26ft by 54ft coaling stage, built in brick and equipped with two half-ton capacity cranes and a 20ft canopy over the coaling road. In a departure from normal practice, the shed's water tank was not mounted above the coaling stage; the tank was a large one for the period - nearly 86,500 gallons capacity - so the 8ft high edifice stood atop the stone office building mentioned earlier. At the south-west corner of the shed site, near the end of the coaling road, a 50ft turntable was installed and because turntables and coal stages invariably meant the heaviest weights, spread over a relatively small area, those at Bradford required the deepest foundations - 24ft 6in. This probably also explains why the coal stage and turntable pit were made in brick, that being a lighter construction material than the York stone used in all other buildings. The shed's facilities were completed by a sand furnace and dock on the outside of the western wall, served by a siding.

The repair, or erecting shop was based on the pattern evolved at Doncaster (Carr) shed in 1876, and repeated at Colwick the year before Bowling Junction shed opened. Equipment for the Bradford repair facility was similar to that provided at Colwick and had been ordered at Stirling's behest, on 24th March 1882. On that date, the Locomotive Engineer had detailed his requirements as follows:

5ft 6in wheel lathe for locomotive wheels, from Messrs. Hunt & Sacre: £425

12in piston turning lathe: £170
Self-acting lathe, driven by corn pulleys: £70
Radial drilling machine: £125
A Smiths fan: £20
Shaping machine: £125
Hand-powered 25 ton overhead travelling crane, for lifting engines, complete: £600

Added to the above, Stirling said: "...it will be necessary to construct in the company's workshops at Doncaster a steam engine, boiler, shafting and pulleys, at £500..." The total of all this was £2,035.

First developments to affect Bradford's new shed came in April 1884, when the Thornton-Keighley line was completed and at Ingrow, provided a second out-station for which Bowling Junction had to supply engines. The first out-station, Halifax, had been subordinate to Bradford since 1854, but would disappear around 1887, to be replaced in 1890 by Holmfield. Such new lines and services brought ever increasing traffic to Bradford, with consequent additions to the locomotive fleet stationed there. In 1896 ninety-five locomotives were allocated, of which six and four were out-stationed at Holmfield and Ingrow respectively. The eighty-five remaining at Bowling Junction were causing problems over water and coal consumption - the first because of the cost and the second because of demands made upon the shed's coaling stage and its method of operation.

First to be tackled was the search for an alternative to the expensive Bradford Corporation water supply. On 28th July 1899, a contract for a borehole was let to the specialist firm C.Islar and by 2nd November 1899, boring had reached 127ft without success. The next mention comes from no less than three years later, 2nd December 1902, when the Minutes record that drilling had reached the huge depth of 772ft, with water being present but not at exploitable level! Undaunted, the GN carried on and with the passage of a further year, to Christmas Day 1903, Ivatt was able to report: "...the bore hole has reached 894ft through grey shale; water level stands at 232ft from surface, having risen 5ft since last report. 13ft of boring has been done since last month and 36½ft done since boring recommenced on 12th October..." Quite when drilling had ceased before October 1903 is not clear, but it was to be suspended again, as recorded on 23rd January, 24th June and 26th November 1905, when it was noted that recommencement of drilling for water had been "postponed again." After that, the Minute books are mute but a subsequent GN register of water suppliers still shows Bradford Corporation feeding all the GN's operations in the city, so after what must have been a very considerable expense, the company had obviously admitted defeat. However, there were to be further developments!

Savings were more easily predicted and achieved with regard to Bowling Junction's coaling operations. On 2nd November 1899, Ivatt noted: "...the coaling arrangements at Bradford are old-fashioned, with coal being wound up in tubs. There is sufficient space to make an incline up to the coal stage and alter it the way we did to the one at Ardsley. The cost of this is estimated at £1,500 and I can guarantee a saving (annually) of 10% of the outlay..." The expenditure was approved next day and the job completed around mid-1900.

Efficiency was greater increased in 1902, when a telephone line was installed between Bradford and Leeds (Copley Hill) engine sheds - this facility is more fully described in the chapter on Copley Hill. The same year saw the first record of roof repairs being necessary at Bradford shed. Quite what caused the problem

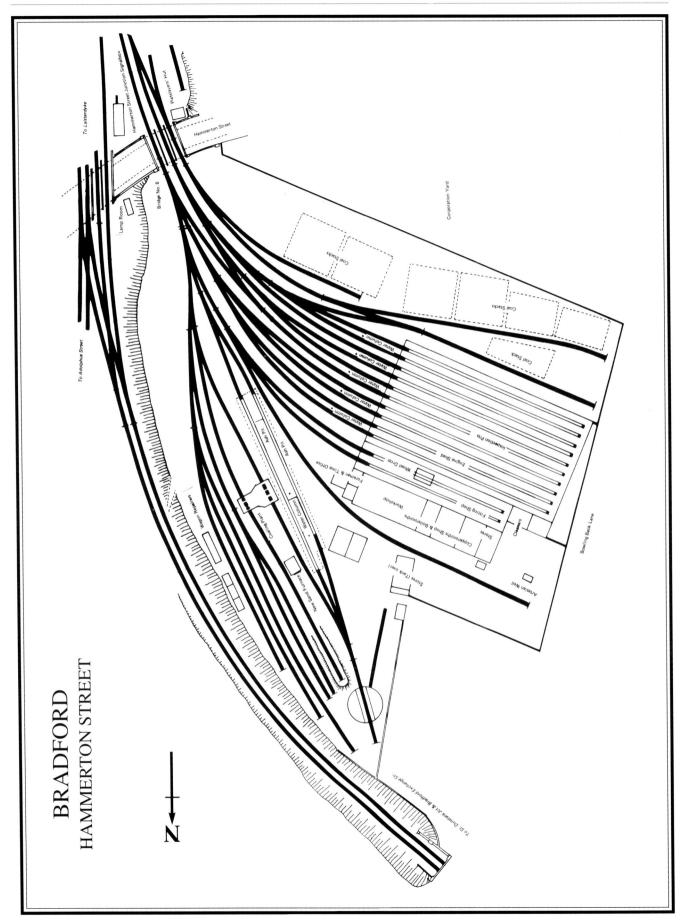

BRADFORD
HAMMERTON STREET

was not noted - the usual northlight syndrome perhaps - but whatever it was cost £176-6-8d. to rectify. Nearly seven years later, on 25th January 1909, the Minutes announce more expenditure on roofing work. That particular job involved rebuilding of the roof over the Locomotive Stores, at a cost of £135. Again, the reason was not stated, although it is safe to assume a fire was the cause of damage, because on 25th June 1909, a further £90 was spent on provision of a new fire main and hydrant "near the locomotive stores."

Seven more years were to elapse before mention of Bowling Junction shed next appears in the archives. By the middle period of World War One, that conflict's drain on manpower had necessitated widespread employment by Britain's railways of women, mainly for engine cleaning work. The GNR was no exception and on 25th November 1916, approval was given for expenditure of £107, to provide a mess and lavatories for those women working at Bradford depot. The result was a building of 'permanent' nature, which was taken over by Bowling Junction's men, when their erstwhile female colleagues returned to more normal pursuits.

The immediate post-war period brought improved conditions of employment for Britain's railwaymen, with one major factor being a reduction in working hours. The knock-on effect was increased engine turn-rounds, which placed greater burdens upon shed facilities. Bradford was so affected and late in 1919, Gresley commented upon the need for more engine pit accommodation at the shed. The Locomotive Engineer stated that: "...overtime is necessary to get the engines away on time, which is costing £240 per annum..." Estimated cost of the ash pit extension was put at £956, which was finally approved on 1st July 1920, with completion of the work on 25th February 1921.

A further alteration was sanctioned on 7th October 1920, when costs of £2,236 were approved, for enlargement of Bowling Junction's turntable, from 50ft to 55ft. The job actually involved removal of the 1903 table from Grantham shed, its overhaul and re-installation at Bradford. Of course, most of the cost of the work was for alteration of Bowling Junction's turntable pit with its deep foundations, and to keep the price down the whole job was carried out by GN employees, with completion during November 1921. That was the last recorded GN alteration to the depot, so before considering the LNER and BR periods, let us pass briefly over the shed's locomotive history.

Engine types stationed were dictated, to a large extent, by the city's position as a centre point of a number of hilly railway lines. Earliest examples would have included the 2-4-0s of 223 class, specifically designed by Sturrock for the West Riding and delivered by Hawthorn's Leeds factory in 1855/6. These were followed in 1858 by eight "small passenger engines" taken from earlier GN stock and modified by Sturrock for "300 pounds each." During the period of estrangement between the GNR and LBHJ, the latter's fleet of six 0-6-0's were working from Bradford, continuing to do so after absorption by the GN in 1865. At the same time, the GN absorbed the West Yorkshire Railway (ex-Bradford Wakefield & Leeds Railway), and that small company's engines too were to be seen at Bradford. In fact, one of them, 0-6-0T No.470, was allocated to Bradford until withdrawn in 1872. Interestingly, No.470, as 'rebuilt' by Stirling to Class J19 0-6-0ST - using only the wheel centres of the original 470 - returned to Bradford as shed pilot, in the early years of the 20th century.

Other tank engine classes were the rebuilds of early Sharp and Bury locomotives, being joined in the late 1860's by the

first of Stirling's 0-4-2 tanks. None of these types found particular favour with West Riding enginemen, largely because of the poor protection offered by their open cabs. However, in 1881 there came from Doncaster Nos.658 to 661, a departure from previous GN designs, an 0-4-4T with side tanks and an enclosed cab that set new standards in comfort for footplatemen. The engines had been designed by Stirling for the explicit purpose of working in the Bradford area, so it is not surprising they soon became known as the "Bradford Bogie Tanks." Sixteen of the 0-4-4T were constructed, with ten - Nos.658-661, 682, 683, 762-765 - being allocated to Bradford and the other six going to London. At Bradford their 5ft 1in wheels and power - they were also nicknamed "Wolves," on account of their distinctive exhaust bark - were great assets over the district's difficult railway routes. For other, 'traditional' tank engine pursuits - shunting, banking, local goods work, etc., Stirling 0-6-0St were long a feature of the West Riding, followed by Ivatt's J13 (LNER J52) model.

Goods duties on Bradford shed's roster were for many years purely local in nature; for example, the GNR's 1889 WTT shows no main line goods working from the depot. Engines used were Sturrock, then Stirling 0-4-2 and 0-6-0, both types frequently appearing on passenger turns, which were also mainly of a local nature. But, by the early 1900's, things had changed somewhat as the following collection of notes illustrates. The notes come from the records of Dr. John Sykes, a well known student of the GNR in West Yorkshire, and the writers are indebted to him for permission to reproduce them here:

In the period from 1903-7 the average allocation of Bradford shed was 90 engines, including the following:

Class	Type	Numbers
C2	4-4-2T	1015, 1016, 1017, 1018, 1020
D2	4-4-0	1301, 1302
F2	0-4-2	35, 37, 75, 105, 106, 200, 325, 584, 587, 589, 591, 952, 954
G3	0-4-4T	658, 659, 682, 695, 697, 762, 765
G4	0-4-4T	661, 763, 764
J5	0-6-0	323, 334A, 360A, 640, 797, 1089, 1090, 1146, 1147, 1148, 1149, 1150
J6	0-6-0	150A, 163, 171, 300A, 372, 427A, 723, 733, 741, 742, 750, 835
J7	0-6-0	484
J14	0-6-0ST	929, 978, 980, 1052, 1053
J15	0-6-0ST	397, 494, 495, 496, 497, 616, 634, 635, 636, 680, 681, 779, 780, 852, 853, 904 913, 914, 916
J19	0-6-0ST	470, 471
L1	0-8-2T	130, 131

Plus two GCR 0-6-0's, outstationed from Gorton and Grimsby. At the two out-stations of Ingrow and Holmfield, available records show only the following engines allocated during the period in question:

Ingrow:

Class	Type	Number
G2	0-4-4T	128
J15	0-6-0ST	619

Holmfield

Class	Type	Number
F7	0-4-2ST	631, 632 (631 withdrawn February 1904)
G2	0-4-4T	657

Several Bradford crews had knowledge of the road to Peterborough, for the depot's main line turns to Peterborough and March (GER) (it is not clear if Bradford men and/or machines worked throughout on all duties). Special workings were also taken through to London, in which case Ardsley shed provided pilotmen who knew the road south of Peterborough.

The L1 0-8-2T came to Bradford in 1905, with one of the class' first duties being a football special from Leeds (Central) to Horton Park (for Park Avenue) via the St Dunstans curve. After that the big tanks were put into a link with the re-boilered J15 No.913. One of the link's duties comprised:

1515   Goods Bradford to Keighley.
1915   Goods Keighley to Wrenthorpe (a non-stop working - the "Keighley Wringer" [*see* Ingrow])
          Wrenthorpe to Laisterdyke
Another duty involved the 0610 goods Laisterdyke-Morley, followed by shunting at Morley, Soothill Wood Colliery and Batley.

Bradford's 0-6-0's saw use on numerous local workings, such as the "Thornton Shunt":
1130   Light engine to Thornton.
          Whole day on Keighley branch.
2030   Pick-up goods Keighley-Bradford.
Bowling Junction's top link passenger turns at that time were as follows, worked by D2's 1301 and 1302, sent to the shed 1903 specially for the services:
(a)
1410   Light engine to Bradford Exchange.
1435   Bradford to Retford (King's Cross train), via Morley and Wakefield (Westgate).
          Turn engine at Retford.
2057   Retford to Halifax (train from King's Cross), via Doncaster, Wakefield (Kirkgate), Mirfield and Brighouse (note working over L&Y lines).
2240   Arrive Halifax.
          Light engine to Bowling Junction.
(b)
0910   Light engine to St Dunstans sidings; propel train to Bradford Exchange.
1000   Bradford to Doncaster (King's Cross Luncheon Car train), via Morley and Wakefield (Westgate).
1110   Arrive Doncaster
          Turn engine.
1241   Doncaster to Bradford (train from King's Cross - the fastest working between London and Bradford).
1338   Arrive Bradford. Then:
          Bradford to Leeds.
          Leeds to Leeds (circular working).
          Leeds to Bradford.
1845   Light engine to Bowling Junction.
Local passenger trains involved Bowling Junction's 0-6-0's on such duties as the "267 Guard's Working:"
1715   Light engine to Bradford Exchange.
1735   Passenger Bradford to Keighley.
1837   Passenger Keighley to Halifax.
          Goods Halifax to Bradford.
There were also such special workings as race trains to Doncaster and in summer, from Halifax to the East Coast, particularly Scarborough. 0-6-0 from Bradford took these trains, which usually loaded to nine coaches, working over the hills unassisted. A very special 'one-off' train of the period was the "Showvan Special", which the GN took over from the Midland at Keighley. From Keighley to Batley, via St Dunstans, where it was taken over by the LNWR for passage to Longsight (for Belle Vue), the train was worked by double-headed 0-6-0's, with a third as rear banker, to Dudley Hill.

Such was the pattern of things until Grouping, with the notable exceptions of the 1914 departure of the L1 and the 1912

arrival of Ivatt's N1 0-6-2T. They were used on locals to Halifax and Keighley and to Leeds, via both Pudsey and Stanningley. By the 1930's N1 monopolised Bradford's No.2 link (see below), and continued through until the last survivors were withdrawn in April 1959. One long term member of the class at Bradford was LNER 4574 - BR 69474 - taken out of service in March 1959 after 47 years in the West Riding. Four N1 were provided by Bradford for the last day services over the Bradford, Keighley and Halifax, via Queensbury lines, on 21st May 1955; until the 1933 and 1936 closures of Holmfield and Ingrow sub sheds respectively, N1 had been out-stationed at both places.

N2 appeared around 1931, partly replacing N1, but never entirely succeeding them; one of the N2's duties in the 2 years prior to World War Two, was in double-harness on *THE WEST RIDING LIMITED* between Bradford and Leeds. Other 0-6-2T working from Bradford were N7 Nos.7991, 7996 and 7997 for a short time in 1924, with eight of the class returning for twenty months, early 1942 - late 1943; as in 1924 the class was not popular. Better liked were ex-GC N5, of which Bowling Junction had a brace, from 1935, with the complement doubling to four by Nationalisation., but to disappear by the early 1950's.

Smaller tank types saw the demise of Stirling's 0-4-4T by 1926 and the gradual decline of Stirling and Ivatt 0-6-0ST, including the last J54 in the district, No.3908, leaving late in 1933, and the last West Yorkshire J55, No.3859, going in February 1944. J52 also reduced, and all these types went in favour of Gresley's J50/1, a class designed with the West Riding in mind and nicknamed the "Ardsley Tanks:" an allocation of two in the early 1930's had risen to a peak of twenty by the 1950's. Ivatt's C2 (LNER C12) were very long-lived, first appearing in 1898/9 and remaining in West Yorkshire until the mid-1950's. Further ex-GC tank engines came in the guise of A5 4-6-2T during the 1937-42 period, and from 1950-54, three C14 4-4-2T; both types shared in local passenger workings during their sojourns at Bradford. Lastly, for a short time in 1949, Thompson L1 2-6-4T No.67762 was tried out at Bradford, in use on the through Bradford-King's Cross portions as far as Wakefield - the class was not retained.

Bradford's passenger workings reduced after Grouping, the shed losing the regular turn to Retford. Nevertheless, the Doncaster duty remained and with the summer East Coast excursions, Bradford-Wakefield, Bradford-Leeds portions of King's Cross workings, kept the depot's passenger engine busy. Ivatt's 4-4-0 and 0-6-0 continued to monopolise such workings until 1929/30, when a trio of ex-GC Class B6 4-6-0 arrived in the West Riding - Nos.5052, 5053 and 5416 - they spent some time working from Bowling Junction until mid-1934. Two years later, K2 2-6-0 came to Bradford, with three being present by the end of 1938 and staying until 1942; the class made a brief re-appearance in 1945/6. Further GC passenger power returned in 1941, with B4 No.6101, which stayed until 1943, working mainly on London trains between Bradford and Wakefield. Shortly before Nationalisation Thompson B1's arrived and mostly took over all the N1's Bradford-Wakefield duties; by 1952, eight B1 were allocated, most staying until the depot closed to steam.

Goods duties remained the preserve of 0-6-0's in the main, but O4 2-8-0 were seen from 1924 to 1927 and again from 1947 for a short time. Then, in 1950, a single O4 came on the scene again, and after several members of the class had worked from Bradford, No.63920 became resident from December 1953, until January 1958. Prime use seems to have been made of the O4 on

An April 1939 picture of the mechanical coaling plant provided by the LNER in 1937. Note that although the coaler has electric lighting, the yard lamps are still gas-powered. Other improvements carried out at the time included raising the two existing disposal pits with an appliance for the removal of ashes. The total expenditure of the 1937 scheme came to £9,000. *British Railways.*

May 1948 - Bowling Junction's northlight roof has been modified, but after 5 months of BR ownership, it has little time left. *B.Hilton.*

The shed's roof has been removed in readiness for its new covering. This will be applied "on the cheap" though, because the original cast iron supporting columns have unusually been retained for re-use. Former GN locomotive types, with a mixture of liveries, dominate the stabling roads. *H.L.Overend.*

such duties as the Hull goods. That working had mainly occupied a pair of ex-GC Q4 0-8-0, between 1929 and 1941, with No.3217 of the class returning to the job in 1946, finally going in 1950. GNR 0-8-0's of Class Q1/2 also worked from Bowling Junction, they were employed on workings within the district - to Ardsley and over the Keighley and Halifax branches. In LNER times, J39 came in 1928 and an average of three was allocated during the latter period of the 1930's, disappearing after WW2, to return around 1955, until 1958. Of former GNR 0-6-0 classes, J1 and J2 had left by 1943, J3 and J4 stayed until the early BR period, while a handful of Gresley's J6 were resident at the end.

It is interesting to note the ebb and flow of Bradford's locomotive allocation, rising from forty, in the late 1870's, to ninety-five by 1896 and staying around ninety engines through to Grouping. By September 1931, Bradford's roster had been cut back to seventy, but a visit to the shed, on 6th April that year found only thirty-one inmates; these were:

B6	5053
C12	4009A, 4013, 4017, 4020, 4528, 4539, 4540
J1	3004, 3005, 3006, 3008, 3009
J2	3071, 3080
J3	4036, 4097, 4098, 4119, 4134, 4135, 4146, 4150
J4	4084
J39	1289
J50	3223, 3233
J52	4053
N1	4564, 4568, 4569, 4572, 4593, 4594, 4595
N2	2589

By September 1933, numbers had reduced by one, falling again in March 1936 to sixty-three. Dr. John Sykes has again been of immeasurable assistance to the authors and below is listed Bradford's links for the mid-1930's period:

No.1 Link Express Passenger to Wakefield, Doncaster, Leeds and Halifax - 6 turns.
No.2 Link Local Passenger work on Leeds-Wakefield-Bradford services - 12 turns.
No.3 Link Local Passenger and Mixed Passenger and Goods diagrams, covering Keighley, Halifax and Shipley lines - 24 turns.
No.4 Link "Special B Link" - Express Goods work - 6 turns.
No.5 Link Tender Goods Link, including Ballast diagrams, Banker turns and 'Q' turns - 26 turns.
No.6 Link Tank Goods Link - 20 turns.
No.7 Link Shunt Link. Includes several Control sets, used for Relief purposes - 24 turns.
No.8 Link Shed Enginemen, 6 Drivers, 3 Firemen.
No.9 Link "Demic Link" - 4 turns (approx.).

The "Demic Link" is an intriguing name, the origins of which appear to be entirely local. Apparently in Bradford to be Demic means to be unfit for normal duty, due to illness or injury. In other words, the Demic Link was worked by men unable to undertake any but the lightest duties.

In the Spring of 1939, the shed was still operating 55-60 engines, yet a visit on Saturday 29th May that year found only twenty-nine engines 'at home'. True, it was the Whitsun Holiday weekend, so the number of engines 'off shed' was larger than would normally have been the case:

C12	4018*, 4517*, 4530*, 4536
J1	3005, 3008
J2	3071, 3079
J3	3398, 4134, 4153*
J4	4041
J39	1487, 2973

J50	589, 591, 3159, 3164†, 3166, 3170
J52	4053
K2	4670
N1	4568
N2	2583, 2585
Q4	6135, 6178

* - Stored; † - Repair shop.

By January 1947, the number of locomotives working from Bradford had diminished to fifty, with one fewer by August 1950. The decline in numbers continued until the last days of steam at the shed, when about thirty-five engines were present - classes B1, J6, J39, J50 and the faithful N1 remaining to the end.

Going back to LNER days, no improvements were recorded before 1934, when a wheel drop was installed in the repair shop. This was the such only facility to be provided in the West Riding District and it is frankly surprising that it was not fitted at Ardsley, which had a much larger allocation of locomotives. Then, in 1936, it was recorded that coal consumption at Bowling Junction shed had reached 35,000 tons per year and this was deemed sufficient to justify provision of a mechanical coaling plant. Accordingly, in 1937, a 175 ton capacity coaler was erected on the depot's west side and the 1883 coal stage, with 1900 ramp and other modifications, dismantled.

Consideration of the new coaler brings us back to that early 1900's search for an alternative water supply, which had figuratively and literally "dried up", about 1905. This makes it impossible to explain a 28th August 1937 plan of the mechanical coaler's foundations, clearly endorsed to the fact that "standing water" had been found at a depth of 19 feet below rail level! Then comes a 1939 plan which shows that an artesian well had been bored at Bowling Junction, sited at the rear of the repair shop. When that well had been bored is not known, but the fact that it was "artesian" in principle, plus having standing water at only 19 feet, makes a mockery of the GNR's expensive and fruitless quest at the beginning of the century!

The next works concerned the shed's northlight roof, which had virtually expired after 56 years service, i.e. by the start of the Second World war. Blackout precautions made replacement doubly necessary and this was done as speedily and cheaply as possible, using asbestos sheeting laid on the original cross ties and columns. That sufficed, with frequent patching up, into BR times, during the early part of which the shed saw some very distinguished visitors. That was in 1951, when re-wheeling of East Coast Pacifics was being carried out on quite a large scale. Bradford's wheel drop was pressed into service and it is noted that during October 1951, the following 4-6-2's came to the depot to be fitted with new wheel sets: A1. - 60123, 60144; A3. - 60065; A4. - 60007, 60028, 60034.

It is known that other Pacifics did come to the shed for attention to their wheels, but not in the same numbers as in 1951. A couple of years later the decision was taken to house first generation diesel multiple units at Bradford, Bowling Junction - or Hammerton Street, as it was then officially christened. Steam was not considered finished just then though, so when during 1953/4, a new steel and asbestos roof, with brick end screens was fitted, the depot's hot ash pit underwent a much needed rebuilding. To accommodate the new diesels, an internal wall was constructed between the 4th and 5th roads on the eastern side and new doors were fitted across the width of the four partitioned off roads. However, the fourth road was 'lifted' inside the shed to allow space for specialised repair equipment, with the track ending at a buffer stop just outside; the remaining six roads and repair shop continued in use by steam locomotives.

First of the "Derby Lightweight" DMU's arrived in 1954, to be followed in 1955 by announcement of the BR Modernisation Plan. One of the results of impending wide-spread dieselisation was the decision to turn over Hammerton street to all-diesel working at an early date. Initially £12,430 was spent to receive these first units in 1955 but a greater amount was expended during 1959 and 1960 conversion. In January 1958, the shed lost its last steam engines to the nearby ex-L&Y depot at Low Moor. The ensuing influx during 1959/60, of further DMU's and diesel shunting locomotives, saw additional modifications to buildings and facilities at Hammerton Street, amounting to a cost of £106,350. New electric lighting was installed, all but one of the inspection pits inside the former 6-road steam section of the shed were filled in and the redundant turntable, water tank and coaling tower dismantled.

Work was completed in time for the 1961 debut of the Calder Valley DMU's, designed specifically for the railway along that valley and a type that became synonymous with Hammerton Street depot. As with many BR diesel designs though, there were early problems with the new units, particularly in regard to their heating boilers. However, Hammerton Street's artisans summoned up their new found skills, tackled, and remedied the faults with a series of modifications that came to be adopted as standard BR practice. Further evidence of the staff's keenness, loyalty - call it what you like - came in 1964, when DMU trailer E59706 caught fire at the shed. In the words of the official report on the incident, several staff, in particular the depot foreman, "risked their lives" to get the DMU's power cars to safety.

After that bit of excitement, about ten years passed until another improvement was made. this concerned the conversion of the repair shop's overhead crane to electric power - and not before time as the laboriously-operated hoist required no less than four men to work it! Another ten years passed, seemingly uneventfully, except for the fact that West Riding train services dwindled, lines and yards were closed or "rationalised," and the motive power fleet reduced accordingly. Even though during recent years there has been a dramatic resurgence of rail travel within the West Riding, due largely to action by enlightened local authorities, Hammerton Street diesel depot had, by 1984, become surplus to requirements. Accordingly, on 13th May that year, the shed was formally closed, two months into its 102nd year, 75 of which had been spent in service to the steam locomotive. At closure, all remaining DMU's (locomotives had disappeared some time before) and men not taking retirement terms, were transferred to Leeds (Neville Hill) depot.

The authors visited the shed in August 1990, to find it prominently marked with "For Sale" signs. All the buildings were still complete although it was evident that the 1954 asbestos roof covering the one-time six road steam section had been missing for some years: even so, the 1883 cast iron columns still stood and had obviously been used to support the BR-built roof. The last of the six internal pits was still present and the original four road diesel portion retained not only its roof, but also its pits, internal rails and doors. This section of the building had housed a preserved Class 506 EMU for a time, from April 1985, in the hope that the building would form the nucleus of a transport museum. This did not come to pass, however, and the EMU was moved away, finally leaving the shed empty. At the time of the visit, the repair shop, also empty, was virtually untouched still featuring its pits and overhead travelling crane. The offices at the rear of the depot were in use for second-hand car sales and

the former single road diesel inspection shed was employed for car repairs.

In 1991 the decaying depot was finally demolished, leaving either Hornsey, or the remaining half of Doncaster (Carr) shed as the largest ex-GNR engine shed still in existence.

Bradford shed's sand-drying house is seen here in diesel days - by then, disused of course - while a worker goes in search of a quiet place to drink his cup of tea. Note how the railway wasted nothing, by re-using old sleepers and rails with which to build and retain a ramped line of rail. *Syd Outram.*

A 1979 interior shot of the erstwhile "steam section" of Hammerton Street clearly shows, at the bottom of the inspection pits, the tops of the arches upon which the entire building was supported. *Syd Outram.*

(*above*) **Bowling Junction was known as Hammerton Street during BR days and the shed is seen here in September 1961, displaying the roof received some years before and with the building as later modified for the introduction of diesel traction. Initially, this comprised the four shed roads seen at left segregated for the new regime, with the right hand road actually taken out to allow more space for repairs etc. By 1961 the shed was all-diesel in content, but still the six right hand roads remain separated as they were for steam locomotives, for the few years before they were moved away.** *W.T.Stubbs.*

(*right*) **Seen in 1984 the interior of the high-roofed repair shop waits for the demolition men. In essence, little has changed after 101 years' use.** *Authors' collection.*

(*below*) **By 1984 Hammerton Street had been mostly abandoned and once again lost the roof over the former steam section. This was the time when it was hoped to use the shed as the basis for a museum, but this was not to be and the building was demolished eight years later, at the age of 109 years.** *Authors' collection.*

The south end of Doncaster station in August 1909, with a marvellous array of signals and showing in the centre, carriages parked on the site of the town's first "permanent" engine shed. Note also, on the left, the south end turntable and the small engine shed-style building that formed Doncaster Works' test house, and in later years at least, a refuge for the Works' pilot engines. *British Railways.*

DONCASTER.

Destined to become the hub of the Great Northern system, Doncaster lacked a substantial engine shed for the first quarter of a century of the company's operations. Plans for Doncaster's "main engine house and workshops" were requested of Messrs. Cubitt and Bury, by the Board, on 4th May 1848, but as services were soon to commence, recourse had to be made to temporary facilities in the first instance.

Doncaster's train services opened on 7th September 1848, with completion of the line from Stockbridge, later to be renamed Arksey. For the initial period, up to 1st August 1849, all workings were in the care of Lancashire & Yorkshire Railway engines and it was not until 4th September that the GN-worked services were expanded by opening of the line southwards, to Retford. That was followed, on 1st October, by first workings to Wakefield and Leeds and, on 7th August 1850, the start of the service to York; finally on New Year's Day 1851, came commencement of services to Barnsley. All these trains used temporary station buildings at Doncaster while the 'permanent' premises were being built on the same 460ft long platforms.

The makeshift station facility was complemented by a temporary engine shed sited on a dead-end spur some 175 yards south of the Up platform; it was positioned on the Retford side of the level crossing that was replaced in later years by Hexthorpe Bridge. Undoubtedly built of wood, the single road shed scaled 100ft by 21ft and was of the 'through' type, with a spur projecting to the rear for a short distance. Halfway between the shed and station a 16ft turnplate was inserted in the spur, with one other short road radiating from it. Engine facilities were completed by provision of a coke stage, water tank and 38ft inspection pit on another dead-end spur, this time about 75 yards north of the Down platform. All this detail comes from a plan dated 1848 and it is fascinating to speculate whether L&Y engines used the shed - or perhaps, even that it was built by the "Lanky". In the absence of more information it is impossible to be certain.

As planned, Doncaster's permanent engine shed was to be integral with the station buildings and several references appear in the Minutes about progress of construction. First, from 7th January 1850, comes a note that the station roofs were being erected, followed on 12th February, when Cubitt's letter of 8th was read out. It said "...In return for the Minute of this committee for 9th January, I do not see any sufficient advantage to justify the proposed substitution of iron for timber roofs over the shops and engine houses of the Doncaster station. Now that considerable progress has been made I recommend that roofing be proceeded with according to the original plans..." It was resolved by the committee "...that these roofs on the Doncaster station be proceeded with of timber and slate as designed, and that Mr Goddard the architect be instructed to adopt iron roofs in the future in preference to wood, when applicable..." (only ever done at New England). Six months then passed, until 11th August, when Sturrock reported that Doncaster engine shed was "nearly ready", so it probably came into use not long after, at which time the temporary locomotive depot was almost certainly removed. However, it is just possible the shed did not open until mid-1851, when the station buildings were finally brought into use.

In its completed form, Doncaster engine shed adjoined the Down station building, running the length of its west side. Constructed in brick with a slated gable roof, the locomotive depot occupied only the northernmost 205ft, and the 36ft wide building contained three dead-end roads which were accessed from a 40ft turntable near the depot entrance. Running south from the engine shed portion was a 125ft long smiths' shop, a 20ft "engine house", 30ft office, 20ft boiler house and lastly, another "engine house", this being 85ft long. The small engine house obviously contained a stationery engine for powering the smiths' shop and possibly pumping, but what the purpose of the larger "engine house" was, is not clear. It could have been a locomotive shed, but the northern portion of the building would have held some 12 engines, as designed. The answer is not known - neither is it evident what coke and water facilities were laid on for those dozen machines, but some word about water can be obtained from a Minute of 15th April 1851. That was when Sturrock recommended that a steam pump be obtained from Messrs. E.B.Wilson of Leeds, for use as an auxiliary to the existing pump, "to ensure water is always being obtained". Estimated cost was £50, which was approved. Water for Doncaster engine shed came from the River Don, a source (literally) of much trouble in the coming years.

All train services mentioned earlier were enhanced on 1st August 1852 by completion of the Peterborough-Retford section of main line when the GN commenced through running of trains to King's Cross. Traffic generally expanded at a fast rate, requiring more engine power, so on 24th May 1853, Sturrock made his first request for additional locomotive shed space at Doncaster. His plan was estimated to cost £2,350 for provision of covered accommodation for another 12 engines, plus £400 "to make the present shed a through building." The Locomotive Engineer's plans were approved and it seems fairly obvious that a brand-new building was not put up. Rather, the smiths' shop, boiler house, office and two "engine houses" were converted into a locomotive shed, with the original portion being made 'through.' In the absence of contemporary plans the authors cannot be certain about this, but it seems the only logical conclusion that can be drawn, and more than enough space for 12 engines would have been created. The authors' theory is perhaps confirmed by a request made while work was in progress on the above. The request was presented to the Board on 10th January 1854, by Cubitt, on behalf of Sturrock, after the Locomotive Engineer had asked for an additional coke stage, engine pit and water crane which, with the necessary lines and standing space for coke wagons, was estimated to cost £750. The General Manager added his endorsement to the plea, which was approved and the coke stage and associated facilities duly appeared at the south end of the station area, where it would have been ideally situated to serve the converted ancillary accommodation of the original shed. It was also around this time that Doncaster got its first accident crane, a hand-powered 8-ton capacity machine; it was purchased following the success of a similar device introduced at Peterborough in 1853.

Within a year, on 27th May 1855, Sturrock is again saying that "...there is now not enough covered room for engines now on order. The cheapest method (to create more room) would be to roof over the space between the engine shed and workshops, for an estimated cost of £1,500 to £2,000; this is needed before next winter..." The matter was referred to Cubitt to prepare more detailed estimates, which he duly gave to the Way & Works Committee on 17th April. He said that it would cost £1,950 for roofing and alterations between the running shed and the repairing shop, together with other works costing £2,400 for the shops themselves. It was resolved that tenders be invited for the whole project, but details are lacking of the contractor involved and when the work was completed. As to scope of the work, again, no plans are available, although from March 1865 references in the Minutes (see below), it would seem this extension provided covered space for only another six engines, to add to that existing, for 24 locomotives; unfortunately the exact position, dimensions and layout of the extension have not been ascertained. Returning to 17th April 1855, authorisation was also given for purchase from Messrs. Whitworths of a screwing machine for Doncaster running shed and here it should be remarked that in these two Minutes come the earliest use yet found by the authors of the term "running shed."

After that, things went quiet for five years, until 8th may 1860, when Sturrock said that as the Lancashire & Yorkshire, Midland, and South Yorkshire Railways were already running into Doncaster, "now to be joined by the Manchester, Sheffield & Lincolnshire," and all wanting to take water from GN Company cranes, the water tank was no longer large enough. Accordingly, the Locomotive Engineer asked for the tank's depth to be increased by four feet, at a cost of £108, which was sanctioned. Events then moved to 1863 before Doncaster shed got another mention in the Minutes, with a request on 28th January, for a new band saw, for a cost estimated at £90; this was approved.

Towards the end of 1864 the north coke stage was found to be in the way of proposed new lines, so sanction was given for its removal. The job was completed in February 1865, as a lead-in to the next 2 years, when there were other alterations at Doncaster, and much talk about even greater change. It all commenced on 3rd March, with a report to the Way & Works Committee by the Locomotive Engineer, pointing out that there were 112 engines allocated to Doncaster with 33 on order, yet he had covered room for only 30. He said a new shed was required, which the Engineer estimated would cost:

Shed building:	£7,650.
Two turntables:	£1,000.
Traveller:	£500.
Sundries:	£200.

A total cost of £9,350, which did not include rails and "alterations to the road." This was passed to the Board on 7th March, when it was resolved that the matter be referred to the Station Committee for the North District, to report its recommendations. That committee reported back on 21st March with a recommendation that provision of accommodation for 20 additional engines be carried out.

What transpired is not recorded and the next reference comes from the 7th July 1865, when Sturrock made this observation "...Five months ago Mr Johnson removed the coke stage at the north end of Doncaster station to make way for new lines, with the understanding that it would be added on, fully provided with all appliances, to the coke stage at the southern end of the station. The original stage had a pit, water crane, gas, etc., but Mr Johnson advises me that he cannot provide them now, without additional instructions accompanying other documents concerning it..." This bureaucratic bungle was not resolved, however, until after the Locomotive Engineer made further representations, on 9th January 1866, about re-provision of the north coke stage at the south end of the station, for which approval was given (again?). Then, from 3rd February comes a most significant comment, when the Locomotive Engineer "...begged the Board's attention to the engine shed sanctioned

10 months ago - i.e. April 1865 - to be erected on the Crimpsall and to state that it is necessary to being completed this year. Should it not be so, and if the winter proves severe, then it will not be possible to work the number of engines that will then be stationed at Doncaster..."

The matter was taken up by the Locomotive Committee which, on 10th March 1866, called attention to the fact that it would be necessary under the present scheme for every engine to go up to, and perhaps through Marshgate level crossing at Doncaster, before it could return to the engine shed. The committee suggested that the scheme should be reconsidered and also called attention to the "serious expenditure" that would necessarily be incurred in filling up a large area of ground to gain access to the proposed new running shed. The committee then asked if the present locomotive depot could be extended or not and if any of these schemes could be cut, to alleviate the cost involved. Sturrock was then asked to give the committee detailed statements of the work done by engines in Doncaster District, especially pointing out the necessity for the extra engines he had asked for, with consequent demands for more engine shed space. The Locomotive Engineer apparently came straight back on this point by stating that the North Eastern company was still working all coal traffic from York to Doncaster, performing a mileage which would require about 6 or 7 engines more if undertaken by the Great Northern company. He added that at any time, the North Eastern "might decline this work so it would be expedient for the Company to be in a position to carry it out."

What resulted from the Locomotive Committee's penetrating observations and queries is not known, but on 24th July comes a mention that the Company's land at the Crimpsall would have to be raised to rail level before it could be utilised. Mr Johnson, the Engineer, said this could be done by utilising spoil excavated by the contractor making the Doncaster to Gainsborough line, of which there was a large quantity, and this could be done for about one shilling per yard. It was resolved that the work be carried out if lower term could be obtained. Lastly, in vindication of the by then retired Sturrock's representations, Stirling quickly got involved when on 3rd December 1866, he remarked: "...the Company are very much pressed for engine power at present and at least ten engines are wanted at Doncaster, to reduce the mileage now at that depot, to a standard which experience has shown to be the most economical for the efficient repair of the rolling stock..."

So, what was the outcome of all this? Without plans the authors can only offer theories. First, it is extremely unlikely the proposed shed on the Crimpsall was proceeded with. As that area was progressively occupied over the next 25 years, for expansion of the "Plant," it is evident that land-filling, to an average depth of 4 to 5 ft, was put into effect. When this took place is unclear, but in view of the cost cutting sentiments expressed at the time, it might be reasonable to assume the work was only undertaken in phases, as the works grew in size. Regarding the existing locomotive depot, it is possible that extension works were carried out, but only a year later, in 1867, expansion of Doncaster works, in preparation for the start of locomotive building activities, caused encroachment upon the engine shed space anyway! Therefore, the authors tend to the idea that the already inadequate locomotive shed was left to soldier on, with items being renewed as required. For example, on 18th September 1868, when Stirling said the turntable at the south end of the station was "worn out" and he requested its

Patches of snow mingle with the dirt at the south end of Doncaster Carr engine shed, about 1900, with a group of enginemen posing around 2-4-0 No.209, which was built at Doncaster Works in December 1884 (Works' No.378). In 1907 the locomotive would receive an Ivatt domed boiler to become Class E1, eventually to be withdrawn in November 1922. *R.Tarpey collection.*

The south end of Carr shed in a picture packed with detail from 1911. Visible are the south end coaling shed, the immense coal stacks with carefully whitewashed edges, spare turntable girders, double-post telegraph pole and in the distance, the eight road LNWR shed of 1881, which had in fact, been taken over by the GER, from 1893. It would be interesting to know what message(s) were carried by those two very prominent notice boards. Doubtless something very firmly worded! *Authors' collection.*

replacement on a new site (unspecified), at an estimated cost of £872. The work was approved and very swiftly executed as by 28th November, Stirling was able to report that the new turntable and engine sidings ordered on 18th September were complete and the old table was being taken up. This reveals that some form of shed extension was effected, by provision of more locomotive standing room, probably uncovered. The Minute also indicates there were two turntables at the station; doubtless the second was provided with the 1853 shed extension and scaled 40ft; diameter of its replacement was 45ft.

The mists of time obscure things once again, until 30th May 1871, with the Board asking "Mr Stirling and Mr Johnson to report on the proposed widening of the engine stables at Doncaster..." Given all that has gone before, and what we know about the cramped state of affairs at Doncaster station, this request is inexplicable and in the absence of any further mention in the archives the matter must be left. Suffice it to say that it confirms the authors opinion about nothing significant being built in 1865/66 and furthermore, it can safely be asserted that the engine stables were not widened on this occasion either. But, only two years later, on 3rd July 1873, comes the first mention of renaissance at Doncaster. That was when the Engineer displayed to the Way & Works Committee plans he had prepared, "...for the preliminary examination by the Directors for the additional accommodation at Doncaster Station, involving construction of new engine sheds and sidings on the Carr, and extensive alterations to the passenger station, waiting rooms, offices etc., and three additional lines..." The committee resolved that "...the plan be applied to the Board, for a special committee to visit Doncaster to see which of these schemes it is essential to proceed with at once..." The site suggested for the new engine shed on the "Carr" lay exactly one mile south of the station, on the Up side and at that time, was nothing more than an area of marshland which would therefore require considerable preparation to enable it to accommodate a locomotive shed. After visiting Doncaster, the special committee formed of Directors recommended to the Board that the go-ahead be given for an estimated £80,000 scheme for "works on the Carr;" Board approval was given on 9th January 1874.

On 17th April came the resolution to issue tenders, these being returned during the same month. Successful contractor was Messrs. A. & R. Neill & Sons, with the following schedule of charges:

Engine shed:	£32,320
Two coke stages:	£ 2,454
Pits in front of stages:	£ 566
Turntable foundation:	£ 455
Engine/boiler house with tank over:	£ 1,399
300ft ashpit:	£ 524
250ft ashpit:	£ 347
Total:	£37,995

The remaining £40,000 of the original estimate must largely have been in connection with preparing the site. The authors were informed that landfilling was effected by the use of ash, but no precise details have been found of the work involved, or who carried it out. Messrs. Neill started building operations in May 1874 and in the next August received the first of nine instalments totalling £17,000, with the last being paid in May 1875. Meanwhile, at the station shed, improvements

were still being made! In July 1874, plans were drawn up for fitting the depot's coke stage with a half-ton bucket crane; cost of the operation and date of completion have not been discovered.

Back on the Carr, Messrs. Neill worked all the way through 1875 and into 1876 and because of the nature of the ground, the work involved all of the shed's structures, including ashpits, being supported on brick arches. The only two progress reports discovered come from 1876 - first from 11th January, with the Way & Works Committee noting: "...Doncaster new engine shed on the Carr is now nearly completed and Messrs. Neill & Sons have promised that all shall be ready for occupation. including the offices, by the close of February. The finishing of the work has been very troublesome, as Messrs. Neill & Son have had the greatest difficulty in dealing with their joiners, carpenters and bricklayers..." Seems that even before the days of organised unions workers could cause problems, but in those days the men were more likely to have *genuine* reasons for instigating such disruption. Anyway, there seems to have been little further trouble as on 14th March the Engineer reported that "...the new engine shed on the Carr is ready for occupation and I have requested Mr Stirling to take possession so that we may be in a position to pull down part of the old sheds at Doncaster Passenger Station..."

Stirling complied and Carr shed was formally opened over the weekend of 25th to 27th March 1876. By the 6th April, he was able to report all men and machines had been removed from the old shops and engine shed, to which the Engineer added that he had commenced clearance of those buildings to put in two lines of rail for the MS&LR and NER companies' coal and goods trains. He continued by saying that the water tank would also have to be removed and he intended to construct a new tank close to the river, to hold an amount similar to that erected on the Carr. The Engineer then turned his attention to final payment to the contractor, submitting Messrs. Neill's final account "for construction of the engine shed and other works." It was accepted at £37,000, inclusive of additional works not in the contract, which amounted to £1,061. The Engineer recommended the balance of £2,911 should be paid, which was resolved - not surprising when the job costed-in at below tendered price, including extra works!

To continue with the history of the station shed: although the building was quickly redeveloped as described above, a locomotive yard was retained, complete with north and south turntables and the coal stage, so the investment in providing the latter with a crane was not wasted; the GN's 1881 WTT shows a whistle code of '1 short' to be given to French Gate Junction signal box by engines coming "From the Loco. Yard west of the Down Main Line." Then, on 2nd November 1898, there was a requirement for a small alteration to a turntable road. It would appear to have affected the south table, and work involved removal and refixing of a water crane. In addition, there were changes to buffer stops, permanent way and signalling - all must have been only slightly affected as the total estimated cost was but £287, which was approved.

Moving forward to 10th April 1907, Ivatt asked that the two 45ft turntables at Doncaster station be resited and enlarged, one to 60ft and the other to 52ft. Approval was recommended to the Board by the Way & Works Committee and it is interesting to note that at some unknown date, the north turntable had been enlarged to 45ft - possibly in the 1876 rearrangements. Two progress reports were given in the Minutes: July 1907, when the 60ft turntable foundations were complete and ready for the table; cost £1,230. Signal rods and wires etc., were being moved clear of the site of the 52ft table. Then, in the next month we learn that the 60 footer had been installed and tested on 29th July, while the 52ft table's pit floor had been built of concrete and was ready for the cast iron plates to be fixed. It was added that foundations of an engine pit were also in hand.

These works are thought to have written finis to the coaling stage, and as to the sites of the two new turntables, Appendices to the 1912 and 1947 WTT's show that the 60ft model was placed "Near engine weighhouse in front of Plant works," (for use exclusively by engines on test, after shopping). The 52ft table was used by locomotives in traffic, being sited "Near 'B' (later 'North') signalbox," close by the site of the original shed's turntable. It is thought the 60 footer was removed early in the BR period, but the 52ft device apparently survived until the end of steam - or at least until the practice of a standing pilot engine was discontinued. Finally, it should be noted that the 1912 WTT Appendix shows another 60ft turntable, near the Down carriage shed, which had been provided in a job authorised on 22nd May 1904. Completion was delayed until 1907, at a total cost of £1,230, but by the mid-1920's, another WTT shows that this table had been taken out again.

DONCASTER CARR

In 1876 Doncaster Carr was the GN's biggest engine shed, its 12 roads not being equalled - by Colwick - until 1882, and exceeded, again by Colwick, in 1897. The through building, which could hold nearly 100 engines, was brick-built and measured 420ft long by 180ft wide. There were four slated hipped roofs, each covering three roads and a similar roofing style adorned the office, workshops and stores block along the eastern side, and also the 160ft by 40ft two-road repair shop at the south eastern corner. That shop was dead-end in layout and set a GN standard which would be repeated later at Colwick, Bradford and Ardsley. It had a high roof, to enable a 25-ton hand-powered overhead travelling crane to be fitted - it is said this required "an army of men" to operate - and was equipped with a full range of machine tools, powered by a stationary steam engine and line-shafting. That steam engine was fed by a boiler that also supplied two stationary pumps, each with a capacity of 10,000 gallons per hour, that fed water (still from the River Don) into an elevated 130,000 gallon tank. Two brick-built coaling sheds were provided, one at each end of the north and south locomotive yards. The coaling floors were provided with half-ton bucket cranes and covered by slated gable roofs that extended into canopies over the coaling lines; the latter were equipped with ashpits and had water cranes adjacent. To complete the engine facilities, a 45ft turntable was installed near the south coal stage. Originally a similar table was planned for the north end, but for some reason was deleted before tenders were invited; events were soon to prove the decision to have been short-sighted. Lastly, mention should be made of the large clock installed in a tower at the depot's western side. Its four faces were 4ft 6in. in diameter, which were soon found inadequate, being enlarged to 6ft in 1879.

In the same year that the clock faces were changed, the London & North Western Railway sought some land on the Carr, upon which to build an engine shed. Prior to that the LNWR had kept the Locomotives handling its Doncaster services in the GN sheds, but expanding traffic had caused motive power requirements to increase to such an extent that a separate shed

was justified. No doubt the GN was glad of the opportunity to get the interlopers off its property and quickly concluded the sale of four acres of land for a price of £1,910. This was located several hundred yards east of the GN shed and on it, the LNW erected an 8-road, dead-end northlight shed, complete with turntable and coaling shed. Although this was the then standard LNW design of engine shed, Doncaster was most unusual in that the building was constructed in wood. The use of wood was probably necessitated by overall weight and foundation considerations in the marshy ground. Opening of the LNWR shed occurred in 1881 and its siting resulted in a complicated track layout at the south end of the GN depot, with many conflicting locomotive movements. Because of this, a single-line staff was used between the GN's Carr signal box and the LNW building, to ensure the presence of only one engine at a time on the complex of lines.

At the GN shed certain deficiencies became apparent, leading on 13th January 1883, to a 45ft turntable being ordered, for installation in the north locomotive yard. Then, six years later, Stirling obtained approval for a new ashpit along the eastern side of the south coaling shed, following that on 23rd February 1892 with a request for similar work at the north coaling point. On that occasion, Stirling observed that the sheer volume of engines using the coal stage and ashpit was causing delays and he proposed enlarging the pit, providing a new crossover road to the coal stage and alterations to other sidings, all at an estimated cost of £455, for which approval was given.

Later in the same year, on 1st October, Stirling had to report about a collision at Carr shed the previous night. He said: "...engine No.298, which had been standing in the shed, was interfered with by persons unknown and set in motion and it collided with Bradford engine No.352, which was coming into the shed tender first. Three men were injured, none of them seriously. The Company is placed in very great difficulty in the management of this shed by reason of the large amount of foreign engines and men being allocated there. On the night of the accident, which happened at half past midnight, 25% of the men on duty were from other companies and over these we have no control..." Presumably Stirling had dismissed as unthinkable that the incident could have been the result of a GN employee's carelessness, but his thinly-veiled accusation of some other company's servant must have ensured there was a negative outcome to the affair.

To further illustrate the magnitude of the GN's 'foreigner' problem, we turn to a Great Eastern Company Minute of 14th April 1893. This noted that on its own, the GE was keeping 26 engines at Carr shed, 8 of them under cover, so possibly one entire shed road was allocated to the company. The GER also had use of turntable and water facilities (at the south end), and in 1892, had paid the GN £1,498-10-0d for "board and lodging." In addition to the GER, other railway companies stationing men and machines at Carr shed at that time were the L&YR, and NER. (The MS&LR and Midland also ran into Doncaster - the former had five yards in the town, while the latter had its own goods depot at Cherry Tree Lane. With a big shed at Mexborough, only 6½ miles away, the MS&L had no need to visit Carr depot and it seems unlikely that Midland engines used GN shed facilities either).

The matter was soon eased though, as later in 1893, after only twelve years in its own shed, the LNWR moved its entire stud of engines away from Doncaster and immediately leased their depot to the Great Eastern. Even so, it seems the GER was

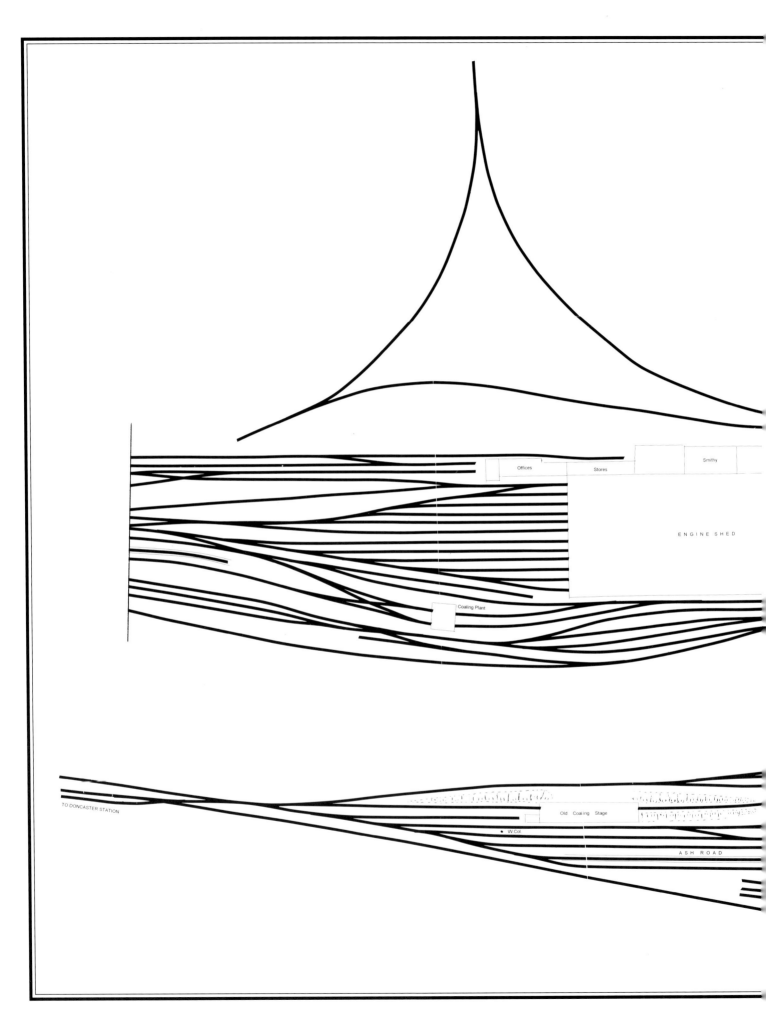

Offices   Stores   Smithy

ENGINE SHED

Coaling Plant

TO DONCASTER STATION

Old   Coaling   Stage

• W Col

A S H   R O A D

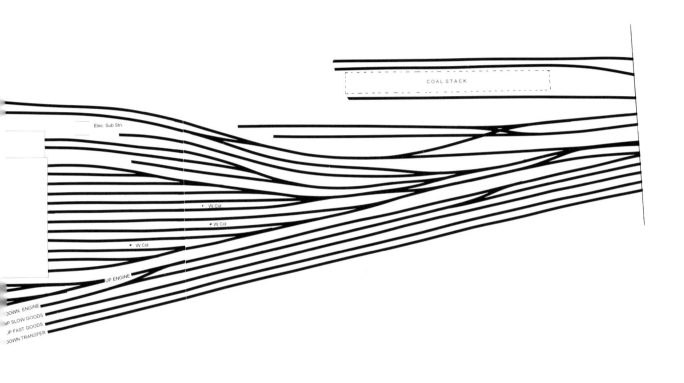

COAL STACK

Elec. Sub Stn.

W Col

W Col

W Col

UP ENGINE

DOWN ENGINE

UP SLOW GOODS

UP FAST GOODS

DOWN TRANSFER

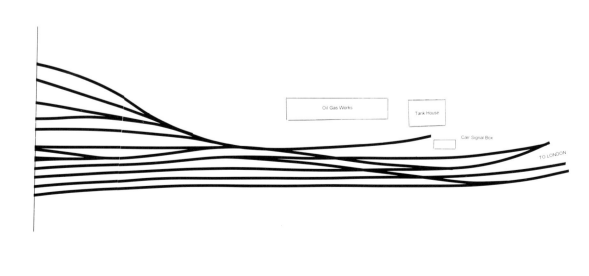

Oil Gas Works

Tank House

Carr Signal Box

TO LONDON

not quite 'off the GNR's books' for a time, as on 28th November 1895, a valuation was made of the south coal stage "as used by the Great Eastern Company." The valuation totalled £3,712-10-0d, with a note that "this does not include water cranes and mains thereto, cranes and other fittings on the stage." The reason for making the valuation was not stated, but at a guess, it had something to do with a final payment by the GER, for use of GN locomotive facilities. Regarding GER occupation of the LNWR premises, this continued until the Grouping. In fact, even after 1923, engines from the Great Eastern section of the LNER maintained their presence in the building until 1924, when it was closed for locomotive use. After that the shed was taken over by the wagon repair firm Messrs. Bell & Co., for something like three decades, finally to be abandoned and allowed to deteriorate until demolished in 1965.

Returning to 1895, £258 was spent on clearing and levelling ground, and laying a siding, for expansion of Carr's coal stacking ground - this was situated in the area of land between the GN and LNW sheds. Then, not long after, a borehole was sunk close to the Red Bank Viaduct, at the extreme south end of the shed yard, in an attempt to ease the problems emanating from use of the Don's increasingly polluted water. Some water, no doubt expensive, was already being taken from Doncaster Corporation, for domestic purposes, and this had to be continued, because the borehole proved unsuccessful. As an aside, it is interesting to note that the 1897 plan showing the well also reveals a GN-owned oil-gas works beside the locomotive yard, between the viaduct and shed. When the gasworks had been installed is not known, but it continued in use into the 1950's, until all gas-lit rolling stock was withdrawn. This had a direct affect upon Carr shed which, because of its close proximity, retained gas lighting until 1957, thus making it a very late candidate for conversion to electricity.

Doncaster shed's coaling facilities came into focus again on 2nd May 1898, when Ivatt sought permission "to alter the coal stage at Doncaster and make provision for a drivers' room at the same shed." He said "...the stage should be made to work the same as the coal stages at Ardsley and Grantham, to considerably reduce cost of handling the coal and, the present driver's mess is much too small for the number of men. Mr Ross has estimated the cost of the whole work at £7,360 and I estimate I can save at least £400 per annum on labour at the coal stage..." The scheme was approved on 6th May, with tenders subsequently being invited, for opening on 28th July. On that day, the contract for "making alterations to the (north) coal stage and locomotives offices" went to Messrs. Arnold & Son, with a bid of £3,668; work started almost immediately. Apparently, the staff amenity portion of the job had been deleted, but this was not the case; the coaler works involved provision of a wagon ramp, leading to an elevated coaling floor and a drivers' room was provided beneath. The result was an almost total demolish and rebuild of course - hence the considerable cost involved, even though it was less then half the original estimate.

While the coal stage work was in progress Ivatt turned his

attention to Doncaster's 1850's vintage breakdown crane, requesting its replacement by a Cowans Sheldon 15-ton steam crane; the cost of £1,795 was approved. Delivery of the new crane was affected later in 1899, but before that comes another of those completely inexplicable entries in the Minute books. It was typically complicated - a Way & Works Committee note of 13th April 1899, titled: "Doncaster engine shed, extension of," and stated: "...Reported that as part of the Executive Committee meeting of the 23rd March sanction was given to the appropriation of funds for the extension of the new engine shed at Doncaster. Reported recommendations from the Traffic Committee on the 16th March..." So, we have a case involving three of the GN's committees, including the prestigious Executive one. With no prior mention, an extension to the shed is sought on 16th March, seeking funds sanctioned a week later and first actioned by the Way & Works Committee 20 days after that, to then disappear into obscurity again! What caused the request for the extension and its seeming precipitate demise? And look at use of the word 'NEW' to describe Carr shed, then into its 23rd year of service - titles associated with railways seem always to have long-lived connotations!

However, the next expenditure at Doncaster was genuine - and considerable. The River Don's water had for long been totally unsuitable for locomotive use, costing the GN thousands of pound a year in boiler maintenance and therefore loss of revenue-earning mileage. So, with tapping of supplies from the River Idle at Bawtry, for the new Scrooby troughs, it was decided to pipe that water, which was good for engine use, to Doncaster. Some eight miles of pipeline were involved and because of the distance, exceptionally powerful pumps and therefore a high output boiler. All in all, the costs came to £20,000, being sanctioned in 1904, but when the job was completed two years later, the GN immediately started recouping its investment all round. In LNER times a water softening plant was installed near Red Bank Viaduct to treat the River Idle water; sludge from the plant was taken in old tenders to a dump north of Ranskill signal box, on the Up side. Incidentally, parts of the Bawtry water main can still be found today under certain lineside inspection covers.

It was 25th April 1911 before Carr shed gets its next mention in the archives, with Ivatt asking for provision of more storage accommodation at the shed, at an estimated cost of £1,120. The job was approved in the next month, tenders were issued and the contract let on 7th July to a Mr H.N.Noel, after a bid of £1,130-15-0d. However, Mr Noel quickly fell by the wayside for some unknown reason and the job was re-let on 28th July,

A panorama of the north end of Carr shed in 1928, showing the original hipped roofs seemingly still in good condition, and the huge recently completed mechanical coaling plant. *H.C.Casserley.*

The coaler in detail, seen from the main line side. Note the looped rails by which the raised wagon is inverted to discharge its load into the hoppers. See also the massive balance weights that ran down each side of the tower. The entire plant was operated by one man, with engine crews simply pressing a button to take on coal as required. The cost of this huge plant was quickly offset by the consequent laying off, or reduction in "rank", of no less than three shifts of eight coal handlers. *Syd Outram.*

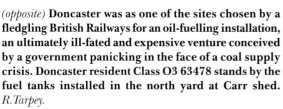

(opposite) Doncaster was as one of the sites chosen by a fledgling British Railways for an oil-fuelling installation, an ultimately ill-fated and expensive venture conceived by a government panicking in the face of a coal supply crisis. Doncaster resident Class O3 63478 stands by the fuel tanks installed in the north yard at Carr shed. *R.Tarpey.*

As well as being seen from all angles, the coaling tower itself provided a superb vantage point as witnessed here, with no less than twenty-four locomotives being wholly or partly seen in this view of Carr's north yard. Locomotives representing pre-group companies such as the GCR, GER, GNR, NER, LYR share stabling room with LNER engines comprising mainly Pacifics. Note the period (1935) open-top motor car by the depot offices. *Authors' collection.*

for £1,139 to Messrs H.Arnold & Son. A progress report by the Engineer, on 23rd December, gave the news that extension of the locomotive offices was completed northwards, except painting, and the walls of the old offices had been raised ready for the new roof. So, once again, we have the locomotive offices being extended, but there is no reference to the original request for more storage space! Perhaps such additional space was provided, by conversion of existing offices, but it only serves to prove how the terminology employed in the Minute books can be very misleading.

By 1915, the south turntable at Carr shed needed replacing. On 27th January Gresley commented that at 52ft diameter, it was too short for the largest locomotives and was getting in "bad order." He had obtained a quote from Ransomes & Rapier for a 65ft model for the same price as charged two years earlier, at Ferme Park - i.e. £546. He estimated additional expenses of enlarging the turntable pit and making a "slight alteration to one road," as £550, giving a total of £1,096. The job, which was authorised the next day, raises a question - when had the 52ft table been installed, in replacement for the original 45 footer? Turntables of 52ft had only become necessary after the introduction of Ivatt's Atlantics, so presumably the change was made in the early years of the 20th century, but record of this has not been found. In any case, usage must have been intense if the table was nearly worn out by 1915! As to progress, a Minute of July 1915 records that the foundations for the new turntable, being constructed by Messrs. Mullins & Co., at a tendered price of £452-19-6d, had reached the stage where the concrete centre block, two end blocks, and the pit floor had been finished. Assumedly the 65ft turntable came into use later that year.

At the same time, Messrs. H.Arnold & Son were building a temporary wooden office for female clerks, employed at the shed during the First World War manpower shortage. In the £278 job Arnolds had, by July 1915, completed the water supply, lavatories, and drains, and the walls were waiting for a corrugated iron roof to be fixed. (The structure proved less 'temporary' than imagines; it still stood at the eastern side of the shed in 1952 and probably was not removed until the latter part of that decade, during the depot's rebuilding.)

That completed works carried out during the war and it was 10th July 1919 before the next improvement commenced. On that day, £220 expenditure was authorised for provision of additional glazing for the roof of the engine shed, the work being finished before a series of locomotive yard rearrangements came about. They were first promulgated on 12th April 1920 and can best be summarised in chronological order of appearance in the Minute books:

1920:-

12th April - Gresley complains that "...there are no engine pits outside the locomotive shed at Doncaster. In consequence drivers have to prepare all engines over the pits inside the shed where the light is bad and there is the danger of engines being moved. To provide pits on each road outside will cost about £1,830..." (Proposed location of the pits was at the southern end of the shed.)

15th April - The Way & Works Committee consider Gresley's request and recommend it to the Board.

16th April - A meeting of the Board resolve to defer the matter.

11th May - Proposals for alterations to the track layout at Carr shed, the making of a new engine pit and moving of a water crane, all at an estimated cost of £3,158. Matter to be investigated further.

7th July - Proposed to install a new water crane near to the south coal stage. Estimate of £80, approved.

18th August - Alterations to the locomotive sidings and extension of the ash pit at Carr shed, around the north coal stage; cost re-estimated at £2,786. Deferred for further reports.

1st October - Gresley comes back once again to say that the plan for increasing pit accommodation for locomotives 'finishing work' from 4 engines to 9 engines and he calculated that he would be able to reduce the number of men 'putting engines away' by at least 3 sets. That would save £22-10-0d a week and a further saving of one man's labour would be effected in the loading of ashes, as he would not now be required to come in occasionally on Sundays, for the clearing of ashes - equal to saving about £4 per week. In all, Gresley estimated he could save £1,300 per year, for the previously advised layout of £2,786. However, the Locomotive Engineer wasn't finished. He then said a new foreman's office was required for the south locomotive yard and he asked for sanction of a further £550 to build such an office.

7th October - After digesting Gresley's statistics, the Board authorised the ashpit extension but deferred building of the foreman's office.

1921:

25th February - Extension of ashpit by 150ft and associated alterations to sidings - in progress.

27th July - Erection of office for foreman approved, at the revised cost of £290.

25th December - Foreman's office nearly complete - "final cost will be £175."

It would seem there were four separate jobs involved in this flurry of activity, with the first - proposed provision of new preparation pits - being refused, rather than "deferred," as the Minute book parlance would have us believe. However, installation of a water crane by the south coal stage went ahead, as did extension of the ash pit at the north coaling point - albeit after a lot of convincing on the Locomotive Engineer's part! Even then, it seems Gresley had to delete the move of a water crane to effect a token price reduction from £3,158 to £2,786. Lastly, a new foreman's office was built, after having first been deferred, then agreed following yet another cost-cutting exercise, to finally be completed at an amount 40% less than the revised price!

Not surprisingly, things then went quiet for a while, during which time the GNR gave way to the LNER. First thing the new management did was replace Doncaster's 15-ton steam breakdown crane with a 35 tonner. Then, in 1926 came a major improvement scheme for Carr shed, the costs of which have unfortunately not been ascertained. Over a period of nearly two years, the following works were carried out:

Provisions

(1) 500-ton mechanical coaler, replacing the two coal stages; the southern stage was removed, but that at the north end was retained as a stand-by.

(2) Large capacity hot water boiler washout plant.

(3) Hydraulic wheel drop (for No.15 road in the repair shop - there was no Number 13 road inside the shed building - it and No.16 road terminated at buffer stops in the south locomotive yard).

(4) Rotary sand dryer - incorporated in the mechanical coaling plant.

(5) Disposal pits doubled in length, to accommodate 18 engines.

(6) Twelve preparation pits, outside the southern end of the shed.

(7) 12 inch water main installed, bringing soft water from a Doncaster Corporation supply. (A main of that diameter would have been much too large for purely domestic purposes so it is assumed it supplemented the Bawtry feed for locomotive use.
(8) 45 ton steam breakdown crane, replacing 35 ton model (actually stabled at Doncaster carriage sheds).

Deletion

(1) 45ft turntable from the north locomotive yard - it was not replaced.

After such a wide-ranging modernisation scheme it was natural that Carr shed did not feature in the Minute books for many years. Some alterations occurred around the period of the Second World War, the first, about 1939/40, when the depot's 25 years old 65ft turntable gave up the ghost. Rather than provide a new table , however, the LNER repeated New England's facility of an engine-turning triangle, laid out on land formerly occupied by the Civil Engineer, east of the engine shed and north of the coal stacking ground. An emergency 'light tunnel' was erected alongside the east wall of the shed during the period of hostilities. This particular facility was built to a standard design and allowed repairs to be completed at night in properly lit conditions, the doors being sealed so that the 'black-out' could be maintained. Besides the Doncaster 'tunnel' there were similar structures at New England, March and certain other LNER main depots. The only other wartime change noted was a minor one - the removal of all doors from the depot entrances - the LNER finally getting fed up with constantly having to repair them! Perhaps the 'light tunnel' facility helped bring on their demise. The final LNER addition to the shed was the provision of two large storage tanks and filling facilities in the abortive oil-firing "panic" of 1947/48. The tanks remained in situ, in the north locomotive yard, for many years and even until recent times their circular bases, along with base of another tank not actually erected, have been prominent features.

Thus did British Railways take over Carr depot, to do little until the mechanical coaler was extensively overhauled, in 1954. During the time it was out of use, the north coal stage was resurrected, but on completion of the overhaul the old coaler's ramp was dispensed with, leaving an earthen incline that eventually grassed itself over. Soon after, BR was forced to replace Carr's 80 years old hipped roofs. The £60,000 project was approved in November 1956, with work starting early the next year, but replacing the roof was not all that was done. Inside the shed, No.10 road (reading from the west) was taken up, the pit filled in and the alignment used for a new steel and asbestos wall. Roads No.11 and 12 were thereby separated, with the intention they be used for the forthcoming diesels; in the meantime they were given over to steam maintenance purposes. In addition, a diesel fuel tank was placed in the north yard, between the office block and the site of the north coal stage, while inspection pits Nos.3, 7 and 8 were rebuilt, and numerous other small jobs carried out. With regard to the roof replacement, this was comprehensive, involving a shortening, by 90ft, of covered space at the north end. Four separate roofs were retained, but this time gable-ended, and comprising steel frames, covered by asbestos sheets and wire-reinforced glass panels, with asbestos cement smoke chutes over the nine roads of the 'running' shed. Lastly, electricity replaced gas, for lighting purposes and the whole scheme was brought to completion during the winter of 1957.

Just over two years later, in 1960, the Civil Engineer re-claimed the land space occupied by the triangle so, once again,

resort had to be made to a turntable. In what was one of BR's last ever steam days installation of a turntable, room was found near the north east corner of the shed, a pit was dug and a refurbished 70ft table installed. That came from Southend Victoria ex-GER shed, where it had probably never been used to its full extent and had recently been rendered redundant by an electrification scheme. After that, the ever increasing fleet of diesels caused installation of more fuel tanks, in 1961, and it was then simply a question of waiting for steam's demise. An interesting incident occurred in 1963, when Alan Pegler rented No.14 road - i.e. in the repair shop - to house his newly purchased A3 Pacific No.4472 FLYING SCOTSMAN, a spare boiler, and other parts. But, for steam in general the end came in April 1966, when Carr shed was turned over exclusively for use by diesel locomotives. Part of the conversion to serve the new motive power involved opening out and deepening the pits at the north end of Nos.6 to 12 roads. However, the original building plans were no longer available so the brick arches supporting the pits came as a surprise - and an awkward one at that, making the pit enlargement very difficult! Other steam age trappings were removed at the same time - the turntable and boiler washout plant, the steam-driven hydraulic pump for powering the wheel drop, the two stationery boilers supplying the last named facilities, and eventually, even the massive coaling tower. However, the wheel drop itself was retained, still hydraulically operated but with an electric pump, while the overhead crane in the repair shop was derated to 7½ tons capacity and also converted to electric drive. That hoist was, nevertheless, taken out during a July 1980 reroofing scheme, with the aid of the depot's breakdown crane; the repair shop was thereafter used for crane maintenance purposes. In the meantime, the engine shed continued to serve diesels, also to house some of the Civil Engineer's rail-borne machinery, and be used for wagon repairs. Carr shed is still in use today, with an allocation of diesel shunting locomotives, but the building has been reduced to the two easternmost sections, now housing only four tracks and such heavy plant as a Hegenscheidt wheel profiling machine.

Doncaster was created the centre of a Locomotive District in 1858, but for more than half a century the town provided the District's sole engine shed(s). That changed from 1st June 1912, when the post of District Locomotive Superintendent (DLS) at Retford was abolished and that shed came into Doncaster District. Then, around the period of the First World War, Doncaster also absorbed York Locomotive District. Prior to all that though, at the beginning of the 20th century, when some new train services were introduced through Harrogate, Doncaster supplied a few locomotives to an outstation at the North Eastern Railway shed at Starbeck.

The outstationing of locomotives at Starbeck was substantively rendered 'redundant' by Grouping, but GN locomotive types were still allocated to Harrogate in the early 1930's, for working the HARROGATE PULLMAN. The Grouping witnessed an 'explosion' in Doncaster District's significance with the addition of the ex-GCR depots at Mexborough, Keadby (replaced by Frodingham in 1932), Barnsley and Retford. A further increase came some time between the end of the war and formation of British Railways. The LNER took over a wartime Royal Ordnance Factory at Ranskill, for use as a wagon works and there erected a wooden engine shed for the resident shunting engine (usually a Y3 Sentinel); this little depot was made an outstation of Carr. Late in the same period, on 13th July 1947, Retford 'regained' its sub-shed at Newark - 'lost' to Grantham in the June 1912 re-shuffle - but that marked the pinnacle, because BR could only effect transfers away and closures. These commenced with the early 1958 move of Mexborough and Barnsley sheds to a new Sheffield Division. Closures started with Newark, on 5th January 1959, followed by Retford (ex-GC) in January 1965, Retford (ex-GN), June 1965, and finally Frodingham (to steam), in February 1966. Doncaster itself also closed to steam two months later, since which time, such 'anachronisms' as Locomotive Districts have been of no importance.

The history of all the many locomotive types based at Doncaster is vast, but as noted earlier, the first train services into the town were handled by L&YR engines. However, from 1st August 1849 the GNR took over responsibility for its own workings and the first allocation appears to have comprised "Small Hawthorn" Singles mostly; with the odd Hawthorn 0-4-2 'Luggage' engine and possibly Bury-type 0-4-0. From 1855 the 223 Class of 2-4-0, designed for the West Riding lines, were also seen at Doncaster, although none were allocated there. Singles continued to dominate passenger duties, whilst goods work was largely in the hands of Sturrock 0-6-0. with his designs giving way to those of Stirling and of Doncaster 'Plant' construction. In 1870 the first 8-foot Single, No.1 arrived, to be followed in the next year by No.33, and then ten more during the years up to 1882. By 1895 there were thirteen 8-footers at Doncaster, together with another eight of the 7-foot and 7ft 6in varieties; the stud comprised:
7ft 0in.55.
7ft 6in.232, 235, 236, 238, 239, 240, 876
8ft 0in 1, 33, 34, 47, 546, 547, 548, 550, 662, 664, 667, 669, 670.

Allocations did not tend to change much during Stirling's office, but Nos.33 and 47 of the above were moved to Leeds for a time, to handle a short-lived Leeds to London passenger working. 0-4-2 and 2-4-0 types worked the other Doncaster passenger duties until Ivatt's appointment as Locomotive Engineer. His 4-4-0 classes appeared in the late 1890's and came to dominate the lighter express duties to Leeds, York, Lincoln and Peterborough besides working fast perishable goods traffic.

The last 4-4-0 at Carr shed was actually a Boston engine, a stored D2, No.2190, which departed just after the formation of BR. During WW2 ex-GC D9 and D10's were used by Doncaster on various duties, mainly over former GC lines.

Ivatt's first C1 Atlantics (LNER Class C2) were allocated to Doncaster from August 1900 and by 1912 nine were on the books. The large-boilered C2 appeared from 1904 and by 1911 no fewer than thirty-four of these were at Carr working the major passenger turns. Many of the Doncaster large-Atlantics spent most of their lives at the shed with No.1435 (4435/2865) holding the record for the longest stay of 38 years and 1 month.

In turn the Atlantics gave way to the Pacifics on all the important duties and the GN's prototype No.1470 was first allocated to Doncaster in April 1922, soon joined by No.1471. These two settled down to regular work on London trains and by the end of 1925 some thirteen Class A1 were based at Carr shed: 2543, 2544, 2549, 2554, 2555, 2561, 4470, 4471, 4472, 4473, 4477, 4478, 4481. At that time these engines were working eight return King's Cross trains daily. Fifteen A1's seems to have been the peak number allocated to Doncaster, during 1935/6, when the shed took over working the *YORKSHIRE PULLMAN* from Copley Hill shed.

1938 saw A4's being allocated to Doncaster and on the eve of WW2 four of the streamliners (4467, 4468, 4900, 4903) had joined eleven of the A1/A3 there. However, during the War the A4's moved away never to return.

Various other Pacifics were based during the period from the end of the LNER to the early 1950's; A2 and A2/3 and Peppercorn's A1. At the end of 1959 some nineteen Pacifics were shedded at Carr and these comprised: A1 - 60114, 60119, 60122, 60125, 60128, 60136, 60139, 60144, 60149, 60156, 60157, 60158; A1/1 - 60113; A3 - 60046, 60064, 60067, 60102, 60104, 60108, 60112. These were gradually washed away by the tide of dieselisation, the A3's going in October 1963, followed by the A1's during 1964 and 1965.

Other large noteworthy engines stationed at Doncaster include the solitary 4-6-4 of Class W1, which ended its days there after a near six year stint when its regular duty included the 1006 Doncaster to King's Cross express and 1550 return. The Class P2 2-8-2's were run-in from Carr during the 1934-36 trials of these huge engines.

Nearly every type of LNER 4-6-0 tender engine, both pre and post-Grouping types, have been stationed at Doncaster over the years from 1923 up until the end of steam.

No mention of Doncaster's engines would be complete without reference to the V2 which first came to Carr in 1937 and growing in number to twenty-six by the outbreak of war. The number peaked at thirty by the end of the LNER period but declined steadily during the BR years. The V2 took on most of the fitted freight work from the K2 and K3 engines but were equally at home hauling express passenger trains.

We return now to goods workings, which we left in the 19th century, when 0-4-2, 2-4-0 and 0-6-0 dominated the scene. Things didn't change for the first few years of Ivatt's office - his J5, J21 and J22 0-6-0 classes merely continued the tradition. But, 1902, his K1 0-8-0 - the "Long Toms" (LNER Q1 and Q2), made their debut. They were used on the heaviest coal trains to Peterborough but their numbers at Doncaster were never more than a handful and by 1912 they had all left.

After Grouping the 0-8-0 type returned in the shape of the ex-GC Class Q4 but they were short-lived at Carr and were gone by 1925. Of course the ex-NER Q6 and Q7 worked into Doncaster daily on mineral trains from York and Selby.

From 1912 to 1923 the GNR 0-6-0 type held sway at Doncaster and by Grouping no less than seventy of them were allocated out of a total of 189 engines at Carr; they were made up from the following classes: J4 (LNER J3) 19; J5 (J4) 22; J21 (J2) 1; J22 (J5/6) 28. Of these the J6 remained in strength until the mid 1950's. Other none GN types which arrived during the LNER period included ex-GE J15 during WW2; ex-NER J23 for most of 1937 and a solitary J21 in the same year. The J21, No.432, stayed for virtually twelve years shunting the carriage works and hauling the staff train from Doncaster station to the wagon works, situated opposite Carr shed.

The ex-GC J11 were ever popular, though only a few were allocated during BR days. On the other hand the LNER built J39's were forever associated with Doncaster, the first seven built being sent to Carr and even though that number soon dropped to five, it was boosted during the latter period of WW2 until a maximum of 21 was reached in 1946. they remained in double figures at Carr until complete withdrawal in 1961.

Of the heavy goods engines, perhaps the ex-GC 2-8-0 of LNER Class O4 was most prominent during the LNER era; from 1924 they literally swamped the shed so that by 1930 there were

By 1957 Doncaster shed's roof had its slates replaced by asbestos sheets, but this was already showing signs of wear! Ex-Plant A4 No.60017 SILVER FOX, adds a graceful relief to the scene. *N.E.Preedy.*

(below, middle) In mid-1958 Carr's mechanical coaling plant was once again undergoing repair, bringing the old ramped coal stage once more into temporary use. The less appreciated costs of running steam locomotives are amply illustrated here, with the doubtless numerous extra manpower required to run the manual coaling. Then, in the sunken ash road, although wagons are provided for its removal, tons of ash must first lie on the ground to cool. Double-handling required and therefore all very labour intensive and expensive, not to mention by then, highly undesirable as an occupation. *N.E.Preedy.*

(below, bottom) British Railways had eventually to replace Doncaster shed roof and did so in comprehensive fashion, with one eye on forthcoming diesel traction. The steam section of the depot was reduced to nine roads with the other three roads partitioned off for the New Order. This 1959 view from the south shows the then new roof to advantage. *N.E.Preedy.*

fifty of the type allocated. Their numbers remained fairly constant between 35 and 45 up to the early BR period when they were suddenly all moved away. However by 1959 six of the class had moved back to Doncaster and four of them were amongst the last steam locomotives working from the shed.

The GN 2-8-0s do not appear to have been present in any number until the mid-1930's when Class O1 appeared to reach a total of ten by 1940, twenty by 1945 and none by 1946! They came back in 1948 when BR started to gather all the survivors - seventeen, now reclassified O3 - but all had been scrapped by 1952. The three-cylinder O2 also had a somewhat come-and-go relationship with Doncaster, twenty-three coming new to the shed in 1942/43, to join twenty-one of an earlier build. Then in January 1944, all were transferred away, with some returning the next year for the total to fluctuate between two in 1946 to twenty-four in 1951.

Of other 2-8-0 classes, wartime brought 'Austerity' designs, with seven US Army Transportation Corps S160's allocated for a while, in 1943, before they left to eventually liberate Europe. The Stanier designed LNER Class O6 came during 1943 also and worked the heavy trains to and from March. Finally the WD 2-8-0 'Austerity' will always be associated with Doncaster and the other sheds in the Doncaster District; in fact they were so ubiquitous that they were virtually associated with every ex-LNER freight shed during BR days. Admitted, their allocation in any number to Doncaster Carr in BR days came late, the first examples coming in 1955 but by 1959 there were a dozen, and by 1965 no less than thirty-five, many of which were to see out the end of steam at Doncaster in the following year.

The 2-10-0 type wheel arrangement was never seen on Britain's railways in any great numbers until the mid-1950s when the BR Standard 9F 2-10-0 made its debut. Sixteen of these superlative engines were eventually allocated to Doncaster but they came too late, being cut down in their prime, some less than six years old when they were scrapped in the name of modernisation.

Tank engines were, of course, to be seen at Doncaster from the earliest days and their types varied from the 0-6-0 to the huge ex-GC 0-8-4's of Class S1, three of which came in 1954 but saw little use and were gone by 1956. The 0-6-0 however, were the workhorses of the numerous yards around Doncaster and their numbers were always in high figures right up to the period when the BR 0-6-0 diesel shunters took over their work from the late 1950s. In 1923 there were forty 0-6-0 saddletanks working the eleven marshalling yards at Doncaster. By 1927 those yards were dispatching 165,000 wagons monthly, of which 44% contained mineral traffic, employing twenty-five shunting engines around the clock with 75 sets of men.

The earliest allocation detail comes from 1865, when 112 engines were stationed at Doncaster. Ten years before that, the GN's Rule Book showed these daily turns and distances being worked by the shed:

Down - Doncaster to:

Knottingley	15 miles
Leeds	30 "
Methley Jct.	21 "
Rothwell Haigh	27 "
Silkstone	35 "
York	35 "

Up - Doncaster to:

Grantham	51 miles
New England	78 "
Peterborough	80 "
Retford	18 "

With Sturrock reporting over a hundred engines allocated in 1865, and another thirty on order, it is surprising to learn from a contemporary account that only "about 80 engines" were transferred to Carr shed in 1876. Yet, we are also advised that in the same year, coal consumption at Doncaster shed amounted to one 8-ton wagon load per hour, or allowing for a 6½ day week, about 1,250 tons a week - 65,000 tons per year. If we assume only 70% of the shed's allocation was active on any one day, then dividing 70% of 80 engines into 1,250 tons gives just over 22 tons of coal per engine, which over a 6½ day week comes out to 3.43 tons of coal per engine, per day. If we use the same formula for an allocation of 120 locomotives, we get 2.29 tons of coal per engine which seems a little low. Indeed, when we compare that amount to the result of similar calculations upon 1927's coal usage (*see* below), the number of engines stationed at Doncaster in 1876 seems more likely to have been around 80.

As an adjunct to those 1876 figures for coal consumption, that for the entire Doncaster District was quoted as 1,505 tons per week, i.e. 161 tons was being used at places other than Doncaster engine shed. So, where were those other places, when whatever details are available apparently show that Doncaster had no outstation? Of course, there was the coal stage at Doncaster station still, and if the readers refer to the chapter on "Coal," it can be seen that even by the early 1850's Sturrock was asking for a coaling stage to be provided at South Yorkshire Sidings, near Doncaster. So, with the knowledge that there had been a considerable growth in marshalling yard space around Doncaster since this time, then perhaps it may be assumed there were other coal stages in operation. Lastly, it is possible, but not confirmed, that the GN's presence at places like Wakefield may have been as an outstation of Doncaster, rather than Leeds/Ardsley, as most evidence seems to indicate. The matter must unfortunately remain clouded.

By 1899 the GN's WTT was showing 36 main line goods workings from Doncaster, together with the corresponding return empties. Quite how many engines that entailed is not clear, but by 1905, there were 158 stationed at Carr shed, a figure that grew to 175 by April 1912. At Grouping, the depot's stud of locomotives had reached 189 in number, and four years later Doncaster Carr was getting through an average of 3,000 tons of coal a week, with a peak of 3,400 tons. Using the same formula as above, we find that equates to 3.47 tons of coal per engine, per 6½ day week.

Carr's roster of engines had advanced to the peak figure of 199 by 31st October 1931, nineteen days after the depot took over the Warmsworth Pilot duty from Bullcroft Junction ex-Hull & Barnsley shed. The Warmsworth pilot engines, a brace of ex-NER Class T1 4-8-0T, Nos.1658 and 1660, did not however, move to Doncaster. Instead the big tanks transferred to Hull, and Carr supplied 2-8-0s in their place. Such large engines were necessary because of the long, heavy rafts of wagons hauled over the 1½ miles from Yorkshire Main Colliery to Warmsworth. Doncaster's allocation dropped a little, to 190 locomotives, by 31st October 1933 and it was slightly less again by Sunday 25th July 1937, when a visit to the shed found:

A1   2543, 2547, 2548, 2559, 4470, 4473, 4474, 4477

A3	2747, 2752, 4480
A4	4482
A7	1129, 1190
B5	6072
B16	842, 2372
B17	2832, 2833
C1	3282, 4416, 4422, 4435, 4441, 4453
D2	4361, 4390
D3	4080
J3	3329, 4093
J5	3035, 3036, 3037
J6	3531, 3556, 3558, 3570, 3606, 3610, 3631, 3632, 3638, 3639
J11	5197, 5228, 5324, 6048, 6049
J16	8182
J17	8174, 8225, 8230, 8234, 8239
J20	8283
J21	432
J23	2460, 2476
J28	2422
J39	1273, 2707
J50	609, 1086, 2792, 3160, 3169, 3173, 3178, 3223, 3229, 3236
J52	3155A, 3685, 3973, 4049, 4202, 4230, 4236, 4238, 4243, 4244 4245, 4246, 4247, 4248, 4249, 4250, 4253, 4258, 4266, 4271 4286, 4287
J75	2532
K2	4633, 4642, 4646, 4655, 4661, 4664, 4680
K3	75, 80, 109, 111, 146, 202, 203, 1162, 1164, 2445, 2446, 2468
N1	3190, 4594
N2	4756, 4768
N5	3035, 3036, 3037
O1	3462, 3465, 3466
O2	2435, 3477
O4	5217, 5390, 5396, 5397, 6205, 6263, 6282, 6284, 6285, 6333 6334, 6347, 6359, 6495, 6519, 6554, 6555, 6556, 6557, 6561 6566, 6594, 6595, 6633
Q6	1362, 2246, 2297
V2	4771, 4772

LMS types:

5F	2840 (Blackpool)
1F	10689 (Wakefield)
3F	12515 (Wakefield), 12534 (Sowerby Bridge)

Total: 164, comprised of 160 LNER engines, of 34 different classes, plus 4 LMS engines. Of course, a number of the LNER engines were visitors which were either awaiting a return working, such as the former GER and NER types, or were ex-Doncaster 'Plant' after repair.

The War's effect upon locomotive numbers at Doncaster is not known in detail, but by 11th January 1947, the depot's roster had decreased slightly from its 1933 allocation, to 174 engines. However, another visit to Carr shed, on Sunday 23rd March 1947, revealed a situation considerably changed from 10 years previously:

A3	40, 65†, 74, 97, 108
B1	1125, 1127
B4	1486
C1	2817, 2832*, 2850*, 2851, 2866*, 2886
D2	2190*
J3	4113*
J6	4183, 4218, 4236, 4241, 4243, 4255, 4259, 4263, 4264, 4272 4279
J50	8890, 8918, 8926, 8936, 8974, 8979, 8985, 8986, 8987, 8989 8991
J52	8763, 8769, 8775, 8786, 8800, 8804, 8806, 8835, 8836, 8841 8842, 8843, 8844, 8845, 8847, 8858, 8860, 8865, 8870, 8886
J55	8318
K3	1803, 1856, 1861, 1910, 1918, 1934, 1972
O2	3944*, 3963*
O3	3481

O4	3572, 3598, 3600, 3608, 3647, 3649, 3654, 3657, 3692
O6	3156
O7	3087, 3132, 3152, 3185
Q6	3453
Q7	3463
V2	800†, 815, 828, 830, 832, 857, 862, 867, 872, 875, 890, 896 905, 906, 930
WD	77138, 77303

Total: 123 engines of 22 different classes. * indicates engine stored. † indicates engine ex-works.

The BR period saw little change at first; in fact the total number of engines based at Doncaster Carr rose steadily to 180, at August 1950, and 191 by April 1959. Just before that, another Sunday visit, on 28th September 1958 discovered:

A1	60114, 60116, 60119, 60154
A2	60538
A3	60046, 60052, 60056, 60064, 60102, 60103, 60104, 60106 60108
A4	60033
B1	61017, 61060, 61087, 61107, 61114, 61120, 61121, 61124 61127, 61145, 61157, 61162, 61170, 61250, 61266, 61325 61326, 61365, 61377, 61405
B16	61418, 61419
B17	61626
D49	62720
J6	64179, 64209, 64214, 64258, 64261, 64262, 64270
J39	64838, 64876, 64883, 64885, 64972
J50	68946, 68960, 68970, 68980
J52	68862
J68	68654
J69	68556, 68558, 68569, 68587
J94	68020, 68022, 68069, 68071
K3	61804, 61812, 61829, 61860, 61864, 61922, 61954, 61964
O2	63922, 63928, 63934, 63941, 63955, 63956, 63957, 63962 63964*, 63967*, 63969*, 63975, 63981, 63984*
O4	63613, 63618, 63769, 63855, 63858, 63917
V2	60817, 60852, 60857, 60880, 60896, 60909, 60921, 60960
W1	60700
WD	90032, 90108, 90111, 90144, 90175, 90246, 90253, 90538 90569, 90587, 90597, 90636, 90695, 90696
9F	92035, 92037, 92142, 92168, 92171, 92173, 92174, 92175 92176, 92177, 92191, 92192, 92195, 92196
4F	43037, 43059, 43070

Total: 146 engines, of 23 different classes. * indicates engine stored.

Over the next few years, the allocation of steam locomotives slowly dwindled in the face of ever increasing numbers of diesels, until it stood at only 63 engines in May 1965, eleven months before steam finished at Carr.

Doncaster Carr engine shed closed to steam in April 1966 after ninety glorious years. At closure even the active engines went to the breakers yard.

During the 'diesel period' Doncaster's allocation consisted of no more than twenty or so Class 08 diesel shunters. However, at weekends, especially during the 1970's and 1980's, there could be as many as fifty main-line diesel locomotives stabled within the shed precincts, the classes being anything from Class 20, 25, 31, 37, 40, 47, 56, 58. Most of those diesels have now gone the way of the steam locomotive as a new generation of high-horsepower diesels are taking over the freight on today's railways.

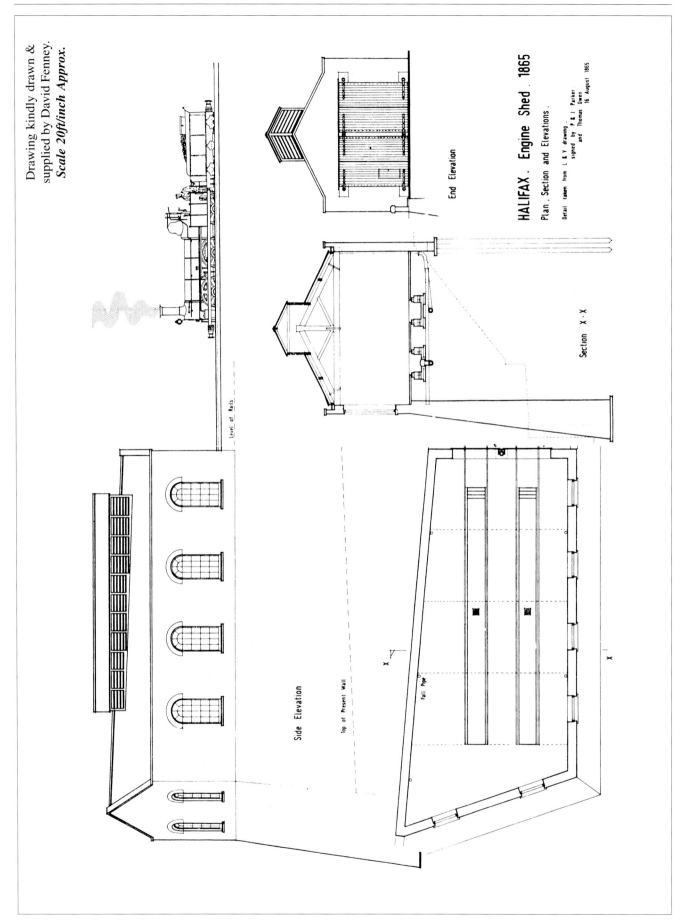

Drawing kindly drawn & supplied by David Fenney. *Scale 20ft/inch Approx.*

End Elevation

Section X - X

Side Elevation

Level of Rails

Top of Present Wall

Fall Pipe

X

X'

HALIFAX. Engine Shed. 1865

Plan. Section and Elevations.

Detail taken from L & Y drawing,
signed by P & J Parker
and Thomas Gwen
16 August 1865.

HALIFAX

The history of GN engine sheds in Halifax is by no means clear-cut and in producing this summary the authors have made a number of assumptions and left some questions unanswered.

Great Northern access to the important woollen and engineering trade centre of Halifax was gained via the Leeds, Bradford & Halifax Junction Railway, which had been incorporated by an Act of 30th June 1852. The GN's working agreement had been signed on 14th July 1854, involving the company in the supply of stock, plant and staff to the LBHJ.

The LBHJ did not build a railway into Halifax. Instead, it made a reciprocal arrangement with the Lancashire & Yorkshire Railway, whereby the L&Y would gain running powers over the LBHJ's line from Bradford to Leeds, while LBHJ/GN trains would run over L&Y tracks from Bradford, via Low Moor, to Halifax. Opening of the LBHJ's route and the L&Y's line occurred simultaneously, on 1st August 1854, with the GN at first using the L&Y's Shaw Syke terminus. From January 1855, the company commenced payment of 50% of the rental, at Halifax, of a locoshed that held two engines. There was a single road L&Y depot at Shaw Syke station (the L&Y's second shed in the town - an 1844 Leeds & Manchester Railway depot having been replaced in 1850), so it is assumed the GN paid for a half share of that building. On 24th June 1855, Halifax's new station on Navigation Road was opened. GN/LY passenger services moved to it, with Shaw Syke subsequently becoming a goods depot: all evidence suggests that the locoshed there remained in use by both companies. The 1855 issue of the GN Rule Book shows Halifax engines having duties to Bradford (11 miles) and Laisterdyke (9 miles).

Disagreement between the GN and LBHJ led to the latter working some of its own services in the period from 1st January 1859, to 30th June 1863. It appears the estrangement affected only the Bradford-Ardsley route, as GN-worked LBHJ trains continued to operate into Halifax, where the station was then managed by a GN/LY Joint Committee. Rapidly growing traffic had, by 1862, caused the Joint Committee to consider enlargement of Halifax station; part of the scheme involved a proposal to "....move the LBHJ stables and engine shed...." However, matters dragged on until 1865 before reconstruction of the station was approved. Specifically regarding locomotive facilities, a Joint Station Committee Minute (No.993) of 16th May 1865, notes that the GN had "....adopted a proposal for a new engine shed at Halifax, to cost an estimated £2,120...."

On 5th July 1865, GN absorption of the LBHJ was accomplished and a month later, Henry Oakley wrote to the L&Y, advising that the GN had accepted a tender for £1,694-10-0d, for construction of Halifax's new locoshed. By 1867, the station enlargement project had been completed - including the appearance at its north eastern corner of a two road brick-built locomotive shed. Study of the associated plan shows the single pitch gable-roofed shed was trapezoidal in shape, roughly scaling 68ftx 32ft (see plan). The tracks extended 60ft into the building, long enough only for one engine on each. Its awkward shape was dictated by its position, which also involved some hefty supporting construction. The west (station) sidewall was carried on twenty eight 37ft wooden piles, while the east side, facing on the road, was buttressed by a 44ft high retaining wall. Coal and water facilities seem to have been minimal and no turntable was installed. Contemporary plans do not reveal the owner/user of the depot, but it can safely be assumed to have been the GN, for three reasons, viz:

1. In 1867, the GNR ceased its 50% rental payments for half-use of an engine shed at Halifax. (Whether the Shaw Syke building had continued to serve, up to 1867, is not known, but if the GN/LY had moved elsewhere, in the years following 1855, there is no indication, in any written document or plan, where they went).

2. A 30th June 1877 "Statement of Worth" of GN-owned buildings at Halifax included: "....engine shed: £3,203-3-3d, ..." (which seems to indicate that the GN's tender price of £1,694-10-0d was for half the actual cost, with the L&Y paying the same amount - i.e., the shed was built as a Joint undertaking).

3. Though seemingly erected as a Joint depot, the L&Y had pulled out by 1879 as an L&Y official plan of that year, showing Halifax station, clearly labels the engine shed as "GN."

Very little else is known, but what throws the whole subject into confusion somewhat, are comments made by the Board of Trade Inspector(s), when surveys were made of the GN/LYR Joint Halifax & Ovenden Railway. That had separate openings and inspections for goods and passenger traffic. At the first, for goods, on 14th October 1878, the B.o.T Inspector said: "....I was much surprised to find that no engine turntables exist either at Bradford or Halifax, two important termini. As these will be the termini of the new service of trains running over the Halifax & Ovenden Railway, turntables should be provided at these stations...." Fair enough - but for the commencement of H&O passenger trains, on 1st December 1879, the Inspector remarked that there was a requirement to build an engine shed at Halifax! Then, on the following 6th December, the B.o.T wrote to the GN and L&Y saying that its Commission no longer objected to the opening of the H&O! It is the opinion of the authors that the B.o.T representative did not at first consider Halifax's existing engine shed facilities to be large enough to cope with the increased traffic brought about by opening of the H&O, but what caused the change of mind is not clear. Regarding the turntable, it is all most confusing, because if one didn't exist in 1878, why, so soon afterwards as 24th March 1880, did the GN Way & Works Committee Minutes record Stirling's observation that "....the turntable at Halifax requires replacement...."? Frustratingly contradictory, but any amount of searching through the archives has failed to provide any further enlightenment.

In the early days of its services to Halifax the GN would have employed its 223 Class 2-4-0, a Sturrock design, built specifically for the West Riding lines. Sturrock's 0-4-2 and 0-6-0 also would have appeared of course - and 0-4-2 and 0-6-0 Saddle Tanks, to be joined in time, by various engines of Stirling's designs. But, Ivatt's creations were never to be residents of Halifax engine shed, because in the mid-1880's Halifax station was again largely rebuilt, resulting in the demise of the GN loco depot, by 1887 at the latest. It seems no replacement was built, or even contemplated by the company. Instead, apparently, Bradford locoshed's diagrams for the Bradford-Queensbury-Halifax route were recast, in such a way as to obviate the outstationing of engines at Halifax. Of course, in 1890, the GN did bring a new engine shed into use at Holmfield, only 2½ miles north of Halifax, but that depot was built to serve the just completed Halifax High Level Railway (*see* Holmfield), although local passenger trains were run from there in LNER days.

So faded another obscure GN loco depot - made more frustrating perhaps, by the amount of tantalizingly inconclusive evidence contained in the company archives!

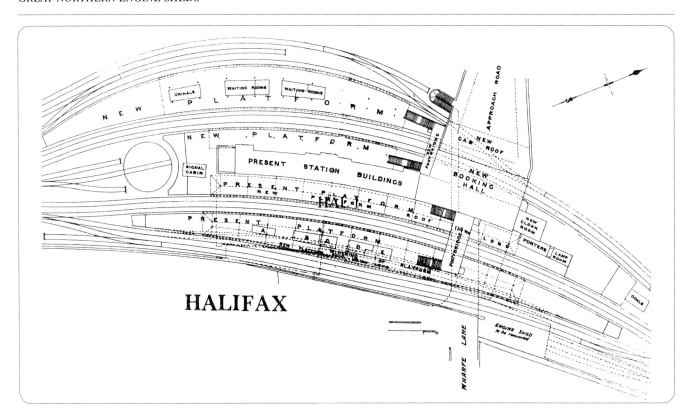

HALIFAX

Seen here to the right of the station platform in 1936, three years after closure, Holmfield shed awaits its fate. The building was removed at a date yet to be determined. *W.A.Camwell.*

HOLMFIELD

Formed in 1863, the Halifax & Ovenden Railway Company promoted a line between Halifax and Keighley. Its Act was passed on 30th June 1864, with initial powers only for the 2½ miles from Halifax, north to Holmfield: the GNR and L&YR each subscribed one third of the £90,000 capital.

Over ten years passed before the short line was completed, for goods only, on 1st September 1874. In the meantime, the H&O's onward aspirations to Keighley had been superseded by the Halifax, Thornton & Keighley Railway's Act of 5th August 1873. It was the GN-worked HT&KR's line which finally connected Holmfield with the other towns to the north, being opened, again for goods traffic only, on 14th October 1878. Passenger trains commenced running through Holmfield on 1st December 1879 and started using a temporary GN station there, exactly two weeks later: the permanent station, when completed, was a GNR/LYR Joint establishment.

There matters rested, until 7th August 1884, when an Act was passed authorising construction of the Halifax High Level and North & South Junction Railway. That company's name was nearly as long as the railway it sponsored, for the GN to work - a 3¼ mile, fiercely graded branch from Holmfield, via Pellon, to Halifax (St. Pauls). This had been promulgated in an attempt to assuage an oft-voiced complaint by the citizens of Halifax, about lack of a railway on the northwest side of their town. It is interesting to recall that this particular section of railway was the only length ever built, that followed a line earlier projected somewhat bizarrely by the Midland and Hull & Barnsley Railways! Their scheme envisaged both companies running over a completely new railway from Cudworth, to a much needed, but never built, central Halifax station, and on, to Keighley.

As may be expected, the HHLR took some years to construct, being brought into use for goods traffic on 1st August 1890 and passenger traffic, on the following 5th September. Until 1st October 1894, the HHLR was pure GN, but from that date it became a GNR/LYR Joint concern, by an Act of 3rd July 1894. Even so, appearances by L&Y locomotives were rare.

It was the coming of the HHLR that caused Holmfield locoshed to be built. Tenders for its construction had been issued in the Autumn of 1889; four submissions were received, to be opened on 31st October that year, with quotes ranging from £3,995 to £4,475. The lowest, from Walter Binns & Co., was accepted and work put in hand straightaway. Records show the locoshed opened with the HHLR, on 1st August 1890, but the final payment to Binns & Co. was not made by the GN until 4th December that year. That last instalment was for £347, bringing total costs of the engine shed to £4047 - £52 over estimate, owing to a post-tender addition of a sand furnace.

Holmfield locoshed had been designed to house six small engines and as completed, it comprised a two road dead-end building, scaling 120ftx 40ft. The depot was built entirely of stone and had a northlight roof that was slated on the unglazed ridges. Immediately outside the shed's eastern portal stood the coal stage, also in stone, which supported a 47,000 gallon water tank. That tank gave some shelter to the coaling floor which was equipped with a manually-powered bucket crane. Small office and stores buildings were ranged around the shed, while the above noted sand furnace stood behind the coal stage - which leaves mention only of the 45ft turntable to complete the depot's facilites. A similar turntable was installed at St. Pauls terminus, which seems to have been more useful than that at Holmfield shed, with the consequence that the latter had been removed by 1912.

Initial passenger services over the HHLR consisted of 12 return trips on weekdays, plus considerable goods traffic to the yards at Pellon and St. Pauls - the former being of notably larger dimensions than that at the terminus. In fact, it appears as if Pellon was the most important station on the line, because the passenger shuttle was quickly christened "The Pellon Bus." To work "The Bus," Holmfield housed a couple of tank engines outstationed from Bradford. At first these were Stirling Class F7 0-4-2ST, and Nos.631 and 632 seem to have been persistent inhabitants of Holmfield shed until the early 1900's, when withdrawal of the class commenced. In 1905/6 a steam railmotor was tried out on the line, but what were obviously ideal traffic conditions could not be served, as the steam car was no match for the HHLR's gradients.

Stirling's Class G2 0-4-4WT were also present at this time and another long-term Holmfield inmate appears to have been No.657. No doubt 657 also saw service on the HHLR, ran local trips and did her share of giving goods trains some tail-end assistance up the hill to St. Pauls. C2 Atlantic tanks were housed at Holmfield too, for passenger services to Bradford, Halifax and Keighley; they had arrived about 1899 and would be seen on those trains until 1944. Shunting the yards around Holmfield would have been in the care of Stirling, then Ivatt 0-6-0ST's, in addition to which the type handled local trip workings. It seems certain no tender engines were allocated to the depot, but of course, visiting 0-4-2, 2-4-0 and 0-6-0 would have been serviced there, on occasion. By LNER days the Class N1 0-6-2T were shedded at Holmfield for local passenger trains, with, from about 1931, some N2 making their appearance - also N5 and N7, but the last-named did not stay long in the district. GN 0-6-0's working goods and summertime passenger trains were joined by LNER J39, while Gresley's Class J50 0-6-0T supplemented, then gradually supplanted, Ivatt saddle tanks on shunting and local goods duties.

So the situation remained, but like the engine shed at Ingrow, whose history is recounted later in this book, Holmfield loco depot was built with an eye to a volume of traffic that rarely, if ever, was realised. So, although the Halifax-Holmfield-Halifax (St. Pauls) section saw quite healthy carryings, Holmfield shed was deemed to be something of a luxury,and the LNER closed it in 1933. The building lingered for a while, before demolition occurred, on a date yet to be determined.

After closure of the shed, passenger services survived until 21st May 1955, after which the line north of Homfield was closed and dismantled. But, four freights a day continued to run via Holmfield, onto the HHLR, latterly with haulage by B1 4-6-0 and LMS 8F 2-8-0. That service finally succumbed on 29th June 1960, when the HHLR too passed into history. When last surveyed, the site of Holmfield engine shed was partly covered by a car breaker's yard, one or two small factory units and a lot of weeds.

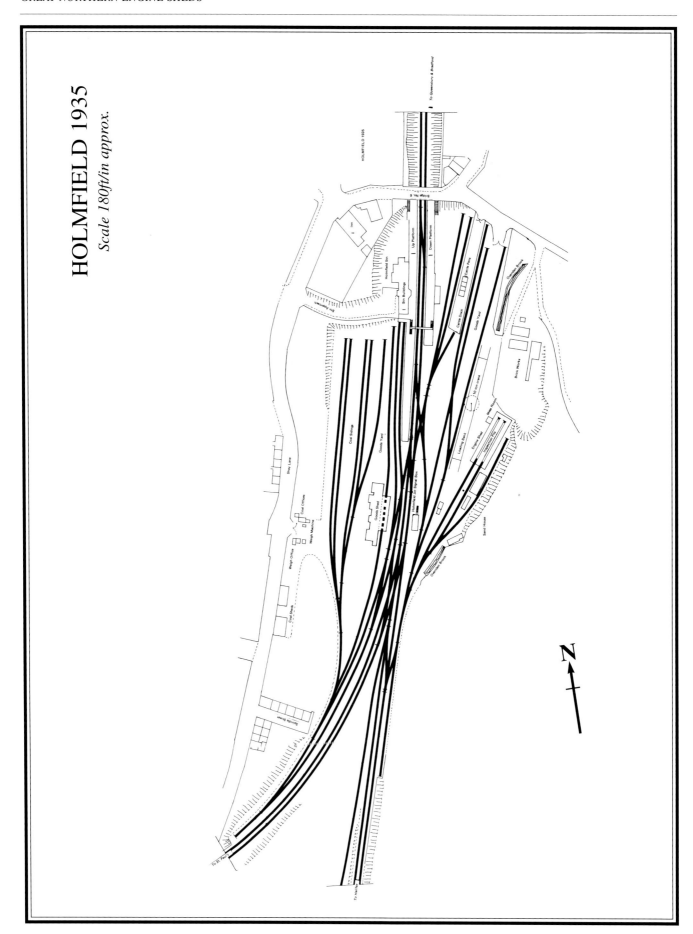

HOLMFIELD 1935
Scale 180ft/in approx.

N

Two pictures of Holmfield in happier times, with what are doubtless the resident shedmen posing with two of their charges. Note the combined water tank and coal platform's buckets behind the 0-4-2T, with the coaling crane's jib visible behind the 0-4-4T. The second picture shows the piles of ash unceremoniously dumped on the ground. Such seeming untidiness is belied by a story that comes from Holmfield, about one particular member of staff who was so conscientious that he reported himself an hour late, on an occasion of oversleeping! *K.Leech (both)*.

INGROW

One of the most uneconomic ventures upon which the GNR embarked was the network of lines linking Bradford, Halifax and Keighley. These were tortuous, hilly and heavily-engineered routes, that surely never paid for themselves and must often have given the shareholders cause to doubt the GN Board's wisdom.

Still, in those far-off days, prospects must have looked rosier and led to sponsorship of the Bradford & Thornton Railway, an independent company that arranged to have its services worked by the GN. The B&TR obtained its Act on 24th July 1871, but was soon to be taken over by the GN, through an Act of 18th July 1872. Construction through difficult terrain delayed opening until April 1878, for goods traffic, and 14th October that same year, for passengers.

In the meantime, another independent company had been promoted and seen its Act passed, on 5th August 1873. The Halifax, Thornton & Keighley Railway proposed two lines, also to be operated by the GN. One would extend the Bradford & Thornton Railway to Keighley, while the other would connect Queensbury, on the Bradford & Thornton, to Holmfield. The difficult to construct Queensbury-Holmfield section (tunnel most of the way) was brought into use first, for goods traffic, on 14th October 1878. Passenger trains did not commence to run through to Halifax until 1st December 1879, making their first stops at Holmfield a fortnight later, when a GN temporary station was opened. On from Thornton to Keighley, the magnificently engineered, hopelessly expensive line was subject to an HT&KR Deviation Act, of 18th July 1881. Slowly though, the railway crept

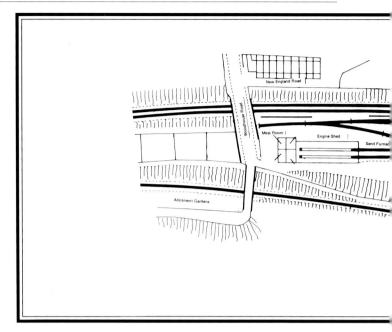

forward, over viaducts and through tunnels, to reach Ingrow on 7th April 1884, and open for all traffic, through to Keighley, on 1st November 1884, over 11 years after construction was first authorised.

Situated on the confluence of the Rivers Aire and Worth, the industrial town of Keighley had a population of 20,000 souls in the mid-1880's, and had for years been well served by the MR's direct Leeds-(Bradford)-Carlisle line. On the other hand,

A close-up of Ingrow shed in 1957, twenty one years after closure and awaiting further use. During its working existence this shed once was able to boast of a depot foreman with a full B.Sc. as a qualification. It is quite intriguing as to why such a well-qualified person should be in charge of a small and remote engine shed like Ingrow! *J.C.W.Halliday.*

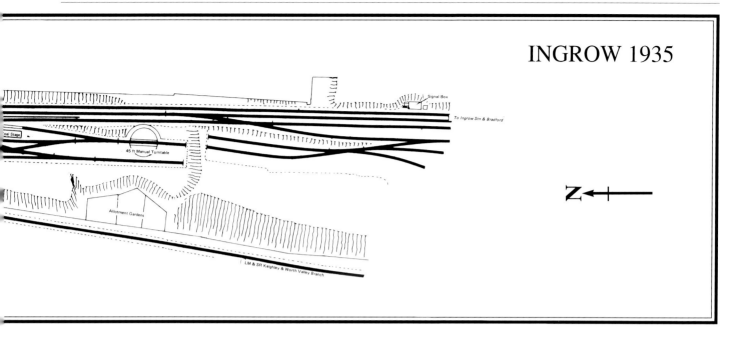

INGROW 1935

Signal Box

To Ingrow Stn & Bradford

Coal Stage

45 ft Manual Turntable

Allotment Gardens

LM & SR Keighley & Worth Valley Branch

A picture taken at the same time as the one opposite, shows the abandoned Ingrow shed's yard, combined water tank and coaling stage, a virtual copy of the Holmfield structure, with just beyond, the sand drying house. The mills of Keighley form a typical West Yorkshire background. *J.C.W.Halliday.*

GN trains between Keighley, Bradford and Leeds would have an incredibly diverse route to follow and quite simply, not be able to compete. Perhaps the facilities provided at Keighley, by the GN, sum up the situation - a fairly large goods warhouse, with smallish yard, was complemented on the passenger side by trains having to share two platforms at the Midland Railway's station!

A connection below Ingrow gave access to the MR, via that company's Worth Valley branch line. It was also at Ingrow that the GNR located its engine shed - had to locate it, to be precise, as there was precious little spare room elsewhere. The result was a long, narrow shed site, on the Down side, just north of Ingrow GN station. A 45ft turntable was positioned at the south end of the yard, with the coal stage at the yard's centre. That stage, which was built in stone, lined with brick, was provided with a hand crane and formed a base for a 50,000 gallon water tank. At the north end of the site a dead-end, two road stone-built locoshed was erected, large enough to hold eight tank engines and measuring 155ft x 38ft. The roof was period northlight in design, with slates on the unglazed areas, but over the office section at the rear of the shed, the slated roof was in transverse single-pitch form.

The shed had opened with the line and before a year was out, cost-cutting ideas were being expounded. In February 1885 Stirling remarked to the Board that the railway was paying the local waterworks company the equivalent of £140 per annum for water - most of which went into locomotives. He calculated that money could be saved by laying a 4in. pipe to the Keighley end of Lees Moor Tunnel, 1,848 yards away from the shed. The water run-off from that bore and the surrounding hills was sufficient to meet all the company's needs and Stirling estimated the cost of pipe, another water tank (at the station) and water cranes to be £970. In other words, after seven years, the GN would be 'in profit' on water costs, so the Board sanctioned the project, on the proviso that the estimated cost was not exceeded.

Ingrow depot was subordinate to Bradford, with the outstationed locomotives' duties centred around shunting the GN goods depot (one engine), while most turns were on local passenger workings, which varied over the years, but involved the three arms of the Queensbury triangle and took in Leeds. Perhaps in the earliest times, local goods trains were worked to Bradford and Halifax, but it would seem that if such trips were run, they did not last for long, as on 1st June 1896, Ivatt goes on record by saying that the allocation of Ingrow consisted of only four engines. By the early 1900's it had reduced further, to two locos, with Nos.128 and 619 Stirling Classes G2 0-4-4WT and J15 0-6-0ST respectively - being noted as almost permanent residents. Presumably, the saddle tank shunted the goods depot and the G2 worked local trips, while both would have given banking assistance, when necessary, from Keighley to Ingrow, up the long hill to Lees Moor Tunnel. Apart from its own allocation the depot would of course, service and house visiting engines, for the short time between inward and outward workings. It was such overall usage, albeit still quite light, that in 1902 caused the shed's northlight roof to require repair. £60-4-6d was spent in remedying the unspecified problem.

Mention is made above of visiting locomotives and their duties. Most would have emanated from Bradford, which sent Stirling, then Ivatt 0-6-0 and 0-6-0ST on goods, and Stirling 0-6-0, 0-4-2, 0-4-2T, 0-4-4T on passengers - these largely giving way to Ivatt 4-4-2T. Also Bradford had some Class L1 0-8-2T for a time, between 1905 and 1914 and these used to appear on goods. A particular duty for those large tanks was the 3.15 pm goods from Bradford to Keighley, returning on the 7.15 pm goods, which ran non-stop to Wakefield (Wrenthorpe Yard). That specific train rejoiced in the semi-official local name of 'The Keighley Wringer,' because usually among the merchandise carried was the daily output from a Keighley factory, making clothes mangles! Another goods turn, featuring an 0-6-0, started at Thornton at 11.30 am (the engine having run light from Bradford), and then spent the rest of the day pottering about on the Keighley branch, returning from there at 8.30 pm, on a pick-up goods. The majority of goods traffic was involved with the woollen mills of course - finished products out, and raw materials like wool - and coal, for the mills' boilers, in. Of the latter, there was a considerable tonnage - so much so in fact that some mills had their own wagon fleet: Ingrow's John Haggas & Co. being a case in point. In addition, Keighley possessed a considerable engineering industry, which gave rise to a healthy traffic in iron and steel castings.

About the time of World War One, N1 0-6-2T superseded C12's on passenger work, some to be sub-shedded at Ingrow and to reign until the line was closed. Not quite supremely though, as N2 and N7 appeared for short times, but were generally not suitable or not liked by the local crews. Better received were 0-6-2T of former GC Class N5, of which Bradford obtained two, in 1935. They were Nos.5525 and 5901 and both were used by Ingrow shed on passenger workiongs and the Keighley shunt/bank duties. On goods, J1, J2 and J3 were joined by the occasional J39 about 1928, but the latter class was mostly seen on summer special passenger workings. Around the same time as J39 first appeared 0-8-0's of Class Q1/2 arrived, the 'Long Toms' especially being favoured for working 'The Wringer.'

Nevertheless, traffic over the route never was very heavy, so it is not surprising that, in 1936, Ingrow shed should become a candidate for closure. It simply meant that goods engines did their own shunting at Keighley and, when necessary, returned to their home stations tender first - though this might have been more onerous for the crews, given the numerous tunnels on the line to Bradford and prevailing weather conditions in the area. So, the depot closed, with the entire Bradford-Keighley-Holmfield network following on 21st May 1955. At that time, buffer stops were inserted at the south end of Ingrow GN station, so that trains operated by BR, over the former Midland branch and connection, could reverse there and still gain access to the former GN goods yard. Eventually of course, even that traffic ceased.

For whatever reasons, neither the LNER, nor the Eastern and Midland Regions of BR undertook demolition of Ingrow locoshed. Thus it remained, trackless, but in surprisingly good order, until it was privately purchased, first for use by Slingsbys Iron Foundry then later as a wholesale groceries warehouse. The latter owner added a small extension at the front, and made interior alterations to the office section, but otherwise the building and site remained in remarkably unchanged condition until the mid 1970s. At that time, the yard, including the turntable's site, was incorporated into a factory estate, to be followed about a decade later by demolition of the coal stage and tank. The shed building continued to serve, however, seemingly indestructible, until with great suddenness, the wholesaler ceased trading and the former loco depot was pulled down, early in 1990. A visit in August 1990 found the floor and filled-in pits still clearly visible and no sign yet, of any redevelopment of the site.

Ingrow shed's final purpose was to serve as a cash-and-carry warehouse, as seen here in August 1984. The building received a front extension, but from the rear appeared largely unchanged. Inside, the northlight roof's cast iron supports mingled incongruously with Messrs Heinz "Noodle Doodles"! Prior to its cash-and-carry role, the shed had formed an annex for Slingsby's iron foundry, which can be seen in the background of the lower picture. *Authors' collection.*

Taken from a contemporary copy of *The Illustrated London News*, is this 1860 view of the Great Northern's original Leeds terminus at Central (Low Level), by then totally turned over to goods use. Through a little artistic licence the engine shed, shown on the right of the foot of the incline, does not appear in appropriate proportion, but official plans of the time confirm that the building on that site was the first GNR Leeds shed. *Authors' collection.*

LEEDS CENTRAL (LOW LEVEL)

The importance of Leeds as one of Yorkshire's largest industrial centres is illustrated by its population, which grew from just over 309,000 in 1893, to 500,000 only twenty years later. Of course, the city had been somewhat smaller when the GNR commenced running into it, but it was the inherent importance of Leeds, even in early days, that attracted the GN in the first place.

GN services to Leeds opened on 1st October 1849, and initially were of a complex nature. Trains ran from Doncaster to the Lancashire & Yorkshire Railway at Askern Junction, and over that company's route via Pontefract, to its junction with the Midland Railway at Methley, then via the MR to Holbeck, Leeds. From Holbeck, Leeds & Thirsk Railway tracks were taken to Geldard junction, where reversal took place, to gain access to Leeds Central station. Under an agreement ratified by an Act of Parliament of 22nd July 1848, the station was jointly used by the Great Northern, Leeds & Thirsk, Leeds & Dewsbury and Lancashire & Yorkshire Railways (the last named starting off as the Leeds & Manchester Railway). Yet, in the very first month of its arrival in Leeds, the GN's engineer, Cubitt, was preparing plans for the company's own station, to be sited close to Leeds Central, but at a lower level.

Cubitt's plans for the station included provision of a 104ft x 43ft engine shed and after due tendering procedure, a contract for the whole project was awarded on 7th March 1850, to Messrs, Wilks, Winn & Pearson. Three months later on 20th June, Wilks, Winn & Pearson's contract was amended to include construction of a coke shed and foundations for a turntable, all works to be completed by 15th September 1850. Because the L&TR was going to share the goods facilities adjacent to Low Level station, that company's Locomotive Superintendent, a Mr. Bourne, assisted the GN by obtaining a quote of £160, for a 36ft 6in turntable from James Lister & Co., of Darlington: "...a turntable large enough to turn engine and tender..." The GN accepted Lister's offer, which probably meant that Mr. Bourne was also able to accept - a small commission from Lister & Co!

So, from 1st October 1849, to 15th September 1850, the GN was apparently without engine shed facilities at Leeds - none too serious a disadvantage as until 1st July 1850, the GNR hauled only its own passenger trains, with the L&YR taking GN goods traffic from Doncaster to Leeds, Hunslet Lane. From 1st July 1850, however, GN goods trains were worked by the company's own locos and the GN partly solved its problem over engine facilities by outstationing locomotives at the L&Y's Knottingley shed. That was not a wholly satisfactory solution though, involving as it did a lot of light engine running - and tender first in the Knottingley-Leeds direction, owing to the lack of a turntable at the former place (see sections on Knottingley and Turntables) But, it seems the GNR probably did make some use of engine shed facilities at Leeds during this time. A former British Railways Manager at Leeds, Bob Oliver, who wrote *Leeds Holbeck, The First Wisp of Steam*, informed the authors that during his researches he had found evidence the GN were visiting Hunslet Lane engine shed, as 'guests' of the Midland Railway.

Hunslet Lane's 8-road shed had been built jointly by the L&YR and MR - or more correctly their forebears, the Leeds & Manchester and North Midland Railways respectively - opening on 1st July 1840. The L&Y and MR each used 4 roads, but the former's occupation was brief, that company having virtually moved out by 1849, to share the LNWR's engine shed at Copley Hill (Wortley). Accordingly, there would have been spare capacity at Hunslet Lane, so it is entirely reasonable that the MR would invite the GNR to use the depot for a short time. (To complete this thumbnail sketch of Hunslet Lane shed, MR engines pulled out about 1873, after which the building became a goods shed, to eventually be demolished as recently as 1980! Even now, some parts of the walls remain).

Whether, Wilks, Winn & Pearson met the target date of 15th September 1850 for completion of Leeds Central (Low Level) station and shed, is not known; if not, the facilities certainly would have been in use not much later than that date. As completed, the engine shed was in some respects different to that which was originally planned. Firstly it was larger, measuring 125ft x 52ft and accommodating three roads under its single-pitch slated gable roof. The building was constructed in a mixture of brick and stone, with all three roads being accessed from the turntable. Between the turntable and shed, on the western side, a coke stage - not coke shed, according to a contemporary plan - was put up, its construction materials being the same as used in the main building.

Although the depot backed onto the River Aire and Leeds & Liverpool Canal, water for engine (and all other) purposes came from Leeds Waterworks Company and that supplier was the cause of the first operational problem at the station and shed, which came to be mentioned in the GN's Minutes. That was on 18th July 1851, when Sturrock gave the following report: "...It is recommended that arrangements be made with the Canal Company for drawing water from that supply and an engine and pump be provided to supply the Leeds station. This need has come about because of the great inconvenience having been sustained on Monday the 7th of July last, when we were in short supply from the Leeds Waterworks Company, from whom at present the water is obtained..." The Minutes note that the Board: "...resolved that the General Manager and Locomotive Engineer be authorised to make an arrangement at the least possible expense for the supply of water at the Leeds station from the canal, using if it can, the pump and machinery of the Leeds & Thirsk Railway Co..." By 5th August 1851, Sturrock was able to report: "...it has been presented to me satisfactorily by the water Company at Leeds that it will be in a position in 7 or 8 weeks, to give a satisfactory supply of water required at the station there at a fair cost. Under the circumstances I have made a temporary arrangement with Locomotive Superintendent of the Leeds & Thirsk Company, to be permitted to wash out the engines and pump at Leeds..." (So GN locomotives also used the engine shed facilities of the L&TR for a while - at the time these consisted of a roundhouse, half roundhouse and two road straight shed, sited on the opposite side of the Aire to the GN depot. The 1½ round buildings still stand, having seen a second complete roundhouse, of NER origin, come and go. Today, the L&TR sheds - well known Leeds landmarks - happily enjoy "Listed" status).

There is no further mention of Leeds' water supply in the archives of the time, so it may safely be assumed the problem was overcome. Before long though another problem came about, when in April 1854, Sturrock reported that the "old" turntable (just 3½ years old!) was "worn out," and he requested its replacement by a new one of similar size. Sited as it was the turntable was traversed by every engine movement into and out of the shed, so it would have been heavily used. Even so, the fact that after only 3½ years it should need renewal was evidence that James Lister & Co. had used inadequate materials - wrought iron probably. So, complete replacement was a *fait accompli*, the

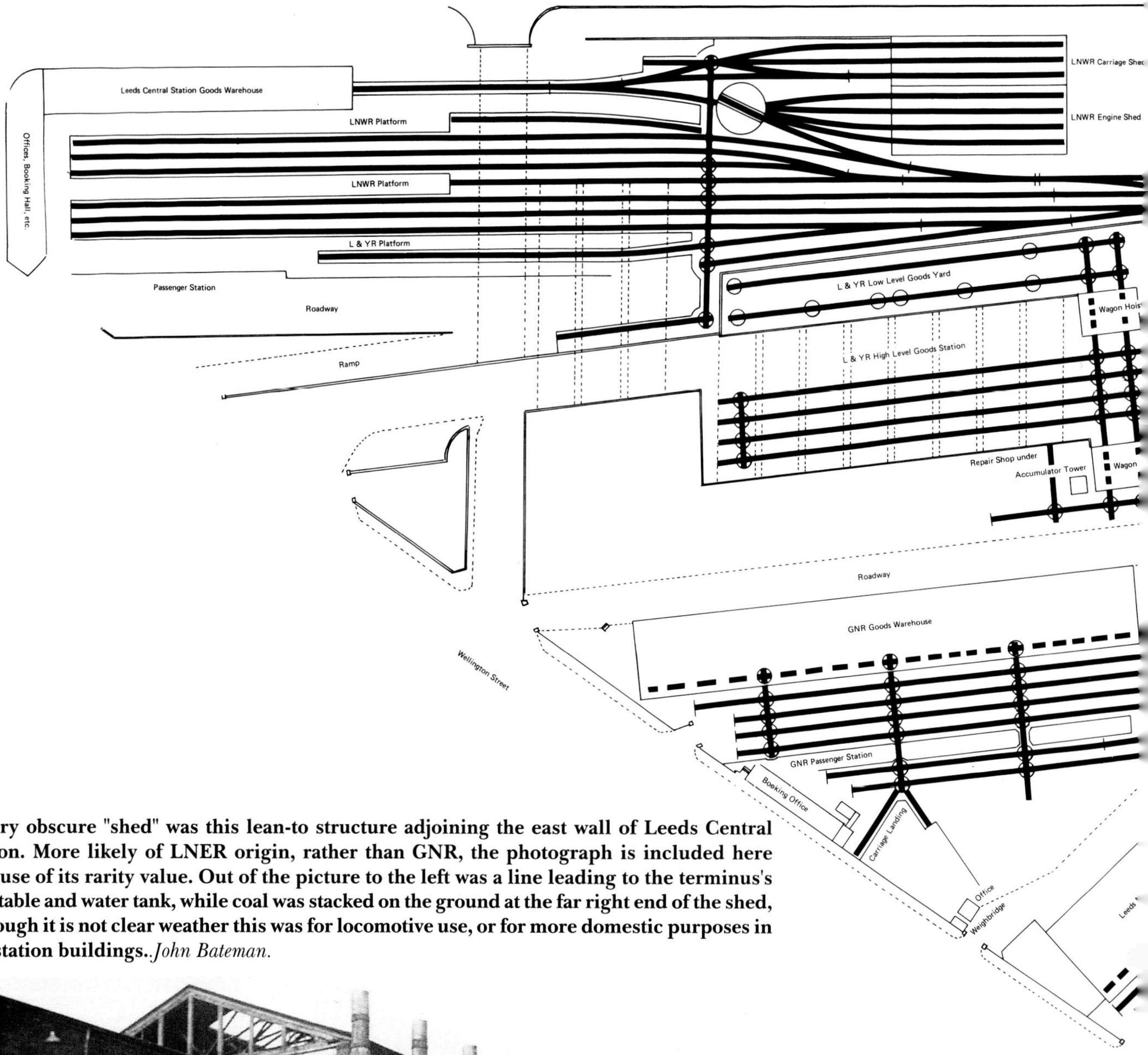
Leeds Central Station Goods Warehouse
Offices, Booking Hall, etc.
LNWR Platform
LNWR Platform
L & YR Platform
Passenger Station
Roadway
Ramp
LNWR Carriage Shed
LNWR Engine Shed
L & YR Low Level Goods Yard
Wagon Hoist
L & YR High Level Goods Station
Repair Shop under
Accumulator Tower
Wagon
Roadway
GNR Goods Warehouse
Wellington Street
GNR Passenger Station
Booking Office
Carriage Landing
Office
Weighbridge

A very obscure "shed" was this lean-to structure adjoining the east wall of Leeds Central station. More likely of LNER origin, rather than GNR, the photograph is included here because of its rarity value. Out of the picture to the left was a line leading to the terminus's turntable and water tank, while coal was stacked on the ground at the far right end of the shed, although it is not clear weather this was for locomotive use, or for more domestic purposes in the station buildings..*John Bateman.*

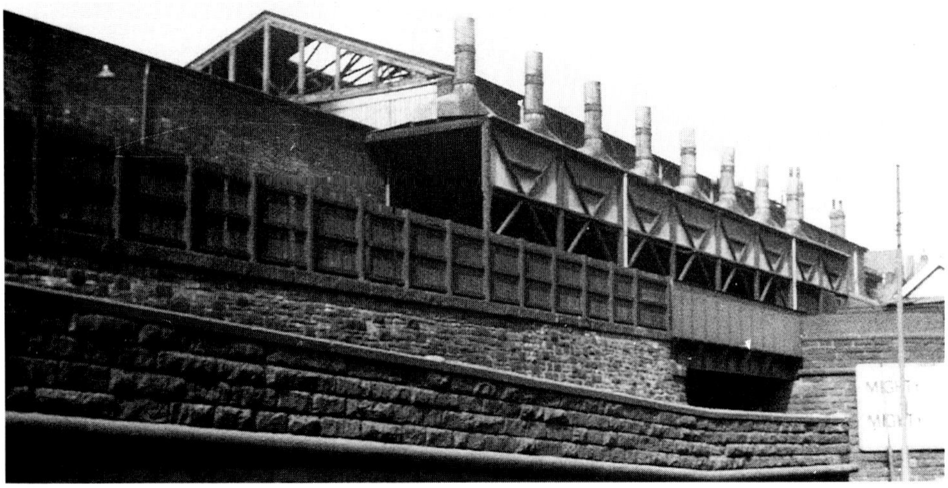

High Level

London & North Western Railway

Shunters

Inspection Pit

Lancashire & Yorkshire Railway

Viaduct

Signalbox

Stables under

GNR Engine Shed

Inspection Pits

Leeds Northern Rly

Ash Pit

Pump

L & YR Low Level Goods Yard

Coke Platform (Water tank over)

Coal Staithes

River Aire

Coal Yard

Stables

Weighbridge

Ticket Platform

Office

Cattle Landing

Leeds Northern Rly Goods Yard

5 ton Yard Crane

Roadway

N

Stores Office etc.

Office

Weighbridge

LEEDS CENTRAL
1854

cost of which the GN Board had to accept.

Although the GN's 1855 Rule Book shows Leeds engine shed as having workings only to Laisterdyke (8 miles), Bradford (10 miles) and Halifax (17 miles), traffic was inexorably increasing and caused the General Manager to remark in a report to the Board, on 9th January 1855: "...the position of the engine house at Leeds is very inconvenient and will become more so but it can be re-erected by removing it to land of about 4 acres valued at £350 per acre, at the junction of the Leeds & Bradford and Leeds & Wakefield railways at Wortley..." The General Manager went on to recommend that the land be purchased in conjunction with the L&YR, which was willing to join in the venture (the GN had suggested a joint engine shed to the L&Y as early as 1849). The Board concurred and resolved that the land: "...be got with the L&Y when necessary..." There is then an added note in the Minute book, which says: "Not to be communicated with the L&Y yet" (!)

As it turned out, the land was purchased soon after, the precise date of which is unknown, as part of the GN plan to return to Leeds Central station. In 1856, plans were laid and contracts let for "removal" of the engine shed to Wortley, provision of a coke stage, engine pit and water cranes at Leeds Central station (those three items to cost £1,250), attention to the approach road (whether this meant the rail approach or *really* the road is not known), and improvements to the station itself. The L&Y was again asked if it wanted to share with the GN in a joint engine shed at Wortley and a plan was produced in December, which divided the shed two thirds GN and one third L&Y. Initial reactions from the L&Y were somewhat chary, the company maintaining that: "...the Great Northern Company would use the shed much more..." It would not be long before circumstances would cause the L&Y to reconsider the idea. Altogether though, the project seems to have been a somewhat confused affair, as on 27th January 1857, Messrs. Kirk & Parry, of Sleaford, expressed their belief that: "...an engine shed which is to be re-erected at Wortley Junction, to be recovered from Leeds, is part of this company's contract for building works at Leeds Central station..." The Board resolved that it must not be admitted the work in question did form part of the original contract - in fact, the shed's construction had been put out to public tender only the month before (the authors have found no trace of this).

Whatever the original plans and wording of contracts at the time, and whomsoever it was that finally built the new engine shed, none of the materials from the shed at Low Level were used in its construction. In fact, the old shed was not taken down for some time, as the accompanying engraving (*see* page 70), which shows Leeds Central (Low Level) goods station about 1860, clearly indicates the erstwhile engine shed in the foreground, still complete with turntable and in use for some purpose. When the building was actually removed is not known, but we must now move on, to consider the history of the GN engine shed at Wortley.

LEEDS (WORTLEY)

Initially known as "Wortley Junctions (Wortley)," the Great Northern's second shed at Leeds was sited in the triangle of lines at Wortley and was brought into use on 30th September 1857. This was very conveniently timed, as the Bradford, Wakefield & Leeds Railway opened from Wakefield to Leeds,

on 3rd October 1857. BW&L trains were worked by the GNR from the outset and completion of the new route meant that the GN had a direct approach to Leeds Central for the first time and reversals at Geldard Junction ended.

Measuring 152ft x 62ft, the new shed building was made in brick, with two gable-ended slated pitched roofs, each covering 2 roads and having a raised central smoke vent. The roof was supported by iron tie rods - an early use of such a method in an era when timber beams were the norm. Layout of the shed was dead-end in pattern, with arched entrances at the front and two workshops, a stores and an office in a 48ft extension at the rear; within the shed each road was equipped with a full length pit. In the yard at the northern side of the shed was a 61ft x 17ft brick-built coke stage, having an 8' wide canopy over the coking road; at first, fuelling was done by hand, but in later years, after coal had been adopted, a bucket crane was installed. Forming a roof to the stage was a water tank made of 4' 9" high plates, therefore having a capacity of about 30,000 gallons - supplies continued to come from the Leeds Waterworks Co. Finally, a 40ft turntable completed the depot's facilities, being sited to the north west of the main building.

During the same year, the L&YR was having engine shed accommodation problems. Since the late 1840's, the LNWR had been housing L&Y locomotives, but now wanted the "Lanky" to leave its 3 road premises at Copley Hill (near the new GN shed, but on a lower level). The matter came to a head during the latter part of 1858, when a number of alternatives for housing the L&Y's Leeds allocation of 3 engines had been considered and rejected. Following that, Captain Laws of the L&Y reported to his board: "...The only safe plan is to build a shed that will hold 4 engines at Wortley, on the joint ground and adjacent to the Great Northern Company's shed. It will be about 100 feet by 30 feet - one wall is built - there will be about 500 yards of excavation, but including all I think the cost will not be more than £800 to £1,000. We now pay £78 per annum for standing 3 engines and we cannot keep a spare one, so that at all times there is great inconvenience when any engine gets out of order. If we had 4 engines the charge would be £104 per annum so that there will be a saving to the company if they build stable room for their own engines. No time ought to be lost as the London & North Western Company cannot let our engines remain with them for more than three or four months..." Quickly, the L&Y Board agreed that tenders be issued and an offer of £492 was accepted in August 1858.

Opening of the L&Y's shed came early in 1859 and Captain Laws' reference to "...one wall is built..." clearly indicates what form the construction took. Quite simply, the L&Y 'added' their 2-road 91ft x 24ft shed onto the eastern side of the GN building. Built in brick, the dead-end L&Y shed had arched entrances like the GN building, but the gable roof was supported by more traditional timber trusses. Few other facilities seem to have been provided but one shortfall was made up almost immediately, when Sturrock got approval for expenditure of £170 for an additional siding for coke and coal trucks - fuel throughput would obviously increase with the L&Y's presence. Then, in 1860 the L&Y built rooms for the enginemen and cleaners and at the same time an external ash pit was added, as there was none inside the shed, so washouts kept it "...in a wet and dirty state..." Later still, interior ashpits were provided on both tracks.

Since August 1854, the GN had been working all services over the Leeds, Bradford & Halifax Junction Railway, but during the time the L&Y were moving into Wortley, the GN and LB&HJ

were involved in a dispute that lasted from 1858 to 1861. Strictly speaking, the railway line between Holbeck and Wortley Junction was LB&HJ property, for the use of which, the small company said the GN should pay. For instance, for the quarter up to 30th June 1858, the LB&HJ claimed £150 for running rights and £35 for watering. By 6th September 1859, according to the LB&HJ, the GN's total owings had reached the sum of £1,982-0-1d and there was a threat of a tribunal if the GN refused to pay - which it did! By 1861, arbitration had been resorted to and a lengthy report, with findings, was published on 6th July that year. The arbitrator was a civil engineer from Westminster, named as Mr Harrison and briefly put, his report found that the LB&HJ could not legitimately seek compensation "...for injuries done to its track by the GN engines entering Wortley Junction Engine Shed..." Mr. Harrison continued by saying that neither could the LB&HJ stop the Great Northern having access to its engine shed at Wortley Junction, over LB&HJ metals. That ended the dispute and exactly four years later, the LB&HJ was absorbed by the GNR. As a result of the LB&HJ's take-over, that company's 'side' of Wortley triangle, i.e. from Wortley North Junction, to Wortley West, became GN property. At a date unknown, but certainly before 1888, the shed's 40ft turntable was removed and engines thereafter used the triangle for turning purposes.

Traffic continued to increase and on 21st April 1868 caused the General Manager to comment that a better supply of water for engines was required at Leeds. He recommended that a 13,000 gallon iron tank should be provided, which with necessary timber work, was estimated to cost £185. The Board agreed to the provision, but it is not clear from the Minutes exactly where the tank was installed - since Wortley engine shed had a large tank already it is assumed the new one was put up at the station.

Further improvements came in 1873, when on 3rd July, Stirling recommended to the Way & Works Committee that three additional locomotive sidings be provided at Wortley shed, at a total estimated cost of £1,398. The General Manager, however, thought that only one siding should be laid and the Committee concurred - for one siding, at £200-250, for 17-20 wagons! What happened to Stirling's locomotive sidings is not known, but the coal sidings were certainly needed. By September 1876, the Locomotive Engineer was reporting a weekly average coal consumption at Wortley of 235 tons; it is not clear if the L&Y's usage was included in that figure - probably not. Next, on 7th August 1877, the engineer recommended that extra sidings, for 40 carriages, should be put down at Wortley Junction, at an estimated cost of £500. This was approved.

Two years later, on 8th August 1879, Stirling was trying to come to grips with the ever-growing workload at various engine sheds, with specific comments about the West Riding, as follows: "...additional engine shed accommodation is required at Leeds and Bradford, the facilities at each place providing for the accommodation of 8 engines only, whereas in the former district there are 60 engines and in the latter, 40 engines, for which proper shelter cannot be given or the requisite repairs be efficiently carried out..." The Way & Works Committee, which heard Stirling's request, resolved that the matter be referred to a sub-committee comprised of Lord Colville, Mr. R. Tennant and Mr. J. Shuttleworth, who were to report their recommendations to the GN Board. In the meantime, the company's Engineer was instructed to prepare plans for wooden sheds, with substructures of brick, so as to meet the requirements of the Locomotive Engineer.

Some interesting points emerge from the above. First, it seems as if Stirling was over-exaggerating the space shortages at Leeds and Bradford, as both places had, at that time, four road engine sheds capable of holding at least twelve of the locomotives of the period. In addition, he seems to have forgotten to mention Ardsley shed, which although small, was housing some of the Leeds allocation. Perhaps the Loco Engineer meant that only 8 engines 'in steam' could be housed at the sheds, allowing for one locomotive under repair or washout to be stabled at the innermost end of each shed road? Interesting too, about the suggestion of providing wooden sheds - obviously intended as temporary stopgaps, and as far as the authors have been able to find out, never actually proceeded with. Neither have the results of the sub-committee's investigation come to light, but on 2nd July 1880, Stirling again drew the attention of the Board to "...the great deficiency in engine shed accommodation at Leeds, Bradford (and Colwick)..." The Board were obviously convinced enough to order the Engineer to draw up plans and estimates for submission to the Locomotive Committee on the following 28th July.

Even so, things still appear to have moved slowly, as it was not until 1884 that purchase of land for a new Leeds engine shed was proceeded with. What machinations had preceded this are not known and even then the 1884 record is sketchy, but what seems to have occurred is that between February and August of that year, the GN's Yorkshire Committee negotiated the purchase of 7 acres 3 rods of land at Copley Hill, from Smythes Trustees, at a price 4/- (20p) per yard. This was in conjunction with the LNWR, who were also interested in expanding their operations in that area; an existing footpath was retained and formed a boundary between the GN and LNWR parcels of land, with the latter very quickly utilising theirs. The Great Northern were not far behind, seeing their purchase as ideal for "...easing curves, enlarging the triangle and providing the site for a new engine shed..." and on 4th June 1885, tenders were opened for the job of preparing the site. This involved "...levelling of the land near Copley Hill, to make it suitable for railway purposes..." tender prices ranged from £5,000 to £8,000 and it seems little heed was paid to the need for the land to consolidate before building began, as on 13th December 1885, Stirling requested a carriage cleaning shed be built "similar to that recently opened at Holloway," at an estimated cost, including engine pits, of £6,140. This was approved.

After approval for construction of the carriage shed, further future plans were considered and on 13th January 1886, the Yorkshire Committee put forward a proposal that the L&YR could take over the entire engine shed at Wortley Junction, as tenants of the GN, once the GN had moved to its projected new shed at Copley Hill (Wortley). The reactions of the GN Board and L&YR to this suggestion were not recorded, but as it turned out, this might not have immediately mattered. That was because on 12th October 1886 came a "bombshell" that may or may not have put back virtually all plans for the new installations at Copley Hill by more than a decade. Due to lack of documentary evidence it is impossible for the authors to be certain exactly what did occur over the next 10 to 12 years, so all that can be done is to report what has been found and draw conclusions.

That report of 12th October 1886, by the GN's Engineer, and read to the Yorkshire Committee on 15th October, advised of "...the proposed working by Messrs. Cliffe of the minerals consisting of ironstone, fireclay etc., which underlie the company's property near Wortley Junction. Submitted is Mr. Rowley's plan on which he has shown the new lines of permanent

Views of the original GNR Wortley Junction engine shed are extremely rare. Likewise photographs of Copley Hill engine shed in GN days are also rare. However, this view of Great Northern 0-4-4T No.764 standing with its wheels just on the Copley Hill turntable at the west end of the yard c1890s will hopefully stand on its own merit. Note the upturned BRADFORD destination board on the tank top and the cleanliness of the engine, which was either a Copley Hill or Bradford (Bowling) engine. *K.Leech collection.*

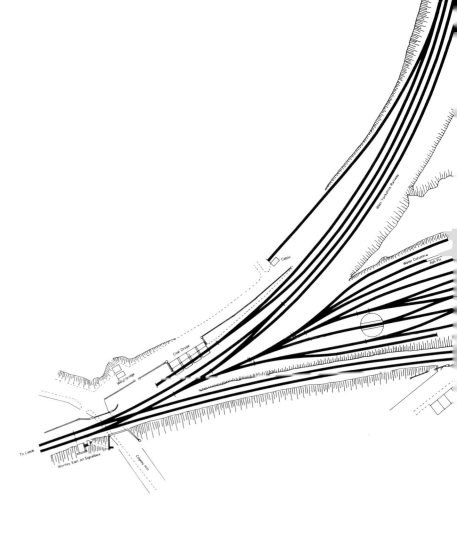

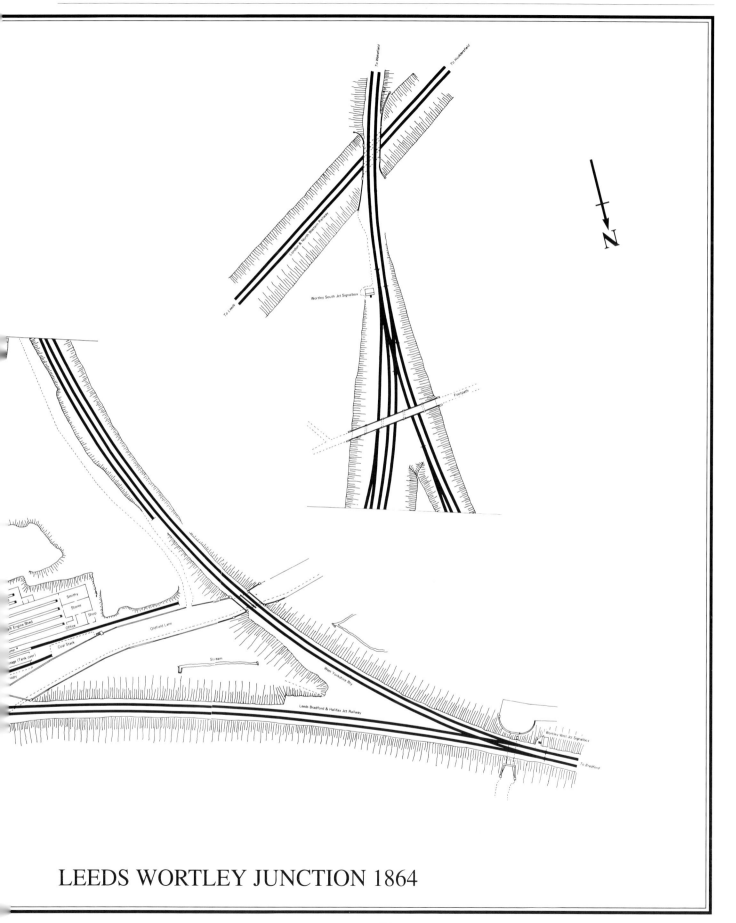

LEEDS WORTLEY JUNCTION 1864

way and sidings, as well as the large engine shed and workshops. Mr. Rowley points out that should the materials be worked, there would be considerable subsidence of the building, for the support of which it would in his opinion be necessary to purchase an area about 14,792 superficial yards, which does not include the area of the proposed carriage shed and coke stage..." the Yorkshire Committee resolved "...to recommend to the Board to proceed with these works and that steps be taken to ascertain the terms upon which the minerals can be purchased..."

No record of negotiations with Messrs. Cliffe has been traced, but if a deal was indeed struck, doubtless that company was adequately rewarded for purchase of the mineral rights. It is not known whether the LNWR's portion of the land was similarly affected, but for the GN the whole business seems to have taken some time, as it was not until 5th June 1890 that Stirling again recommended construction of an engine shed at Wortley, "to hold 30 engines." The next mention was 7th January 1892, when regarding the proposed engine shed at Wortley, the Engineer was instructed to: "...report in respect of the curve at Wortley, as to provision of a 'small' engine shed there..."

Dutifully, Stirling reported back, on 28th January 1892: "...Other works involved would be that the curve would have to be altered from 16 chains radius to 27 chains and the gradient of the line for Wakefield trains, between Holbeck and Wortley East, from 1 in 50 to 1 in 82, which would require the lowering of the road known as Copley Hill Road. The shed for 30 engines, with sidings, coal stage, turntable etc., and sidings for carriage stock, coal and cattle traffic and widening of the bridge over the LNWR are estimated at £92,180. In carrying out these alterations it would be necessary to deal with large quantities of surplus earth and is proposed that the company purchase a strip of land half a chain in width, and about one mile long, so that about 8 acres of land would be created..." The committee resolved that further reports on the matter should be presented to the Board.

Once again though, the subject disappears for more than four years until 1st June 1896, when Ivatt presented a general report about the lack of engine shed accommodation at various points on the GN system. With regard to Leeds, Ivatt said: "...there are 49 engines at Wortley GN/LYR shed, with room for 17 I hope to move some to Ardsley which has spare capacity and think that a new shed for 30 engines would probably be sufficient at Wortley if there is spare room..." Ivatt then specifically mentioned a site "...near West Box, at the rear of the recreation ground, as it would leave room for expansion of the carriage sidings inside the triangle..."

The foregoing raises some points that are not entirely clear. Ivatt does not state whether the 49 engines at Wortley included those of the L&Y. However, when he speaks of a shed capacity for seventeen locomotives, the inference is that the L&Y wing of the depot was being counted, because the GN shed, as built, could hold only twelve engines. Alternatively, the depot might have been extended at some time between 1857 and 1896, but no record of any such work has been found. Next, Ivatt's suggestion of a site for Wortley's new shed lay outside the triangle, whereas all previous plans had concerned the area within the junctions.

These loose ends were further compounded on 15th January 1897, when the Yorkshire Way & Works Committee presented preliminary plans and costs for the new engine shed and carriage shed at Copley Hill, at a total estimated cost of £48,596. The proportion of costs for the engine shed were:
30 engine shed, ash pits, water cranes, workshops, stores - £16,055

Coal stage, ash pit, water tank - £3,850
Sand furnace and mess room for men - £805
Turntable, complete - £1,000
Retaining wall between sidings and main line - £930
Permanent way and land, complete - £6,100
Total - £28,740
Carriage shed for 130 vehicles, 465ft x 80ft, plus washing plant and running lines for engines. (To be made of timber, because the building was likely to be affected by subsidence from coal workings, and to be the project's first construction priority) - £9,970

The confusion comes first with a statement that the new engine shed would be built "on the carriage shed site." In other words, a carriage shed was already in situ in the triangle and the new one was designed to replace it. So, it seems as if some construction at least might have gone ahead as Mr. Rowley recommended in 1886. Secondly, comes the indication that the new carriage shed could be affected by coal mining subsidence. That particular mineral was not mentioned in the 1886 dealings with Messrs. Cliffe, so if that company had been 'bought off' at that time, it seems not all the land had been "made safe" as it were. The authors' conjecture is that some mineral rights were purchased in 1886 and a carriage shed built over all, or some of the sidings that lay above the minerals. Then, after 10 years or so, when engine shed space problems had become acute, the carriage shed had to be 'sacrificed' to make way for a loco depot, being removed to the nearest convenient site, which just happened to be above separately owned mining rights. The fact that the GN were prepared for subsidence problems rather than try to purchase those mineral rights, indicates perhaps that mining was already underway and could not be stopped at reasonable cost.

Whatever, the job was put out to tender on 1st November 1897 with fifteen companies invited to reply. Of these, twelve returned their tenders by the due date of 4th November, with prices ranging from a high of £31,623 and sixteen months to complete, to the lowest, at £25,368, with completion within eight months. That cheapest offer, from Kell Brothers, was accepted on 12th November and work started straightaway. As a last note to the construction of the GN's third engine shed in Leeds, a separate tender was let on 4th November 1897 to Cowans Sheldon, for a 52ft turntable, at a cost of £402. Strangely the cost was not formally approved until 9th June 1898 and not finally paid until 15th June 1899! Before describing the GN's new engine shed though, we must complete the story of Wortley.

As proposed by the Yorkshire Committee in 1886, the L&Y took over all of Wortley shed. What is more, on 26th January 1900, the L&Y produced contract plans for the job of largely rebuilding the depot. The original GN/LY side walls were retained, but in the 4-road former GN sections, the rails were taken through the workshops at the rear. At the same time the two road ex-L&Y 'portion' was lengthened rearwards, to the same 200ft dimension, and a new rear wall was built across the width of the two roads. The original L&Y tracks were not extended from their original length though - the newly created space being used for workshops and a messroom. At the front, the depot lost its arched entrances in favour of square openings and above, a new overall northlight roof was provided. In the yard, the track layout was largely maintained, but on the north side, the GN coal stage was demolished, to be replaced on the southern side of the depot by a standard L&Y ramp-type coaling shed, with water tank above; between the coaler and the engine shed a 60ft

Portraits of Copley Hill shed's original roof are scarce, but a small part of its transverse pitch pattern may be seen in this photograph of Ivatt Atlantic No.3280 with *QUEEN OF SCOTS* headboard. 21st July 1935. *W.T.Stubbs.*

By January 1950, Copley Hill's roof had been somewhat altered - damage during WW2 perhaps? This rather ramshackle state of affairs gave BR yet another major refurbishment job to carry out! Still to receive its full BR number, Ivatt C12 tank No.7372 shares stabling room with an N1, a named B1 and an A1 Pacific - the usual types to be found at the shed during this early BR period. *A.B. Crompton.*

The shed's new roof, with lightweight steel frames, asbestos sheeting and brick end-screens is seen in a July 1961 picture that reeks with smoky atmosphere. Famous for its Pacifics in BR days, Copley Hill is hosting three, seen at left: resident 60070 GLADIATEUR and two visitors from Doncaster, the un-loved Thompson rebuild 60113 GREAT NORTHERN, and 60156 GREAT CENTRAL. Note the filled-in turntable pit; the date for removal of the 'table has yet to be determined. *P.Sanderland.*

turntable was put down. All this was done 'around' the engines using the depot, and must have cost the L&Y a considerable sum. However, the refurbished shed, which was known as "Oldfield Lane," to distinguish it from its GN neighbour, was to see less than 30 years use by locomotives. In 1928, the LMS, having a former LNWR and two ex-MR depots in the Leeds area - Farnley Junction, Holbeck and Stourton - in addition to Wortley, took the practical decision to reduce its locomotive shed facilities. So, Wortley closed in July 1928, to see further use as a repository for old rolling stock and suchlike. To judge by an early 1930's photograph, dereliction had quickly set in and it is thought the building was pulled down before the onset of World War Two, thereby ending a very varied existence of some 80 years.

LEEDS (COPLEY HILL)

The information related above, about purchase of Copley Hill's turntable gives almost certain indication of the time of opening of the shed. Messrs. Kell Bros. were to take eight months to complete their contract, from November 1897 - i.e. July 1898. The fact that costs for the turntable were approved in June 1898 infers the pit, which would have been part of Kell Bros. job, was nearing completion and with it, the rest of the depot no doubt. So, Copley Hill engine shed seems to have come into use about July/August 1898, probably quite abruptly, as the men and machines had only to move across the intervening 100 yards or so from Wortley shed; it was in that space that the new carriage shed had been built.

Copley Hill engine shed incorporated a number of features that were revolutionary for the GNR. First, the brick-built, 5-road, 305ft x 75ft depot was of the through type and featured a transverse pitch roof. In adopting that style of covering, the GN abandoned the then standard 'northlight' pattern in favour of a design used only once before on the railway, in 1862, for the 8-road straight shed at Kings cross "Top Shed." Why the company made the change appears obvious at first glance, because northlight roofs were proving a maintenance liability. Yet for Hornsey shed, which opened a year after Copley Hill, a northlight roof was provided. It serves to illustrate possibly, how much individual responsibility was allowed to the Yorkshire Committee - and perhaps, how 'canny' the members of that committee were! At the front of the shed a fan of tracks led from a single line, while a by-pass line ran down each side of the building. There was a single road beside the ramped coaling stage, which was brick-built, part covered by a pitched roof and part by the shed's 29,000 gallon water tank; timber columns were used to support the roof section, while brick walls held up the much heavier water tank. The 52ft turntable (actually recorded as 51ft 9in. in the *Appendix to the WTT*), was installed at the rear of the shed, but with a large and well equipped workshop a few miles way, at Ardsley depot, the GN did not go to the expense of providing major repair facilities at Copley Hill. So, only basic servicing and running repairs could be carried out there and for any requirements beyond that, engines were sent to Ardsley.

Water was still being supplied by Leeds Waterworks, so with an estimated annual consumption for Copley Hill shed of 47 million gallons, at 6d. (2½p) per 1,000 gallons, the GN was facing a yearly bill of £1,175. Not surprising then, when on 28th July 1899, a contract was let to Messrs. C. Islar for a borehole that hopefully would yield 58 million gallons per year. Messrs Islar's bore had reached 35 feet by 2nd November, with no success,

but then we get another of those inexplicable 'disappearances' from the records! Not until Christmas Day 1903 does another Minute record that there had been "no further progress" with the borehole at Leeds. Frustratingly, it was a further two years before the same comment appears again - three more times - on 23rd January, 24th June and 25th November 1905 before finally fading, seemingly for ever. What stage the bore had reached and at what cost, by Christmas 1903, is not known, but as a 1906 register of the GN's water suppliers records that Copley Hill was still getting its water from the Waterworks, it is fairly obvious the well had proved 'dry.'

Returning to 1st May 1902, indications were given that the Twentieth Century had arrived, and of the close relationships that existed between Leeds and Bradford Locomotive Districts. That was when the Way & Works Committee gave approval for a direct telephone line to be put in, between Copley Hill and Bradford engine sheds. Because Britain's public telephone system was still in its infancy, with few links between towns even as close together as Leeds and Bradford, the GN provided the line itself, running along the company's right-of-way. The total cost was estimated at £160, employing the same pole routes that carried circuits between signal boxes, plus nearly 1-mile of cable carried in underground ducts or through tunnels. The obvious purpose of the telephone was to give a higher speed of communication than existing railway telegraph services and thereby promote even closer co-operation between the district Locomotive Superintendents. This in turn would facilitate a more effective use to be made of the West Riding's motive power, to deal with traffic fluctuations. The Way & Works Committee asked for reports on the telephone's efficaciousness, to ascertain whether future extension was warranted.

Incredibly, that 1902 telephone connection was the last mention for 45 years, of improvements or structural changes made a Copley Hill! The only other point of relevance comes from a Minute of 25th December 1903, when the Way & Works Committee heard that a £1,977 job awarded to Messrs. Kell Bros., "earlier this year" (no record found), for a new tankhouse and foundation for a 55ft turntable at Leeds Central station, had "not yet started." So, we have little idea if and how Copley Hill shed was affected by such things as World War One, or the Grouping for instance. Some small inferences can be gleaned from the records of locomotives stationed at the shed, so it is appropriate now to consider such histories for all three Leeds engine sheds.

The engine shed at Leeds Central (Low Level) would have been capable of holding about nine engines of the early 1850's period. These assuredly were comprised of the first Hawthorn and Sharp types, which were quite adequate for services over the easy route between Leeds and Doncaster. However, during the period when the lines of the Leeds Bradford & Halifax Junction and Bradford Wakefield & Leeds Railways opened, between 1854 and 1857, the GN found need for engines capable of handling traffic over those more difficult railway routes. Accordingly, Sturrock designed a class of 2-4-0 specifically for use in the West Riding - the '233' Class - these being delivered from Hawthorn's factory in 1855. Then in 1857, Sturrock asked for, and got, "...8 small passenger engines from company stock, to be altered for £300 each, for the steeply graded Leeds, Bradford and Gildersome lines..." These locomotives, plus tank engine rebuilds of early Sharp and Bury machines, and examples of Sturrock's 0-6-0 designs, saw service in the West Riding for years. In 1865, or perhaps as early as 1862, some of the tank

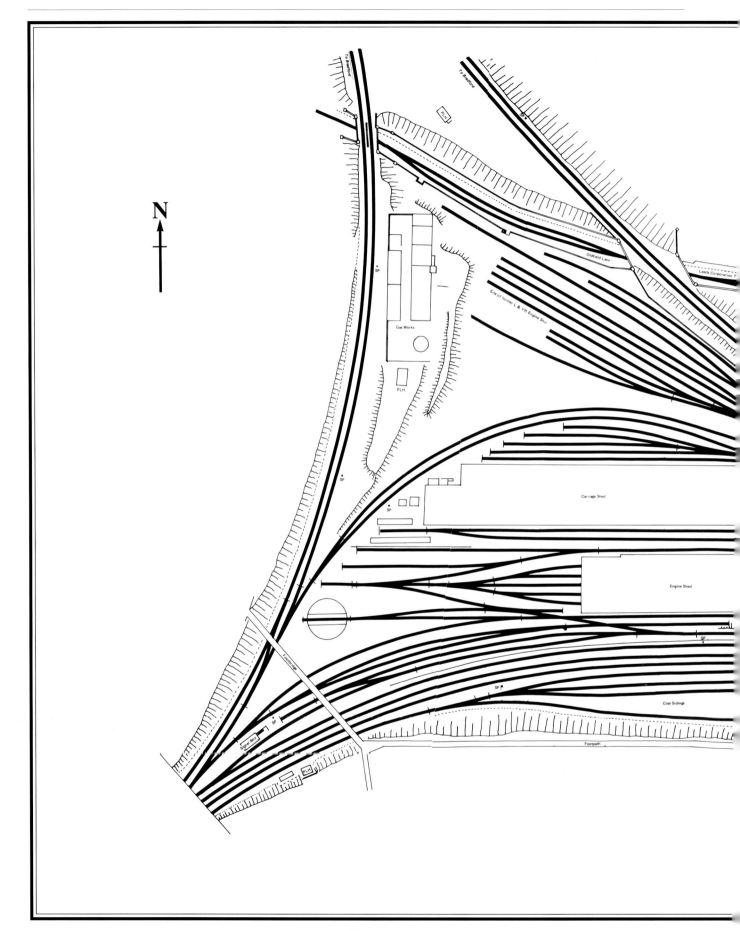

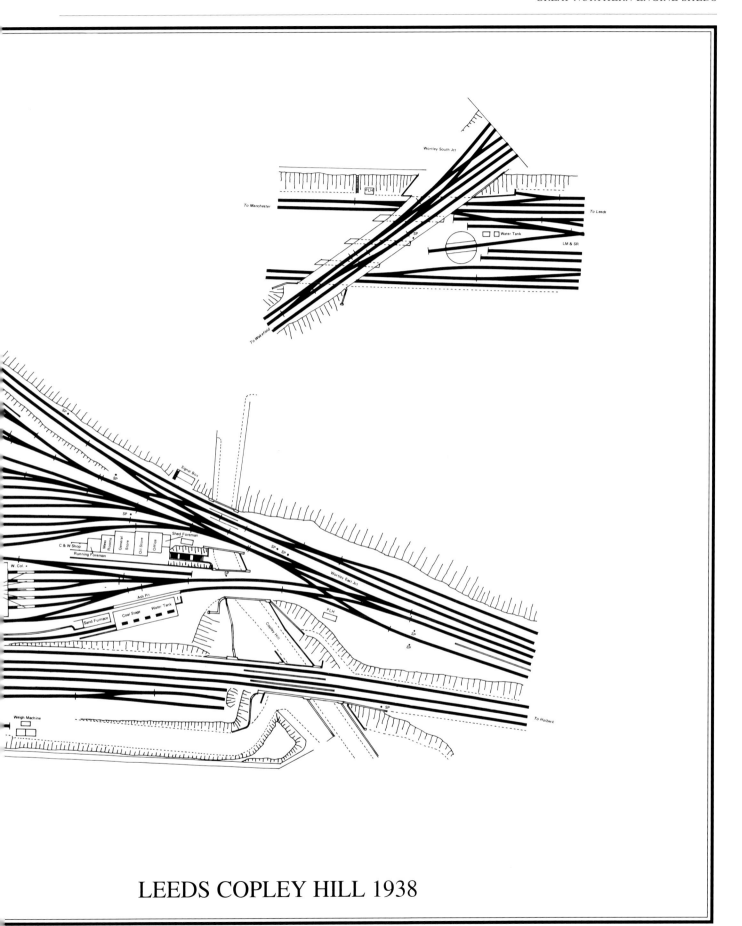

Wortley South Jct

To Manchester

PLH

To Leeds

SP

Water Tank

LM & SR

To Wakefield

SP

Signal Box

SP

SP

Mess Rooms
General Store
Oil Store
Office
Shed Foreman

C & W Shop

Running Foreman

W. Col.

SP SP

Wortley East Jct

Ash Pit

Sand Furnace

Coal Stage
Water Tank

PLH

Copley Hill

SP

SP

Weigh Machine

SP

To Holbeck

LEEDS COPLEY HILL 1938

types and possibly a few goods engines, were moved from Leeds (Wortley) to the shed at Ardsley. That depot was used by BW&LR and LB&HJ engines until 1865, when those railways and their rolling stock were absorbed by the GN; it is quite probable that examples of the absorbed engines used Wortley shed in the years immediately after 1865.

It was not long after Stirling became Locomotive Engineer that first examples of his designs started to appear in the West Riding. For example, it is known that the first two 0-4-2T arrived in 1868. Then, around 1875, two of the famous 8' singles were sent from Doncaster to Wortley, specifically to handle a new London-Leeds express; Nos.33 and 47, however, were destined not to stay long in Leeds. After that, Sturrock types gradually faded as Stirling's designs increased and held sway for nearly a quarter of a century, until Ivatt's first engines appeared. Throughout this period, Wortley shed's duties were almost exclusively related to passenger workings. A good example of this comes from the 1889 WTT, which shows only two main line goods trains worked by the depot, weekdays only:
2000 Leeds - Kings Cross (0420)
2255 Leeds - Peterborough (which continued to London with a New England engine and crew).

Of course, there would have been local goods workings from Copley Hill, but probably these were few in number, and mostly restricted to 'tripping' between Central (Low Level) Goods and the city's plants and mills.

As stated a number of times in this series, the GN's policy of assigning engines to Locomotive Districts often makes it difficult to be precise about an individual shed's allocation. By 1905, when the first comprehensive list of GN locomotive allocations was produced, 145 engines were stationed in Leeds Locomotive District. However, as that District was comprised only of Ardsley and Copley Hill shed, with the former being almost entirely a goods engine depot, it is not too arduous a task to roughly calculate what would have made up Copley Hill's roster of 40-45 engines. First were six D1 and seven D2 4-4-0, for use mainly on services to Wakefield and Doncaster. Of six E2 2-4-0 most were probably at Copley Hill, whereas perhaps, the shed housed only one or two of the District's fourteen F2/3 0-4-2. Passenger tanks comprised six C2 and nine G1/2/3 and probably all based at Copley Hill at that time, for such duties as the Leeds-Wakefield-Dewsbury 'circular' workings. That leaves ten engines which would have been drawn from the 0-6-0 and 0-6-0ST classes, used on local goods, shunting, banking and pilot duties.

Seven years later Leeds District's allocation had fallen to 137, and although the subdivision of class types was the same, the numbers in most classes had changed somewhat. For example, 1912 saw twelve D1 and two D2, and only four 2-4-0 of Class E1. 0-4-2 of F2/3 numbered seven, but whether Copley Hill retained any is doubtful. The various classes of 0-4-4T had increased to eleven, while C2 4-4-2T had fallen to four. Representations of 0-6-0 and 0-6-0ST classes probably had not changed, but there was one newcomer to the District, at Copley Hill N1 0-6-2T No.1953; the type had arrived that year and would not disappear from the West Riding until 1956.

On the day before Grouping the allocation of Copley Hill numbered 45 engines, subdivided as follows: **C2** (7), **D1** (9), **D3** (2), **G3** (3), **J4** (1), **J5** (10), **J14** (1), **J15** (4), **J16** (3), **J23** (2), **N1** (3).

As can be seen, Ivatt's 4-4-0's still ruled as prime passenger power, but the fledgling LNER soon started to change things and Copley Hill began to host 'foreign' engines in some

numbers. First, two former GE B12 4-6-0 spent the first two years of the LNER's existence working from Leeds, mainly on services to Doncaster - they were Nos.1552 and 1561. Towards the end of 1924 the first ex-GC B4 4-6-0 arrived, soon to be joined by four more. They too were used on the Leeds-Doncaster section, usually on the Kings Cross trains, sometimes working through to Grantham, but occasionally London was reached on special passenger workings, which also took them to the East Coast resorts. During the war years of 1941 and 1942, B4 No.6100 was regularly rostered by Copley Hill for the *Mail*, from Leeds Central. Returning in time, 1925 saw a pair of B3 moved to Copley Hill, their use primarily being to participate in the Leeds-London Pullman trains which were shared with engines from Kings Cross shed. In 1927 the B3 moved away, to be replaced by what was arguably, Robinson's best passenger design, the Class D11 "Director" 4-4-0. Three D11 came to Leeds and were allotted to regular crews in Copley Hill's "Pullman Link" - drivers Bird, Malthouse and Rogers - for the 372 mile round trip between Harrogate and London - a lodging turn, run non-stop in each direction. In November 1928, the D11 were joined by Gresley Class D49 No.245 LINCOLNSHIRE for trials on the Pullman turns. The trial presumably did not show performances of any marked superiority over the "Directors," as after only a month, the "Shire" moved away again.

During the month of May 1932, the "Directors" were replaced on the Pullman workings by Ivatt C1 Atlantics, as they were themselves being superseded elsewhere by Pacifics. Three C1's were assigned to the same drivers and the distinguished Pullman service continued, to be enhanced in September 1935, when a fourth duty and C1 were added to Copley Hill's roster, Kings Cross having relinquished its single working of the *QUEEN OF SCOTS* Pullman. At that time, which many consider to have been Copley Hill's 'finest hour,' the shed's various Link duties were as follows:

No.1 Link *Pullman Link* - 4 Turns.
No.2 Link *Main Line Express Link*. Doncaster, Grantham - 6 Turns.
No.3 Link *Whitemoor Link* - 6 Turns, Lodge two weeks in six.
No.4 Link *Big Tank Link*, local passenger work - 10 Turns.
No.5 Link *Small Tank Link*, local passenger work - 10 Turns.
No.6 Link *Sentinel Link* - 4 Turns
No.7 Link *Goods Link*, incl. Banker turns, Leeds Cen. Pilot - 8 Turns
No.8 Link *"Johnny Andrew's Link"* - local goods work - 3 Turns.

No.1 Link would retain its C1's until 1937, when A1 4-6-2 Nos.2553 and 2555 PRINCE OF WALES and CENTENARY took over the *QUEEN OF SCOTS* and *HARROGATE SUNDAY PULLMAN* workings. The Pacifics remained at Leeds until about 1944, although their Pullman duties had been stopped with the onset of World War Two. Copley Hill's Atlantics, though losing their prestige working, were retained as standby for the Pacifics and did not disappear from the shed until early BR days. They were used in No.2 Link no doubt, along with various ex GCR classes of 4-4-0/4-6-0 and the last examples of Ivatt's 4—4-0. Of the latter, only one D3 remained in 1942, being the very last GN 4-4-0 in the West Riding in fact.

Copley Hill's "Whitemoor Link" (No.3) had been introduced in 1927, the duty moving from Ardsley shed, because the diagram was altered so that the Leeds engine first worked a passenger train to Doncaster, picking up the Whitemoor goods in the Decoy yard there. Loss of this duty by Ardsley was not without a certain amount of acrimony on the part of staff at the depot! K3 moguls were used on the Whitemoor workings, five

The same vantage point as found in the illustration on page 80 reveals ex-GCR 4-4-2T No.67443 shunting locomotive sand wagons while a railwayman looks on from the rear of one of the elderly departmental coaches in the shed yard. The depot itself seems remarkably deserted, although the pall of smoke hanging over the roof belies that impression. *A.Robinson.*

Copley Hill's large brick-built coaling stage and water tank are seen here, from the "business" side and partly obscured by B4 No.6100. Four or more of the ex-GCR 4-6-0s formed part of the sheds allocation for much of the LNER period and could be seen working anything from express passenger turns to perishable goods. *Authors' collection.*

being shedded, through to the end of the Second World War, when all were moved away. Number 4 and 5 Links' designations stemmed from GN days, when C2 (LNER C12) 4-4-2T were the "Big" tanks and the various marques of G class 0-4-4T were the "Small." By the mid-Thirties though, the position had changed; the 0-4-4T had gone and on average, about four N1 and two N5 0-6-2T, and eight C12 4-4-2T made up the engine complement of Nos.4 and 5 Links: presumably N1/5 were the "Big" and C12 the "Small."

No.6 "Sentinel" Link is a reminder that the LNER re-introduced steam railmotors early in the company's history. The first use of such machines was during the 1906-1914 period, when two steam railmotors worked the Ossett-Batley service; evidence points to their having been based at Ardsley during that period. The LNER's Sentinel steam cars operated various services in the West Riding - again mostly in the Leeds-Wakefield-Dewsbury 'triangle,' and on the Castleford line, until around 1944/5, when declining reliability brought about their demise. Railmotors No.51908 EXPEDITION and No.51913 RIVAL were the last to remain in service, being replaced by ex-GC Class F2 2-4-2T and push-pull sets. Finally, it is interesting to speculate upon the origins of the "Johnny Andrew's" name for Copley Hill's No.8 Link, but this remains a mystery. Suffice it to say that it, and No.7 Link, were largely operated by 0-6-0's in the 1930's. For instance, in April 1936, three J3 and a J39 were based at the shed, together with six J50 0-6-0T and a solitary J52 0-6-0ST; the tanks were favourites for the banking and pilot duties of course, with some local goods duties also being undertaken. Of the 0-6-0's, J39 also found employment on the Whitemoor jobs at times, and excursion passenger trains.

By January 1947 it was evident the war had changed things. Kings Cross and Doncaster Pacifics were working all Leeds-London services, so the only 'sizeable' engine on Copley Hill's strength was a solitary V2, No.853; three of Gresley's 2-6-2 were allocated by 1954, with two remaining after the West Riding sheds were transferred to BR's North Eastern Region control in 1956. Copley Hill's main passenger power in the LNER's last year were a couple of B4 4-6-0 and three Ivatt C1 Atlantics - Nos.2828, 2829 and 2875; ere long these five engines would be replaced by Thompson's B1 4-6-0, a type which remained until closure. Tank engine strength had increased by 1947, to the extent of 23 engines out of a total of 32. An F2 and five C12 worked alongside seven N1 and two N5, while shunting/banking/piloting was in the care of J50 0-6-0T Nos.8911, 8913, 8937, 8945, 8946, 8978, 8984 and 8988, the latter class remaining until the dawn of the 1960's.

British Railways also rang the changes, and Pacifics soon made their presence felt in a big way. May and June 1948 witnessed the arrival of A3 Nos.60046, 60056, 60062 and A2 Nos.60523, 60533, 60536, 60537. These seven were put to work on three re-introduced London workings featuring a short turnround in the Capital. However, in November 1948, the A2 moved away and Copley Hill received brand-new Peppercorn A1 Nos.60118, 60119, 60134, followed soon after by 60136 and in May 1949 by 60128, the latter in BR's then standard blue livery. The A1 were well liked by Copley Hill men and used on four return London workings, involving three crews. These were the QUEEN OF SCOTS/HARROGATE SUNDAY PULLMAN and the unofficially named "Bradford Flyer." Using a 'foreign' crew, the third A1 turn involved an early express to London, returning on the mid-afternoon WEST RIDING express with a Copley Hill crew, that had worked Up earlier in the day with Copley's fourth

A1 turn, the YORKSHIRE PULLMAN. That engine returned on the Down working of the YORKSHIRE PULLMAN, in the hands of crews from other sheds. By August 1950, Copley Hill possessed no fewer than fifteen Pacifics: A3 - 60044, 60046, 60056, 60062, 60112; A1 - 60114, 60117, 60118, 60119, 60120, 60123, 60125, 60133, 60134, 60141.

By April 1959, the A3's had gone, but the same number of A1 was present, out of a total allocation of 33 engines, which included four ex-LMS 2-6-2T, of Stanier's Class 3 design. Presumably these had superseded C12 4-4-2T, but the 'Staniers' were not very popular and spent as much time as possible out of use. Only three 0-6-0 remained - a single J39 and two J6, while nine B1, a pair of V2 and five J50 completed the roster. Largely, this would remain the pattern of things until the end of the shed's history, but before considering that event, we must briefly return to 1946.

By said year, the passage of time had proved that Copley Hill's 47 year old transverse pitch roof was not that much better than a northlight at withstanding the ravages of soot and steam, exacerbated no doubt, by wartime depredations. Accordingly, the LNER was obliged to completely replace the roof during 1946/7, using a steel frame, supporting asbestos sheets with brick end screens. This seems to have been an altogether better combination of roofing materials but wasn't given a full test of time, as the depot closed only 18 years later. That was brought about by Modernisation of course, and the resultant large scale closure of lines in the West Riding. Diesel locomotives - particularly shunting types - used Copley Hill before closure, but the depot was not really required for the new motive power. That situation was made final by large scale rationalisation at Leeds, when Central station was closed and all services were diverted to a rebuilt Leeds (New) station - by then known as "City." Engine shed facilities were also reduced, leaving just two depots, the ex-NER Neville Hill and ex-MR Holbeck; only Neville Hill is still fully operational today.

The end for Copley Hill itself came on Monday 7th September 1964. Eight weeks prior to that, a visit to the depot on the afternoon of Sunday 26th July, found the following engines, which unless stated otherwise, were allocated to the shed at that time:

A1 60117, 60130; **B1** 61013 (Ardsley), 61031, 61274 (Wakefield), 61382, 61385, **LMS 2-6-4T** 42639 (Darlington), **Ivatt LMS 2-6-0** 43101, **LMS Jubilee** 4-6-0 45675 (Holbeck), **0-6-0DMS** D2094 (Hammerton Street) (Carriage Pilot).

The LMS Ivatt 2-6-0 had been added to Copley Hill's strength in January, coming from Wakefield. Its work consisted of various passenger duties and empty carriage work. On closure, all remaining duties and men were taken over by Holbeck, along with some Pacifics, while the balance of the engines went mostly to Ardsley. The fact that Copley Hill never featured in the LNER's 1930's engine shed modernisation programme indicates the relative importance of the depot; 'prestige' passenger workings - yes, but few in number - the real revenue earning work over the GN lines in the Leeds District being done by Ardsley.

So, Copley Hill's laboriously operated coal stage lasted until the end (the small turntable had succumbed some years before, with locomotives once again resorting to Wortley triangle to turn), and was demolished with the shed soon after closure. The wooden carriage shed followed, and with the ex-L&Y engine shed having gone before, the land within Wortley's triangle of lines reverted to zero use again after some 110 years, until latterly, when the whole area was developed for commercial concerns.

The coaling stage is viewed here from the other (south) side in the early 1960s, giving a good idea of its imposing appearance. The separate building at left, with three large openings, appears to be a later addition, and housed the sand drying furnace; it probably provided warm shelter for the coal handlers in between 'jobs'. Copley Hill never was to benefit from mechanisation of its locomotive coaling operation. *J.Bateman.*

Smoky atmosphere again as Class J50 No.68911 shunts an 0-6-0, while A1's 60141 ABBOTSFORD, on No.1 road and 60139 SEA EAGLE, on No.3 road, furiously contribute through their original unrimmed chimneys to Leeds City's hydrocarbon content. Such practices were eventually to bring about the "Clean Air Act". *Authors' collection.*

To prove the point about the "Clean Air Act", this remarkably clear aerial photograph of Leeds, from September 1963, shows Copley Hill shed in the bottom right corner. The picture includes much else of engine shed, and general railway interest. To the left of Copley Hill are the transverse pitches of the roof of the carriage shed and left of that again coaches are parked on the site of the GNR's 1857 six road shed which it later shared with the L&YR and which eventually accommodated the L&Y's own rebuild of the 1857 depot. Moving towards the top left we see the two and a half roundhouses of the Leeds Northern/North Eastern Railways' Holbeck shed, of which the two nearest buildings survive today (2000). Beyond that can be seen a new warehouse at Leeds Central goods depot and just beyond that, Leeds Central station. Moving right, Wellington and New stations are in the process of being rebuilt, to become Leeds City and just visible is the turntable occupying the site of the NER's sector roundhouse shed at New station. Finally, moving two thirds of the way up the extreme right edge of the picture, one can see the coaling tower and gable roof of the MR double turntable shed at Holbeck. *Fastline Photographic.*

A close-up of Copley Hill from the same angle in September 1963, just one year before closure. There appears to be few engines on shed which is not surprising as this was a weekday. The sand train is now in the hands of a tender engine possibly one of those Ivatt Moguls which came late on in the shed's life. *Fastline Photographic*

This 1949 aerial view of the Deansgate area of Manchester reveals the position of the engine shed alongside the main line into Central station which itself dominates the bottom of the picture. The 'engine shed', with its water tank full, appears to be in use as a wagon repair shop whilst there is shunting activity on the lines leading into the warehouse complex. What is clear is that the goods depot's resident pilot locomotives were, at that time, normally stabled at the depot "throat". Judging by the shadows it is mid afternoon and goods trains are being made up for the evening runs. The lack of activity at Central meanwhile would also point to a mid afternoon period when the station was quiet. At the top right of the picture are three viaducts which from left to right are the MSJ&A line from Manchester London Road to Cornbrook and points west; then comes the first of two viaducts carrying the CLC route westwards out of Central. Running across the picture from left to right is the former LNWR link to Ordsall Lane which is still of great importance as a freight and passenger line. In recent years the Manchester Metro has revitalised the area and now uses the middle of the viaducts but the engine shed is long demolished and all trace disappeared. *Airviews (Manchester) Ltd.*

MANCHESTER (DEANSGATE)

GN trains commenced running to Manchester on 1st August 1857, extending to Garston in 1858 and to Liverpool (Lime Street) on 1st September 1859. Next, in the 1860's, in respect of its part-ownership, the GN supplied some rolling stock to the fledgling Cheshire Lines Committee, but after that, for nearly 30 years, the company lost interest in further expansion in Lancashire. During those years, the Great Northern was quite happy to handle the MSLR's southward traffic, in exchange for the other company taking GN traffic from the East Coast main line, to the two main cities of the north west.

However, the MSLR's plans for its London Extension clearly meant an end to this working arrangement and faced with the obvious competition to be offered by the MSL's new line, the GN planned its own Northern Extension - of sorts. The first move was made in 1892, when powers were obtained for GN running between Sheffield and Manchester, over the MSLR's Woodhead route. Then, in 1895, the company set in motion its masterstroke in the effort to develop Manchester traffic of its own. On 27th July that year, an Act was passed empowering construction of a large Manchester goods station.

The site chosen enclosed some nine acres of the Deansgate area of the city, beside the CLC's Central Station. Everything about Deansgate Goods was on the grand scale, starting with the hundreds of residential and commercial properties that had to be purchased and demolished, to make way for the new edifice. Even some long-dead Mancunians had to be dug up and re-interred as part of the £1 million project, which saw over 90,000 tons of debris cleared, to make way for some 60,000 tons of steel and concrete and over 26 million building blocks, in granite, brick and wood. Contractor for the mammoth task was A.Neill & Co., who by June 1897, had at work 190 men, 38 carts and horses, 3 portable engines, 5 mortar mills, 1 steam crusher and 3 steam cranes. Such was the scale of the job though, that it was 1st July 1898 before Deansgate Goods Station was opened - and then on a partial basis only - full operation was still one year and two days away.

During the design stage it was anticipated that Deansgate Goods would provide around-the-clock employment for 2 or 3 shunting engines. The nearest locomotive depot the GN would likely have access to was the CLC shed at Trafford Park, but this was some miles away. So, it made sense for a small locoshed to form part of the Deansgate complex, to avoid a continuous light engine running by the goods depot's shunters. Accordingly, on 3rd December 1897, the Locomotive Engineer presented the Board with designs for Deansgate shed, at an initially estimated cost of £6,320. But, on 9th January 1899, Ivatt was able to report to his Directors that Messrs. Neill's final schedule of costs for the engine shed totalled £3,047-17-4d, which, of course, was gladly accepted. The reduction was due to changed plans for the depot. Quite what changes were involved is not known, because the December 1897 plan has not been found; that presented by Ivatt, on 9th January 1899, bears the date 27th October 1898. Even then, it was further amended, on 16th January 1899 (see below), after which, construction commenced.

The assumption to be made then is that Deansgate locoshed was completed and ready for use, around the end of 1899. But, alas for its cost-saving potential, no engine was *EVER* to pass its doors! All through the planning process, the GN had naturally been keeping Manchester Corporation advised and

the Council had, in turn, been passing on information to the St. Johns Ratepayers Association. At that time, St. Johns, to the north of Deansgate, was a fairly well-off district and its residents included numerous professional people - doctors, lawyers, etc. The Ratepayer's Association presented a petition, it seems, on 24th October 1899, at a meeting with Manchester Corporation and a deputation from the GN. While the Council's Buildings and Improvements Committee's Minutes of that session are not explicit, it is definite the railway company had certain planning permissions withheld - or withdrawn - as a result of the meeting. All that can be gleaned is the Ratepayers, in an undoubtedly well presented case, were protesting about smoke from standing engines, backing up their petition with concern over a possible accident, involving a runaway locomotive.

As originally planned, the shed's north wall and that at the rear (west), were to be continuations of a corner retaining wall, that formed part of a viaduct, on which all the shed and part of Deansgate Goods were built.Possibly sensing some trouble, one of the GN's 16th January 1899 amendments to the plans of the depot, deleted the offices that would have linked the shed's north side to the viaduct's edge, and moved them as a separate block, further down the yard. This gave a break in the building line and is actually how the depot/offices were finally erected.

However, the rear wall was the cause of the GN's downfall with Deansgate shed, because the ratepayers seem to have convinced Manchester Corporation there was extreme danger of a locomotive running away through that rear wall, to plunge 30 ft into "busy" Collier Street below. As consent for the shed's erection had already been given and indeed, the building was by then in an advanced state of construction, only legal action could prevent its use, and the Council were successful in convincing the Judiciary that a real hazard existed, and an injunction was granted, banning the GN from putting engines in the shed. No record has been found of any GN attempt to have the injunction removed, or to seek recompense for having been caused to incur unnecessary expenditure. So, the locoshed remained a monument to what some people might call bureaucratic bungling.

Some GN devotees claim that the shed was used, because it was 'officially' closed by the LNER, in 1928. The authors' answer to this lies above, which admittedly is part assumption, based on sketchy historical fact. However, another pointer - more definite in the authors' view - concerns the shed's coal stage. Another of the amendments made, on 16th January 1899, to the depot's plans, inserted the coal stage at the east end of the shed yard. In the event, the stage was never built. Planned to be of simple construction, its erection would have been left until late in the building programme, by which time the GN had been told it could not stable engines at the shed. So, why build a coal stage that was destined never to be used? Then, even more conclusive is an article, entitled "The Great Northern Railway, and Manchester" carried in the January-June 1907 volume of the *Railway Magazine*. On page 392 there is a categoric reference to the engine shed at Deansgate as a repair shop for rolling stock. With reference to the 1928 'closure' of Deansgate engine shed, the authors' contention is that this was nothing but an administrative exercise by the LNER's Locomotive Department, at a time when the company was going through a period of financial retrenchment.

Regarding the shed that was erected *(see also Volume 1)*, it comprised a two road building, with a roof part northlight in

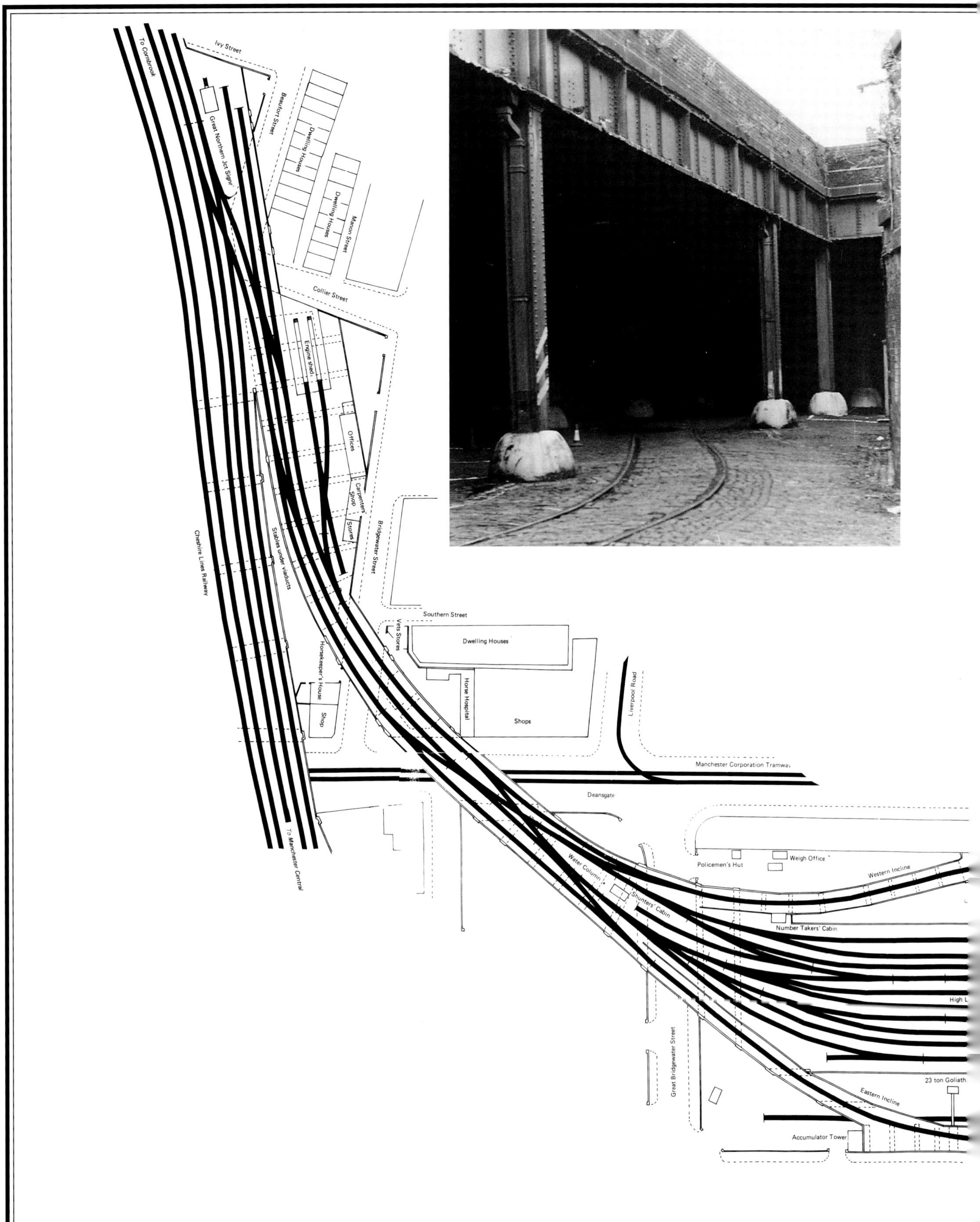

To Cornbrook
Ivy Street
Beaufort Street
Great Northern Jct Signal
Dwelling Houses
Dwelling Houses
Manon Street
Collier Street
Engine shed
Offices
Carpenters' Shop
Stores
Bridgewater Street
Cheshire Lines Railway
Stables under viaducts
Southern Street
Vets Stores
Dwelling Houses
Horse Hospital
Shops
Liverpool Road
Horsekeeper's House
Shop
Manchester Corporation Tramway
Deansgate
To Manchester Central
Policemen's Hut
Weigh Office
Western Incline
Water Column
Shunters' Cabin
Number Takers' Cabin
Great Bridgewater Street
23 ton Goliath
Eastern Incline
Accumulator Tower

(opposite) **A probable further locomotive standing point was situated on Deansgate Goods' low level, where even in August 1984, there remained evidence of heavy sooting of the roof thereabouts and traces of a coal stack on the floor. Sited between the northern ramp and the upper level goods yard, the cover provided shelter and ventilation. There is photgraphic evidence that a Sentinel shunting locomotive was at least tried out here during the early 1950s.** *Authors' collection.*

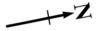

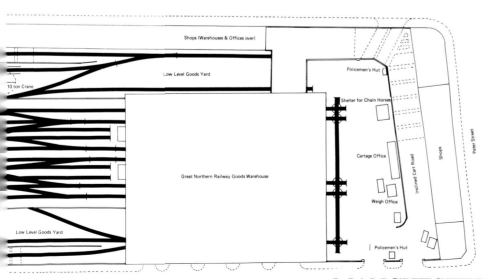

Shops (Warehouses & Offices over)

Low Level Goods Yard

10 ton Crane

Policemen's Hut

Shelter for Chain Horses

Great Northern Railway Goods Warehouse

Cartage Office

Inclined Cart Road

Shops

Peter Street

Weigh Office

Low Level Goods Yard

Policemen's Hut

Watson Street

MANCHESTER DEANSGATE 1900

pattern and part water tank, at the rear. The brick building measured 36 ft in width, with the south side 96 ft in length and the north side 80 ft, resulting in what would have been restricted, but ample enough, capacity for four tank locos. The internal tracks were 80 ft long, with 48 ft pits, and there was a further 40 ft pit outside, in the curved track leading to the proposed coaling stage. That edifice was to have been of wooden construction, on dwarf brick walls, wedge shaped to fit the site and fitted with a wooden shelter. This then was the engine shed so needlessly built, but all was not entirely lost because as stated above, the building saw use as a wagon repair shop and the viaduct extension, built to support it, provided the GN with a ready made street-level stable block, with around 135 stalls being accommodated.

The traffic forecasters were proved right though, Deansgate did provide work for 2 or 3 shunting engines from the outset. The initial timetable of goods trains serving Manchester was as follows:
DOWN
KX (Goods) dep. 4.12 pm SX; Deansgate arr. 2.40 am (GC haulage Retford - Guide Bridge).
KX (Goods) dep. 7.00 pm SO; Deansgate arr. 5.35 am (GN haulage, via Stockport [Tiviot Dale]).
KX (Goods) dep. 7.10 pm SX; Deansgate arr. 4.45 am (GN haulage, via Stockport [Tiviot Dale]).
Clarence Yard dep. 9.18 pm SX; Deansgate arr. 6.35 am (GN haulage, via Guide Bridge).
KX (Goods) dep. 9.30 pm SX; Deansgate arr. 7.05 am (GN haulage, via Guide Bridge).
KX (Goods) dep. 10.45 pm SX; Deansgate arr. 10.40 am (GC haulage Retford - Guide Bridge).
GN haulage continued from point of changeover with the GC.
UP
Deansgate dep. 5.39 pm; KX arr. 4.00 am (GC haulage Godley Jct - Retford).
Deansgate dep. 6.50 pm SX; KX arr. 5.25 am (GN haulage, via Fallowfield).
Deansgate dep. 7.30 pm; KX arr. 5.55 am (GN haulage, via Stockport [TD]).
Deansgate dep. 9.15 pm; KX arr. 7.35 am (GN haulage, via Fallowfield).

These trains were worked in part by an allocation of GN locos at Trafford Park, that will be described later. Those engines also had to handle a GN passenger service for a few years but this didn't last for long. Goods traffic to Deansgate, however, continued unabated, keeping the shunters there very busy. By 1910, the Manchester-London goods services had been altered, with the following workings then in force; use of Midland Railway metals commenced at the beginning of November 1899, an expedient resorted to because of some awkwardness towards the GN, on the part of the GC:
DOWN
KX (Goods) dep. 4.15 pm SX; Deansgate arr. 2.50 am (via GN Leen Valley and GC Woodhead).
KX (Goods) dep. 8.10 pm SX; Deansgate arr. 2.00 am (GC haulage from Retford).
KX (Goods) dep. 9.25 pm SX; Deansgate arr. 4.20 am (GC haulage from Retford).
KX (Goods) dep. 9.25 pm SO; Deansgate arr. 10.09 am (via Brinsley and Hope Valley).
KX (Goods) dep. 10.10 pm SX; Deansgate arr. 4.35 am (via Brinsley and Hope Valley).

UP
Deansgate dep. 7.30 pm SX; East Goods Yard arr. 2.25 am (via GC to Retford).
Deansgate dep. 7.45 pm SX; KX (Goods) arr. 8.35 am (via GC to Retford).
Deansgate dep. 9.45 pm SX; KX (Goods) arr. 6.25 am (via Hope Valley and Brinsley).
Note: 7.45 p.m. runs when required M-F; regularly SO, terminating at Peterborough.

By the late 1920s, there was a gradual drift away of GN types from Manchester and strangers, in the guise of ex-GE Class J69 0-6-0T, took over the Deansgate duties: Nos.7191, 7198, 7273, 7351, 7363, 7371 and 7383 were all noted at varying times. The allocation as at 31st December 1927 was however still GN orientated viz: J52 3962, 4205, 4206, 4216, 4265, 4273, 4274; J54 3919. Like their GN predecessors, the ex-GE tanks were normally limited to 8 loaded wagons when negotiating the 1 in 28 inclines connecting the upper and lower levels of Deansgate Goods, and an eyewitness to activities in the 1930's can vouch for the complete audio-visual experience of movements in the 'up' direction! The same eyewitness can also vouch for the fact that at rest periods, the shunting tanks used to stand in front of, and beside, the shed they were forbidden to enter, with water available from a pipe at the side position. It was further observed that engines 'disappeared' on the low level lines for long periods. Inspection of the site even today, leads the authors to the conclusion that with the shed denied them, engines used to stable on the low level, under cover, for considerable lengths of time. It is also interesting to note that in at least one position, by an incline, there was a supply of coal dumped on the ground for replenishing the shunter's bunkers. Presumably, an engine stood on the incline so that the top of its bunker was more or less level with the coal stack, thereby facilitating loading.

After World War Two, traffic declined inexorably, leading to BR's cessation, in 1953, of nightly goods workings between Kings Cross and Deansgate. Closure of the latter, to rail traffic, came on 29th March 1954, after which it served as a parcels depot, until 6th July 1970. The shed "that never was" survived all this, including the added closure of Central Station, to be demolished a little while after Deansgate Goods was turned over to car parking, a use that continues today, with most of the building's structure intact. On the upper level, including the shed site, car parking is laid out specifically for visitors to the magnificently restored CLC terminus, now serving in its new role as an exhibition centre.

MANCHESTER (TRAFFORD PARK)

This large engine shed, built by the Cheshire Lines Committee, opened partly in 1894 and completely in March 1895, has amply been described already in two books, *LMS Engine Sheds, Vol.2, The Midland Railway* (Wild Swan Publications 1981) and second *An Illustrated History of the Cheshire Lines Committee* (Heyday Publishing Co. 1984). We can do no more than advise readers to consult those works, while adding a few items of our own, specifically covering GNR operations from Trafford Park.

The GN's large-scale entry into Manchester has been touched upon in the description of Deansgate GNR engine shed, above. As mentioned, the company looked to Trafford Park as its main base of operations and when Deansgate Goods partly

An official photograph taken on 10th April 1958, to show the track rearrangements after severing of the lines into Deansgate Goods, fortuitously includes a glimpse of the two road engine shed. Two tracks still enter the building, which only a short time before had been utilised as a wagon shop. *British Railways.*

From street level this September 1970 view of the rear of the engine shed seems quite daunting and it does not need much imagination to realise that a wrong shunt could have brought a lot of metal through that brick end wall crashing onto the street below so it is perhaps easy to sympathise with those who opposed the building's use for locomotives. It is interesting to note that the water tank constituted nearly 50% of the roof (*see* plan/elevation in Volume 1). A grounded coach body has at some time in the past served as a mess room. *R.W.Miller.*

0-6-0 No.316 poses with its crew at the CLC's shed at Trafford Park. Always the least involved partner in the triumvirate that ran the CLC, the GNR nevertheless made much of it's north-west goods traffic, as evidenced by the expenditure at Deansgate Goods Depot. *K.Leech collection.*

opened, in July 1898, the GN, as a partner in the CLC, took up its right to move into a portion of the Cheshire Lines' loco depot. Working arrangements within the 20 road straight shed consisted of the GCR occupying roads 1-10, on the northern side, and having sole use of the coal stage and turntable on the same side. GNR and MR engines shared the remaining roads, 11-15 and 16-20 respectively and both companies used the south side turntable and coal stage - the GN on the stage's north face, the MR on its south face. These facilities did not come free of course and the GN paid a rent to the Joint Committee; in the period around 1909, that rent was £1,241-0-8d per year.

Within three months of starting work in Manchester, GN footplatemen delivered a memorial to Ivatt, which he presented to the Board, on 31st October 1898. The memo concerned the men's difficulty in securing housing near enough to Trafford Park and Ivatt suggested that it would be a good idea for the company to "find some" for them. The Board asked the Company Surveyor to see if land could be obtained and if not, then the matter would be passed to the General Manager, to possibly sanction purchase of existing houses. It is known that by the early part of the 20th century, there was some GN housing at Ardwick, about three miles from Trafford Park, but whether this had been specially built, or bought, ready erected, is uncertain.

On the day following Ivatt's presentation of the enginemen's petition, November 1st, the contractor building Deansgate Goods Station, Messrs. R.Neill & Sons, was awarded a contract worth £3,785, to provide the "...accessory offices required by the GNR at Trafford Park..." Moving with customary swiftness, Neill & Co. had just about completed the job by the middle of April the following year, and GN loco department staff moved in. Their first locomotive charges were Ivatt Class D1 4-4-0 Nos. 1341, 1342, 1343, 1344, 1345 and 1346, Stirling J5 and J6 0-6-0's, with Classes J13 and J15 0-6-0ST's for shunting. The initial goods timetable is given in the section on Deansgate above, to which at first must be added the following passenger turns:

King's Cross to Manchester: 10.20 a.m., 4.15 p.m., 5.30 p.m.
Manchester to King's Cross: 8.45 a.m., 3.00 p.m., 5.20 p.m.
Manchester to Grantham: 12.00 p.m., 3.30 p.m., 10.55 p.m. (Mail).
Grantham to Manchester: Times unknown.

By 1901 though, competition from the GCR, LNWR and MR, for traffic between London and Manchester, caused the GN to cut back its through trains to those between London and Sheffield, leaving only the Manchester - Grantham - Manchester workings. Then in 1905, the GN re-entered the arena, with two afternoon 'fliers' leaving King's Cross at 6.10 p.m. and Manchester at 3.33 p.m. Both trains took only four hours, to complete their journeys, inclusive of a stop at Sheffield in the Down direction and at Sheffield and Grantham in the Up. This service was enhanced in 1906 by provision of brand-new rolling stock, but the competition still proved too great and the passenger workings ceased about 1909.

In November 1905, GN engines allocated to Trafford Park were: **D1** (LNER D3) 1341, 1342, 1343, 1344, 1345, 1346, **J5** 315, 316, 318, 329, 331, 332, 334, 336, 1128, 1133, 1134, 1153, 1157, **J6** 838, **J13** 1205, 1206, **J15** 602, 693. Within two years Ivatt D1 (LNER D2) 1396, 1397, 1398 and 1399 arrived and replaced the older D1's, only to be superseded themselves about 1912, when Gresley's Class J22 0-6-0's came to Manchester. These 0-6-0's were staple power for the remainder of the GN's existence,

with seven being allocated by the Grouping. 0-6-0ST's also increased in numbers slightly, to six J13 (plus two J15), on January 1st 1923. With formation of the LNER, former GN and GC divisions disappeared, as gradually, did GN loco types. The saddle tanks had gone by 1930, being replaced by ex-GE Class J67 and J69 0-6-0T, while the 0-6-0's started to go soon after Grouping, being progressively substituted by ex-GC J11, then LNER J39 types. Of the Gresley J22 (LNER J6) 0-6-0's at Trafford Park, the following are recalled as having been allocated at some time, for varying periods: Nos. 3536, 3537, 3538, 3547, 3553, 3560, 3568, 3569, 3577, 3586.

But, although these classes left Manchester, other engines of GN origin made post-Grouping appearances at Trafford Park. These included a solitary Class J50 0-6-0T, No.587, which was present from July 1940 to May 1943. More numerous and long-term residents were Class C12 4-4-2T, that arrived early in World War Two, for Manchester Central local services. They saw out the war years, with four still being allocated by October 1945, but all had gone before nationalisation. Lastly, Class J1 0-6-0 were also stationed at Trafford Park during the 1940's.

Of the former GN Manchester - London goods workings, a former Trafford Park driver, Harry Halsall, had these recollections of his depot's duties in LNER days, from the early 1920's:

6.50 p.m. Deansgate - Colwick via Woodhead, lodge Colwick and return the following night at 10.45 p.m. Locos were Trafford Park B9 alternating with Colwick B8. Later, the Manchester shed got a solitary K3 Mogul for this diagram which was accelerated, so that the 2-6-0's worked non-stop between Colwick and Guide Bridge, with a stop for water at Sheffield, but no bunker was taken there.

8.22 p.m. Deansgate - Colwick via Midland route, lodge and return on 1.20 a.m. This was a fully fitted train and had engine restrictions imposed by a wooden bridge at Codnor Park, which restricted GN locomotives' successors to Classes J11, then J39, the latter at least allowing the load to be increased from 33 to 40 wagons.

8.25 p.m. Deansgate - Ardsley via Woodhead and Worsborough branch. A lodging turn using Trafford Park B9, but return working details have not been recorded.

10.20 p.m. Deansgate - Colwick via Woodhead. Another lodging turn using Manchester B9 and Colwick B8 turn and turn about. No return working details available.

Lodging for the above turns was in private houses at Colwick and Ardsley, usually run by widows of railwaymen, who charged two shillings a night. At first there was a curfew imposed whereby men could not get into their 'lodge' before 8 o'clock in the morning - awkward, when one considers the 8.22 p.m. from Deansgate was into Colwick about midnight! It appears that while GN men had stoically suffered this inconvenience for years, ex-GC footplatemen drafted onto the duties would have nothing to do with it, and it soon became the practice for a key to be left in the outside 'privy'.

Such was the pattern of things in the LNER era up to World War Two, after which traffic declined. Trafford Park's contribution to workings of a GN origin ended after nearly 66 years, with closure of Deansgate Goods, on 29th March 1954.

In 1900, its year of building, GNR Atlantic No.984 rests between duties on the holding sidings shared with the GER, beside York South's roundhouses. Two of these are visible - at right, No.2 of 1852 and left, No.3 of 1864. *Authors' collection.*

A slightly misty detail lifted from a c1905 panorama of the south end of York station yields, at right, a glimpse of the shed built for the GNR in 1853. With its entrances bricked up the building is seen as closed in 1875 for development of the station, while in a few more years the end facing the camera would be re-modelled to allow access to a new Platform 14. In its latter period, up to demolition in 1936, the shed was used by the signal department as a workshop. *Authors' Collection.*

YORK

The history of the GN's engine shed facilities at York is complicated slightly, by the fact that during its existence, the company occupied at least three different shed buildings, originally belonging to two North Eastern Railway constituent companies.

Access to York was first gained by the GN on 8th August 1850, one day after the route from London (Maiden Lane) opened, via the 'Loop,' Lincoln and Retford, to Doncaster. From Doncaster, GN trains travelled north to Askern Junction, then over the tracks of the LYR to Knottingley, from where York & North Midland Railway tracks were taken to York. At York, the GN ran into the original terminus, which was sited to the southeast of today's station. The terminus was approached in a roughly southwest-east direction by the Y&NM, and from the northwest by the Great North of England Railway's tracks; a connecting chord linked the two companies' lines by-passing the station and forming a triangle.

At the time of the GN's first services, there were already three locosheds at York, all situated inside the triangle. These consisted of one 2 road and one 3 road straight sheds, and a roundhouse. Both straight sheds stood parallel and immediately adjacent to, the lines entering the station. The two road building had been erected by the Y&NMR in 1839 and stood on the north side of that company's tracks, just before they joined those of the GNoER, immediately outside the terminus. The three road depot lay on the south side of the GNoE's lines and dated from 1841, before the company had been incorporated into the York, Newcastle & Berwick Railway in August 1847, having formed part of the York & Newcastle Railway for a short time before that. The roundhouse - a truly circular building - stood between the two straight sheds, closer to, and immediately northwest of the Y&NM straight shed, and had been built by that company a short time before the GNR made its first appearance in the city.

As part of the running powers agreement between the GN and Y&NM, the last-named would be able to stable two engines in the GN shed at Doncaster, while the Great Northern could house up to four locos at the Y&NM's York depot. It is not certain where the GN were accommodated, but four stalls in the round shed is one possibility. However, the favourite assumption is that the two road straight shed was enlarged to three roads, with the third track earmarked for GN engines. At 200ft in length, one shed road would provide cover for four locomotives of the size then in use, and certainly the building was a three-roader by 1855. Support for the authors' assumption comes from within 17 months of the GN starting to run into York. Traffic had grown to such an extent that on 9th January 1852, Mr Gray, Secretary of the Y&NMR, wrote to the GN on the subject of engine stabling at York. He said: "....It appears there has easily been six engines belonging to this company there, although accommodation for four only is stipulated for, in the agreement between the two companies...." Gray went on to suggest that "....the GN should pay a percentage on the additional expenses which will be incurred, accommodating the number required to be kept at York...."

Following this up, Sturrock met with Mr Cabry, Locomotive Engineer of the Y&NMR, on 24th January 1852 and reported to the GN Board: "....I saw Mr Cabry, in accordance with the suggestion contained in the letter from Mr Gray and will arrange, with the Board's approval, for the Y&NM to provide accommodation at York for nine of our engines and conveniences for coke and water. Mr Cabry has undertaken, at my request, to have three lines of rails entering the building and to build it so that extensions can be made at any future date...." The Board agreed with Sturrock's suggestion for space for nine engines because if the company's northern coal trade continued to expand at current rates, then that number of engines soon would be required there. Accordingly, papers were referred to Mr Meek, "....who will enquire as to the costs to the GN for having five more engines at York, accommodated by the Y&NM...."

On 16th March, the Y&NM wrote, stating that the additional engine accommodation could be given for an extra fixed sum of £90 per annum, that being £50 for the room and £40 for water. The GN's reply stated that the company did not want to pay for any more sidings and certainly not any more for water, as it was already paying £1,000 rental for the station, which it regarded as 'high.' On 28th March, the Y&NM again wrote, saying their Board had agreed "....to provide an extra engine shed for the GN Co. to accommodate a further five engines and the cost would be £40 extra per annum and £40 for water...." The Y&NM added that it wished "....to remind the GN that the Y&NM has to provide the means for ensuring all the water at York and this sum is not excessive...."

The GN apparently did think the sum excessive, as on 18th May 1852, the General Manager reported on a meeting with the Y&NM where neither side could agree on water rates for the five additional engines, but both parties had agreed to ask Mr Harrison, of the York, Newcastle & Berwick Railway to arbitrate. He did, and concluded that the GN were entitled to an unlimited supply of water at York, at no extra charge!

That obviously stung the Y&NM into inactivity, as in October 1853, the GN was still having shed problems. Sturrock reported: "....Delays are being experienced by GN engines at York, coming in on empties, returning on coal trains, etc., and wanting to get to water points and coke stages without interfering with engines of the 'amalgamated companies'...."

During all these proceedings, in 1852, the Y&NM opened a second roundhouse, close by the first and the inference of all the above is that the Y&NM intended building a shed for the GN's exclusive use. The authors think this is what happened, but the second roundhouse was not the means, because a further three road straight shed also appeared, between the GNoE building and the terminus, immediately north of the Y&NM's No.1 roundhouse. The date of construction is uncertain but the depot was definitely in situ by 1855, which means of course, that the Y&NM-approved building might have been completed under the auspices of the newly formed NER. In his very detailed book on NER engine sheds (David & Charles 1972), the NER's acknowledged historian, the late Ken Hoole, says the origins of this particular engine shed are very obscure. The authors believe their GNR/YNMR theory, provides a very plausible explanation.

The new three road 160ftx 40ft shed was brick-built, with a single-pitch slated gabled roof. It was a dead-end type building, with arched entrances for each track at its eastern end. Coaling facilities were provided by an uncovered wooden stage sited between the shed yard and main lines, but whether it was equipped with cranes or was totally manual, is not known. The much-disputed water would certainly have been available too, but still fed from the NER's central supply, while turning facilities were provided by the triangle, or the turntables in the two roundhouses.

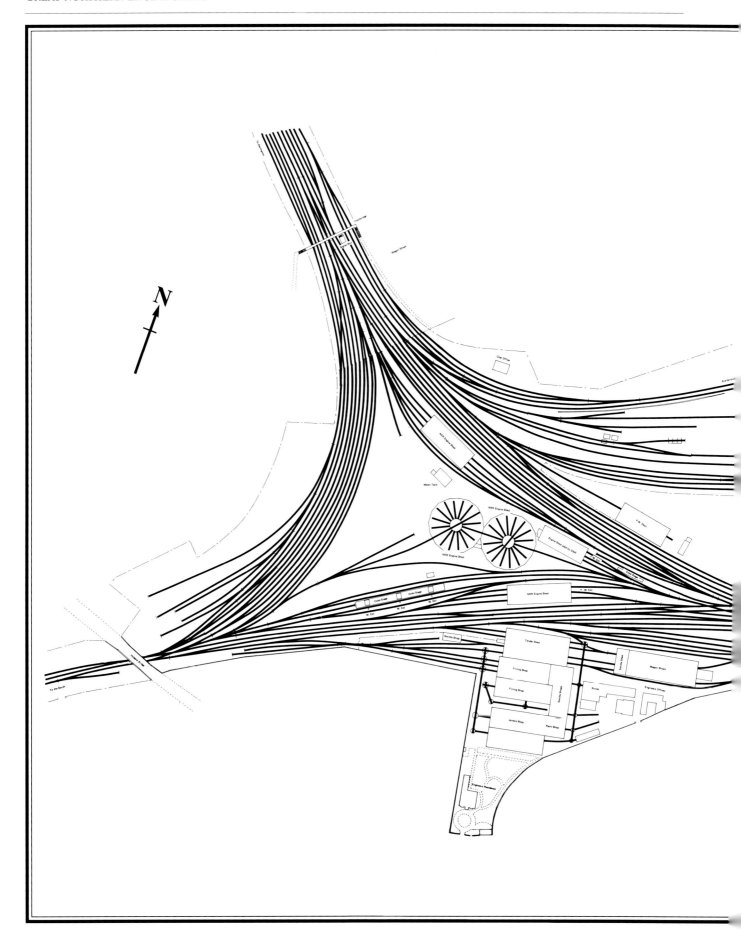

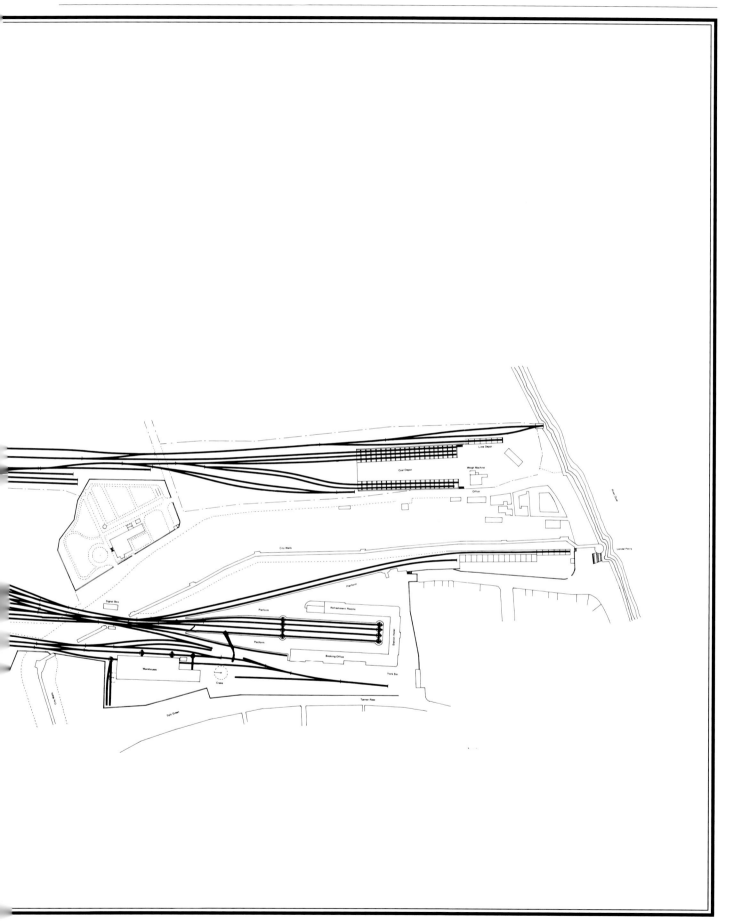

GNR 4-4-0 No.1370 stands outside the GNR's shed at York, about 1900. The depot retains the arched entrances with which it was originally built. *K.Leech collection.*

With a home of their own at last, Sturrock, then Stirling 0-4-2, 2-4-0 and 0-6-0, settled down to a peaceful existence for some twenty years, the only disturbance being in 1859, when for unspecified reasons, the NER was asked to carry out alterations to the roof of the GN's shed: this was approved by the NER, on 28th April that year, at a cost estimated at £240. The forethought shown in providing space for nine engines ensured that expansion of the depot was not required during this time. Which is fortunate, because by 1875, the NER had put into operation a massive development scheme for a new station at York, complete with north-south approaches. In the building works the Y&NM's 1839 shed disappeared under the new station's Platform 11. The GN shed and roundhouse No.1 found themselves in close proximity to the new station - so much so that the straight shed had to have its east end cut back, which drastically reduced its capacity and made engine movements impossible. Before that could be done therefore, the GNR had to move out, so the NER asked the company to take up residence in the ex-GNoE shed nearby, where engine movements would not be constrained by the new station. After the GN's departure, its former engine shed had the entrances bricked-up and saw many years more service, some as a P.W. stores and a signal shop, before finally being demolished in station extension works, in 1936. Of the other sheds at York South, where a third, larger roundhouse had been erected by the NER in 1864, roundhouse No.2 also had a partial "shaving" of its wall to accomodate the new station developments.

The depot to which the GN moved was, as stated above, of three roads. It measured 170ftx 53ft and was a through building, in brick, with arched entrances and a slated hipped roof that was surmounted by a large longitudinal smoke vent. A wooden coal stage, complete with cover and a crane, stood in the eastern yard; the cover and crane were probably late additions (the latter was in situ and steam-powered by 1890), as such luxuries were rare indeed in the 1840's! As such, this was to be home for GN engines at York, until the Grouping, and even after, up to the mid 1930's, engines working into York off former GN tracks were housed in the building (see below).

Even so, the 1881 WTT Appendix contains a whistle codes for GN engines wishing to enter or leave York North shed (In - 1 'crow'; Out - 2 'short'). Why and when that facility had been introduced, if and how many times it was used, and when it ceased, are all mysteries, but mention of York North brings in an interesting aside to the story. North shed - or Clifton as it was also known, comprised three integral roundhouses in 1881 (a fourth was added in 1915), but if circumstances had been different, it might not have been built at all. During their researches the authors came across an NER plan, produced as part of the 1875 station works, which shows that the proposed large new engine shed for York was intended to comprise four circular sheds, in a straight line, adjacent to the existing buildings at York South. As it happened of course, they were not built, but if they had been, what a vista York South would have presented - 7 roundhouses and 2 straight sheds! This information is presented here for what the authors hope is the readers' interest, as it updates data given in Mr. Hoole's *magnum opus*, mentioned above.

Because of its important traffic, York was classed as a separate Locomotive District (GN No.10), until 1st June 1912, when with Retford (GN No.9) it came into Doncaster District (GN No.1). York's GN allocation always was comprised of tender engines only, because the NER, and presumably the Y&NMR

before, was responsible for shunting all GN traffic. By 1905 two 2-2-2, nine 4-4-0 and 10 2-4-0 were stationed at York by the GN. For a short time, just before this, the shed had one of the famous Stirling 8ft Singles allocated - No.33, arriving in 1902, to see out the last couple of years of her life. By April 1912, York's allocation had changed to eleven 4-4-0 and six 2-4-0, with some of the 4-4-0 being replaced later in 1912 by Class J21 0-6-0 Nos.71, 79 and 80 - they were used on the fast night goods to London. By the eve of Grouping the 0-6-0 had gone again and York hosted three 'Klondykes,' and eleven 4-4-0. Then just after Grouping, 'Large' Atlantics Nos.4424 and 4447 went to York, eventually replacing their smaller-boilered sisters, in a stay that would last for nearly twenty years.

As mentioned above, even after Grouping, former GN locos tended to stick to 'their' traditional engine shed, even though in 1925 the allocation became part of the LNER's North Eastern Area and the Atlantics started to venture north of York, turn and turnabout with former NER motive power. As an illustration, an Easter 1926 visit found the following on York 'GN' shed: **B3** 6164; **C1** 3279, 4417, 4447; **D2** 4382, 4387, 4396, 4398; **D3** 4348; **D9** 6031; **J18** 8245; **K2** 4651; **K3** 39, 52, 53, 120; **O4** 5102, 5397, 6194, 6527; **O5** 5010. The former GC and GE types are reminders that both companies also ran into York. Their engines used to be housed along with those of the L&Y, in Queen Street shed, across the line to the east of the collection of depots at York South.

With the Grouping, GC and GE types gravitated to the GN building, leaving the LMS (ex-L&Y) engines to have Queen Street nearly all to themselves. Until 1932, that is, when Queen Street was formally closed and LMS engines congregated in the 1864 roundhouse at York South, which had been leased to the Midland since 1879. Around 1936, the LMS moved out of its roundhouse and took over the 'GNR' shed, whenceforth the LNER's southern constituents' engines found shelter at York North. After the LMS moved out, No.3 roundhouse joined No.2 in housing 'pilot engines' and miscellaneous vehicles (No.1 roundhouse had burned down in 1921). At some time during its GN or LNER use, the GNoE shed had lost its arched entrances at both ends, in favour of steel framed doorways, but the distinctive roof remained, to be replaced by the LMS, with a much lower, curved top variety, sometime in the late 1930's.

In that condition it remained, until 1947, when York South sheds were supplemented by oil tanks and a boiler house, under the Government's oil-burning scheme; they were never used! In very early BR times the GNR shed continued housing Midland Region 'interlopers' into North Eastern Region territory - traditional allegiances to the end. Shortly after nationalisation though, the LMR locomotives began using York North shed, leaving the GNR depot and 1864 roundhouse to the many York pilots and No.2 roundhouse to become a slowly deteriorating store for surplus engines and stock. The end of the one-time GNoE 3 road shed came with demolition in 1963, at an age of 122 years.

LNER 0-6-0T No.1000 stands before the former GNR shed, occupied after 1932 by the LMS - ex-MR 4-4-0 No.727 is partly visible. The GNR had taken over the building in 1875, but typically made no changes to the hipped roof and large ridge vent built with the shed, in 1841, by the **Great North of England Railway.** *Authors' collection.*

With apparently little attention paid to the shed roof during 91 years, it can be no surprise that the LMS had to make some changes! That this was done with economy in mind is evident from this picture of Garratt No.47997, still marked "LMS", standing in the ex-GNR shed yard. The LMS had provided its York outpost with a simple, but rare, "Dutch Barn" style of roof with wooden end fascia. The arched entrances had also gone, in favour of a clear three track-wide portal. 3rd October 1948. *H.C.Casserley.*

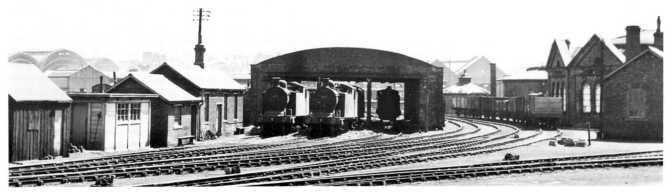

In BR days, former LNER engines once again used the ex-GNR shed, though they were more often than not in store rather than in active service - as here, with an ex-NER 4-8-0T. As a variation at this end of the building, the LMS-provided roof has a brick fascia and retains the door pillars between the three roads. On the right are York South Roundhouses 2 and 3 - the latter with its individual gable roof over each radiating road, as built by the NER and leased to the MR, between 1879 and 1923. *B.K.B.Green.*

THE MEN

The GN's first formal staff appointee seems to have been James Johnson, recruited by Cubitt in early 1848, to set up the organisation for, and oversee, the delivery of the first few locomotives at Louth, for the East Lincolnshire Railway. In August of the same year Bury successfully sponsored Frederick Parker for the position of Foreman at Boston Works and also suggested men to take charge of the locomotives at Peterborough, Lincoln and Boston sheds, at salaries ranging from £120 to £180. Initially these posts were graded as 'Foremen', but after about ten years - i.e., around 1858 - those at the principal locosheds of London, Peterborough, Boston and Doncaster, became District Locomotive Superintendents. By March 1863, salaries for those posts were being increased as follows:

Frederick Parker - Doncaster Works Manager   £450 to £500.
James Johnson - Locomotive Supt., Peterborough   £300 to £350.
John Budge - Locomotive Supt., London   £250 to £300.
Charles Troward - Locomotive Supt., Doncaster   £250 to £300.
R.C. Hornby - Locomotive Supt., Boston   £200 to £250.

Further down the 'family tree' of jobs, men were recruited consistent with the needs of an expanding service - to find employment with a company so demanding that it was 1866 before the GN's uniformed staff gained an annual holiday allowance of three days! Twenty-five years later though, an application from the locomotive workmen, for three days paid leave, with free passes for themselves and their families, was turned down. It seems the only other railway giving such concessions and facilities was the Great Eastern, so presumably some fraternisation between GN and GE staff, at places like Doncaster, had prompted the request. Mention of uniforms above; these started to come about late in 1850, when Sturrock arranged for the GN to provide the footplatemen with caps - drivers having a different pattern to firemen. Then, on 11th February 1851, Sturrock recommended one shilling a week be granted to enginemen in lieu of uniforms. This was sanctioned, but within three months the Engineer asked for £500 to purchase uniforms wholesale, which was allowed, subject to tender; presumably the locomen were using their extra shilling for other purposes!

Moving back to 1866, that year saw the retirement of Archibald Sturrock, who seems to have been something of a martinet when it came to granting improved conditions to the staff. For example, on 29th May 1866 he read out to the Board a deputation petition from the workmen in the Locomotive Department at Doncaster and Boston, asking to finish work at noon on Saturdays, instead of 2 p.m. The Board were guided by Sturrock in declining the request. One of Stirling's first tasks, therefore, was to deal with a request from the drivers and firemen for better pay and terms of employment. He quickly negotiated an agreement for the daily pay of drivers to be increased to 5/6d (27½p) in the first year, rising by 6d (2½p) in the second year, and 1/- (5p) in the third year, reaching 7/- (35p) a day, to be paid thereafter. The daily pay for firemen rose to 3/6d (17½p), (year 1); 3/9d (19p), (year 2); and 4/- (20p), (year 3 and henceforth). The only addition to basic pay applied solely to London District men, who received an extra 6d (2½p) a day,

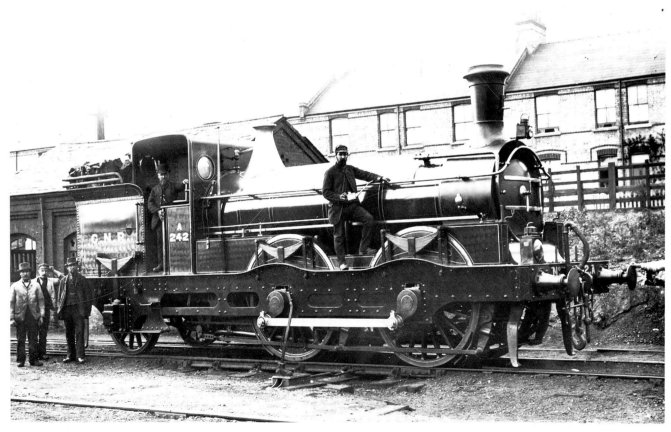

A Hatfield driver proudly poses with his immaculately turned-out 0-4-2T, its condition doubtless due to the labours of himself and his fireman, whose arm may just be seen on the front buffer. From the locomotive's cab the bowler-hatted shed foreman looks out, joined a little sheepishly one feels, by three others of the depot staff. *K.Leech collection.*

Grantham shed's turntable is host to 2-2-2 No.14 and an assemblage of the shed's staff. Ages seem to vary but most appear young, especially the small chap standing on the tender, just to the right of the cab. Whatever their ages though, such men served the GNR - and Britain's other railways - with loyalty and diligence all their lives. What is more, such railwaymen of yore did this for generally poor pay and few, if any, benefits to support them after their working lives were over. It is the authors' humble contention that virtually none of today's workforce would find it possible to appreciate, let alone emulate, such an attitude and way of life. *Grantham Library.*

after completion of five years service. However, for men working lodging turns, a daily allowance of 2/6d (12½p) was granted - a very big increase from the previous lodging allowance of 1/- a day.

All this was in exchange for a ten hour day, with a nine hour minimum break between duty turns. A maximum daily mileage of 210 applied, but this could be exceeded, in an emergency, in which case overtime would be paid. Overtime payment was also given, at the rate of one and a half times, for Sunday duty and each man got half a day off per week!

Stirling was not all goodwill though as when, on 21st July 1871, the Board discussed a memorial from 1,124 workmen at Doncaster, asking for their wages to be paid weekly instead of fortnightly, the Locomotive Engineer endorsed the Board's inclination to deny the request. However, four months later, on 3rd November 1871, Stirling convinced the Locomotive Committee to grant a request from the men in the workshops at Doncaster and Boston for a 9 hour day, with effect from 1st January 1872. His argument was that other railway companies were already working such hours, so the GN could hardly do otherwise and maintain good relations with the workforce.

Following the 1866 wages agreement described above, the next eight years evidently saw little improvement in the pay of the Company's servants who, by July 1874, numbered 3,957 in the Locomotive Department alone. This is illustrated by a specimen "Summary of Pay Sheets," (*opposite*) for two weeks ending 25th July 1874, as detailed in the table. It lists fifty-one different occupations or trades in the Locomotive Department, from Shed Foremen downwards, of which three: "Inspector of Trains, Waggon Cover Repairers and Harness Repairers" were not, at that time, in employ.

Notes on the summary:
1. When averaged out, the emoluments per job title sometimes varied considerably between the Locomotive Districts, with London, as evidenced earlier, generally being better paid. With regard to those men employed only at the locomotive sheds, the situation of the foremen cannot be commented on as, for some reason, the number of foremen in each District was not stated. For footplate staff there was small geographical variance in average weekly pay, with London and Peterborough being very similar, while Doncaster had the worst paid drivers, but the best paid firemen. For the many engine cleaners the wages for such a gruelling task can only be described as appalling,

GREAT NORTHERN RAILWAY LOCOMOTIVE DEPARTMENT
Summary of Pay Sheets. Week Ending: 25th July 1874

Despriction of Men	London Loco. Dept.		Peterborough Loco. Dept.		Doncaster Loco. Dept.		Doncaster Loco. Shops		Doncaster Carr.aige Shops		Total	
	No.	Amount £	No.	Amount £	No.	Amount £	No.	Amount £	No.	Amount £	No.	Amount £
Foremen of Engine Stations		27- 1- 8		46-10- 0		31-16- 8						105- 8- 4
Overlookers	3	9- 5- 1	4	10- 6- 4	8	22-15- 0	7	24- 3- 0	6	16-15- 0	28	83- 4- 4
Engine Drivers	88	209- 3- 1	122	290-12- 5	185	421-11- 4					395	921- 6-10
Firemen	83	115-19- 8	118	161- 4- 7	188	263-16-11					389	541- 1- 2
Engine Cleaners	89	79- 1- 2	151	123-14-10	219	194-15- 9					459	397-11- 9
Cokemen	12	18- 4- 8	17	19- 4- 1	25	28-15- 7					54	66-14- 4
Erectors							115	162-16-11			115	116-16-11
Fitters	33	55- 5- 6	76	84- 6- 7	35	57- 4-10	64	101- 2- 6			208	298- 0- 5
Turners	7	12- 6-10	7	10-10- 7	1	1-13- 0	96	133-11- 0			111	158-11- 5
Machine Men	10	12- 8-11	16	11-17- 7	2	1- 6- 0	99	103- 7- 8	21	26- 8- 6	148	155- 8- 8
Smiths	13	20-13-10	14	17-18- 1	6	9- 1- 5	72	248-18- 8	5	8- 4- 7	110	304-16- 3
Spring Makers							34	67- 8- 1			34	67- 8- 1
Boiler Smiths	14	23- 1-10	12	21- 8- 9	17	24- 4-10	85	150- 5- 1			128	219- 0- 6
Copper Smiths	2	3-15-10	5	5- 0-11	3	3- 2-11	5	4-10- 2			15	16- 9-10
Steam Hammer Men							15	5- 2- 1			15	5- 2- 1
Strikers	13	12-12- 3	17	11-11- 9	7	5-17- 9	201	146-18-11	4	4- 0- 9	242	181- 1- 5
Tinmen	9	11-18-11	1	1-10- 0							10	13- 8-11
Pattern Makers							6	7-13- 4			6	7-13- 4
Joiners	4	4-15- 9	7	9- 9-10			12	16- 3- 5			23	30- 9- 0
Saddlers	8	12-18- 2			2	2-15- 8	2	2- 7- 0			12	18- 0-10
Grinders							3	3-13- 6			3	3-13- 6
Brass Moulders							15	16- 2- 4			15	16- 2- 4
Painters	9	12-11- 9	4	5-16-11			11	10- 0- 8	73	88-15-10	97	117- 5- 2
Bricklayers	1	1-16-10	4	5- 9- 2	1	- - -	5	7- 3- 3			11	14- 9- 3
Gas Fitters							3	4-19- 2			3	4-19- 2
Carriage Washers & Cleaners	80	83- 3- 3	5	4-15- 9	12	12- 6- 6			4	4- 0- 6	107	104- 6- 0
Stationery Enginemen	9	11- 0- 2	12	11- 9- 4	10	9-14- 3	4	6- 3- 5			35	38- 7- 2
Carriage Woodmen									106	123- 6- 8	106	123- 6- 8
Waggon Woodmen	12	22- 2- 5	15	18-18- 0	4	5-19- 5			119	178-10- 6	150	225-10- 4
Carriage Fitters	23	33-19- 6	8	11-12- 7	4	6- 2- 2			43	70- 7- 0	78	122- 1- 3
Carriage Trimmers	2	3- 7- 5							22	27-15- 5	24	31- 2-10
Wheelwrights	14	22-13- 2									14	22-13- 2
Carriage Exams. & Greasers	23	29- 5- 4	29	30-13- 2	43	53-15- 7			24	29- 2- 0	119	142-16- 1
Sawyers									15	22-15- 3	15	22-15- 3
Gas Makers			5	5-17- 0	1	1- 6- 0	5	9- 2- 0			11	16- 5- 0
Iron Moulders							41	60- 8-11			41	60- 8-11
Labourers	76	87- 1- 2	98	99-16- 7	47	50-14- 4	143	133- 5- 7	132	129- 2- 8	496	500- 0- 4
Timekeepers	3	3-13- 0	1	1-15- 0	5	7-10- 0	6	13-17-10			15	26-15-10
Watchmen			1	1- 2- 0			5	5-16- 5			6	6-18- 5
Clerks	2	4- 3- 0	2	4-17- 1	2	3-16- 7	21	88- 5-10	2	2-12- 0	29	103-14- 6
Draughtsmen							2	5- 2- 0			2	5- 2- 0
Inspector of Trains												
Coke Burners							5	11-11- 0			5	11-11- 0
Messengers, Office Boys							8	5- 9- 7			8	5- 9- 7
Farriers	25	36- 8- 0									25	36- 8- 0
Puddlers							39	79- 4- 4			39	79- 4- 4
Waggon Cover Repairers												
Grease Factors									7	7- 7-10	7	7- 7-10
Harness Repairers												
(Coke Premiums)		34- 0- 0		51- 0- 0		72- 7- 0						157- 7- 0
Totals	**667**	1014- 8- 1	**751**	1078-18-11	**827**	1292- 9- 6	**1129**	1634-14- 4	**583**	739- 4- 6	**3957**	5759-15- 4

(Original signed by P. Stirling).

Fortnightly Pay <

26th July 1873 - *3780* *6381-13- 2*

3rd August 1872 - *3697* *4702- 1-10*

at 17/9d (89p) per week, in London and Doncaster Districts and only 16/4d (82p) - 8% less - in Peterborough District. Cokemen were decidedly better paid, but even then, Londoners, by getting £1-10-4½d (£1.52p) a week, were some 34% better off than their colleagues 'up country'. London's fitters too were best off - only marginally so over Doncaster (shed and shops), but some 51% over Peterborough!
2. In the field of office work, Peterborough paid its clerks, on average,

more than its engine drivers - a situation not emulated by London or Doncaster, but even in those Districts clerks were exceptionally well paid. However, it was at Doncaster Shops that being a clerk obviously meant something, with twenty-one of them receiving pay totalling £88-5-10d or, on average, £4-2-6¾d (£4.13p) each - certainly more than locoshed "Overlookers" and probably almost as much as the exalted shed Foremen.

18th August 1919, (for all railway companies' footplatemen and engine cleaners):

Drivers and Motormen		1st and 2nd years	12/- per day
"	"	3rd and 4th "	13/- " "
"	"	5th, 6th & 7th "	14/- " "
"	"	8th year onwards	15/- " "
Firemen & Ass.Motormen		1st and 2nd years	9/6 per day
"	" "	3rd and 4th "	10/6 " "
"	" "	5th year onwards	11/- " "
Engine Cleaners		16 years of age	4/- per day
"	"	17 " "	5/- " "
"	"	18 & 19 " "	6/- " "
"	"	20 and over	7/- " "

Mileage allowance would be paid if any turn of duty exceeded 120 miles, payment being made on the basis that 15 miles was the equivalent of one hour. Distances of less than 5 miles would be dropped, while 5 to 11 miles would equal half an hour and 11 to 15 miles would count for one hour. In addition, 15 minutes would be allowed before going off shed for booking on, reading and examining notices, assuming charge of the engine and taking it to the shed exit signal. Marginal times for preparing engines were adopted. For locomotives with more than 1,500 square feet of heating surface, this would be an hour; for all other classes, 45 minutes. (Typical GN classes with 1,500 sq. ft. or more, were Atlantics, 2-8-0's and the solitary Q3 0-8-0).

From today's well paid standpoint the figures above seem a poor reward for the work involved but despite their undoubtedly hard and dirty lives, the GN's men were no different to those of any other company. Neither did they differ in three other major respects. The first was a fierce loyalty to the company. They also had a strong sense of duty, which led them to place the GN in a position of eminence among its rivals - a situation that became pre-eminence after the formation of the LNER. Such qualities were readily recognised by the beneficent Stirling. For example, in January 1893, he strongly sponsored the award of a retirement gratuity for one Mr Judd, who had retired on health grounds a few weeks before. His last job was Locomotive Foreman at Doncaster, a post he had held since 1868, when he'd moved from a similar position at Bradford. Judd had joined the company in 1849 and completed his 43 years of service - 33 as a foreman - on a wage of 55/- (£2.75p) a week. The GN Board obviously valued such devotion too, as they voted Mr Judd a retirement present of six months wages, i.e., £71-10-0d - a large sum in those days.

Lastly, the men of the Great Northern Railway had a sense of honour, to go with duty. To such an extent that in the cauldron of the First World War, over 10,000 of them served their King and Country, and no fewer than 980 lost their lives in the performance of that duty. The authors hope that this book can, in some small way, be dedicated to the memory of them all.

(opposite, top) **Probably the authors' most stalwart supporter and assistant in the production of this history is Sid Checkley, a mine of knowledge and experience, so freely shared with us. Here we see Sid at the rear of Colwick shed in 1958, with the subject of one of his numerous fitting tasks resting on the ground. Note the "odds and sods" lying around in typical steam shed fashion and behind Sid, the depot's well-head.** *Sid Checkley collection.*

(opposite, bottom) **The best possible picture with which to end our history. The end of a working day in 1954, at the ex-GNR shed at Bradford Bowling Junction - Hammerton Street as it was then known. The men, which really, have always been the most important factor of any and every engine shed, commence their walks home. One has the luxury of a motor-assisted bicycle - very useful for coping with Bradford's hilly terrain.** *Syd Outram.*

3. With regard to some staff numbers, it is slightly incredible to note that only two draughtsmen were employed for the entire Locomotive Department. This seems to indicate that the locomotive. carriage and wagon superintendents were very much their own designers and illustrators.

4. At the other end of the scale, the 'wooden spoon' in the pay stakes indisputably goes to Doncaster Shops' "Steam Hammer Men." For doing what was probably one of the most dangerous, dirty and noisy jobs in the place, those fifteen stalwart individuals each got an average weekly pay of six shillings and ninepence halfpenny (34p)! Such conditions would be unthinkable today.

5. So too would the levels of pay revision be unacceptable today! In 1874, 395 drivers averaged £2-6-8d (£2.33p) per week, and 389 firemen got an average £1-7-10d (£1.39p) per week. Twenty-nine years later, on 2nd November 1903, Ivatt gave staffing details to a Locomotive Committee meeting which showed 1,301 drivers averaging £2-4-6d (£2.22½p) per week and 1,314 firemen, £1-8-11d (£1.45p). On the face of it then, after 29 years, firemen had achieved and averaged weekly pay increase of 3.29%, whereas drivers appeared to have had their wages CUT by no less than 8.57%! Not even Victorian employers were that hard though, so it is obvious the 1874 wages must have included considerable levels of payment for overtime.

Mention above of 'Lodging Turns' brings into focus another of the GN's somewhat austere attitudes towards its staff. Unlike many other railway companies, the GN did not provide dormitories for its footplate men, although in 1906, the company did come under pressure to build one at Hornsey. On the other hand, this may have been a blessing, as most companies' dormitories were often sited in the noisiest and dirtiest places, whereas GN men were expected to find 'digs' for themselves. This doubtless led to many a 'comfortable arrangement' up and down the system.

The coming of the Unions gradually brought about proportionately greater improvements in the men's conditions and payments. The Conciliation Scheme was a good example of this, with typical results being seen in the pay rates agreed on

SERVICING & STABLING POINTS

On completion of its duties a steam locomotive did not necessarily have to retire to an engine shed, if all that was required was basic servicing, like turning, fire cleaning and taking on fresh supplies of coal and water. Indeed, for locomotives in use on duties like shunting and empty stock workings, servicing needs were minimal and they could, therefore, spend sometimes days away from their home sheds. In addition, intensive diagramming, particularly of goods engines, such as on out-and-home turns, often precluded their spending long periods at distant sheds, before making the return journey.

The solution therefore was to provide servicing and stabling points, away from the main sheds. There, the engines could be turned, coaled, watered, oiled, have their fire cleaned and the crews could find shelter for meal breaks, etc. That was the servicing aspect; by definition the stabling part meant some engines spending considerable amounts of time operating from that location - this would apply particularly to those employed on empty stock and shunting duties.

Such servicing/stabling points were common sights on all of Britain's railways and the GNR was no exception. The first recorded mention of a need for one was on 20th April 1853, when Sturrock asked for a water point and coke stage at the South Yorkshire Coal Sidings, because: "...GN engines are being inconvenienced by a lack of supplies..." His request for action was postponed by the Board on 3rd May 1853, but goods yards were the most usual place for the siting of servicing/stabling points. This was particularly so where the yard was at an 'end of the line' situation, like Burton, and especially London, where the very heavy goods and coal traffic into the capital eventually made necessary the installation of two such facilities. They were at Clarence Yard and Ferme Park, which were opened in an effort to reduce pressure on the heavily burdened sheds at King's Cross and Wood Green. On the passenger side too, short turn-round locomotives did not always need to go on shed between trips. The servicing/stabling points at King's Cross station are well known, but because they sported engine sheds for many years, are covered in detail in a previous section of this history. Then, such was the traffic in empty coaching stock (e.c.s.) to and from the London terminus, that a basic servicing/stabling/turning facility was, in time, provided at Holloway Carriage Depot, for e.c.s. pilots.

All in all then, the servicing/stabling points were an economic and sometimes strategically necessary alternative to the working of every locomotive, on every occasion, to 'proper' engine sheds, often for what were minimal purposes. The following is a list, with brief histories, of the most important places where the GN set up such facilities:

BURTON-UPON-TRENT

Promulgated under the Derbyshire & Staffordshire Extension Acts, of 1872 and 1874, the line into Burton saw its first GN goods trains in January 1878. At first, they used the Midland Railway's Wetmore Junction sidings, until the GN's own sidings opened on 1st April 1878, to be followed by the Hawkins Lane Goods Yard exactly four months later. Prior to that event, on 1st

July, the GN's passenger service started - that always used the MR's station, normally arriving at the main Down platform and departing from the north east end bay platform.

Great Northern engines might initially have received attention on Midland premises, as the GN servicing point was not formally opened until 24th October 1878; alternatively, the GN may have provided some wagons of coal. Whatever, the servicing facility comprised a 44ft. 7in. turntable, with a wooden coal stage, 44ft. ash pit, water tank and water crane. All these stood on a siding in the goods yard, north west of the grain shed. Records show that construction of the turntable pit and foundations were contracted out to Messrs. E.Wood, for a tendered price of £172; Wood won his job against one other bid, for £190. The remaining facilities - turntable, coal stage, ash pit, tank supports, water tank, pipes and column, all came from the GNR's own material and labour sources. In 1887, the water tank evidently was in something, or somebody's way, as on 5th October that year, the Way & Works Committee approved expenditure of £670 to move it - such cost including the necessary pipework.

By December 1912, ten return trains each weekday were running into Burton, from Derby, Nottingham and Grantham; these would have been in the care of the various classes of 4-4-0 and 0-6-0. The main goods imports were grain and malt, from Nottinghamshire and Lincolnshire - especially Sleaford, where the Bass brewery had extensive maltings - while Burton's joyous main export was beer - which reached all parts of the system! Initially, goods engines carried out shunting duties between trips, but by 1900, locomotives were sent light engine from Derby each weekday, exclusively to shunt Burton yard: the regular duty left Derby at 1700, with an extra turn leaving there at 0650 hours, Monday only. Eventually, two sets of men were 'permanently' outstationed at Burton, operating from the Midland shed. They used J52 saddle tanks mostly but sometimes an ex-GCR Class N5 0-6-2T officiated. This practice continued well into BR times.

The 1947 WTT showed Burton's turntable diameter to have been 46ft. 7in., so presumably 2ft extension rails were in use and probably remained so, until Hawkins Lane yard and servicing point closed on 6th June 1966.

CLARENCE YARD

The first London stabling point per se (King's Cross station had sheds until 1893), Clarence Yard opened about 1890. It was meant to cater for shunting engines only, it seems, as no turntable was provided to accompany the coal stage, engine spur with pit, and water standpipe. Construction had been undertaken by the contracting firm of Messrs. Mattock & Brothers, at a tendered price of £1,733.

Soon complemented by the Ferme Park facility, Clarence Yard satisfactorily, and quite unspectacularly, performed its duties for generations of shunting engines and their crews, from King's Cross and later, Hornsey sheds. Wood Green depot's five pilots also operated between Clarence Yard and East Goods, until 1899. It is thought to have gone out of use soon after the first diesel shunters arrived in London, in 1952. Later, BR built their diesel locomotive depot nearby, but traces of the coal stage and several small brick buildings were visible well into the 1960's. In its day of course, the diesel depot acquired a mystique all of its own, largely due to the "Deltics" allocated there. Now they too, and the diesel shed, are just memories.

FERME PARK

Opened, like Clarence Yard, to mitigate delays to locomotives due to chronic congestion at King's Cross Top Shed, Ferme Park was first mooted in a Locomotive Engineer's report of 2nd April 1891. Tenders were quickly prepared and let, with Mattock & Brothers again being the successful contractor, with a bid identical to that for their Clarence Yard job - i.e., £1,733. For this, the GN were to get a coal stage and engine siding with pit, as at Clarence Yard, but Ferme Park was also to be supplied with a 44ft. 8in. turntable, so the railway company either provided the necessary foundations themselves, or got a good bargain from the contractor. A water standpipe completed the initial facilities, but by 23rd July 1891, while Mattocks were in the process of erecting the coal stage, they received a supplementary order to put up a sand furnace, at an estimated cost of £350.

Opening was during the latter part of 1891 and Ferme Park was soon proving its worth by assisting in the more punctual turn-round of goods locomotives arriving from the north. So much so in fact, that on 29th September 1896, Ivatt proposed the provision of an additional locomotive siding and pit, as: "...we are much crippled for want of siding accommodation..." He continued by pointing out that the 1891 plans for Ferme Park had made allowance for such expansion and he asked for, and got, sanction for expenditure of £510 for the additional facility.

There matters rested, until 1st April 1913, when Gresley declared that his new 2-8-0's would be too long for Ferme Park's turntable, so he asked for it to be enlarged to 65ft. The estimated costs were £560 for a Ransomes & Rapier table, and £550 to recover the old turntable and enlarge its pit. These were approved on 2nd May 1913, with completion of the job on 15th December of the same year.

Ferme Park's busy existence continued through World War One, up to the period around Grouping, when it achieved 'star' status for a couple of years. That was when Gresley's Class A1 Pacifics first appeared in London and had to run to Ferme Park to be turned, as they were too long for the turntables at either King's Cross shed, or station. Such exalted visitors continued to use the 65ft turntable until a 70-footer was installed in 1924, at King's Cross station, at which time Ferme Park resumed its humdrum duties.

The opening of Hornsey shed nearby, in 1899, increasingly overshadowed Ferme Park and with traffic levels dropping after the Grouping, the servicing point's days were clearly numbered. The end effectively came in 1929, when the 65ft turntable was recovered for re-use at Hornsey, where it replaced a 52ft specimen. After that Ferme Park served only the shunting engines from the adjacent yards, until even those turns were moved away and the servicing point closed at a date still to be determined.

HOLLOWAY CARRIAGE SIDINGS

The carriage sidings at Holloway were opened for use about 1885 and employed a considerable number of pilots on the empty stock workings. For a few years the to and fro of pilots from Top Shed for servicing, was a tolerable necessity, but by the time the 1890's dawned, it was clear the main shed was overloaded. So, in 1893, with the large new Holloway Carriage Shed due to open the following year, it was decided to create a minor servicing point. This would also assist the company in its efforts to speed up the turn-round of e.c.s. pilots and thereby improve the failing

punctuality of their workings, which had been the cause of late departures of numerous services and adverse comment from the travelling public.

The request for the facility had actually come from the Locomotive Engineer, on 1st June 1893, when he asked for a 50ft turntable (49ft 7in, according to the WTT), which, with foundations and two locomotive sidings with pits, would cost an estimated £1,250. The request was passed to the Board who, seeing the success of Clarence Yard and Ferme Park installations, quickly approved the expenditure and the servicing point was opened in late 1893. No coal stage was provided, but water was obtainable from two existing standpipes, situated near the carriage sidings signal box.

Quite why a turntable was required is not clear, as e.c.s. work was invariably in the care of tank engines, including in 1919, the re-allocation to King's Cross of six Class L1 0-8-2T, specifically for carriage pilot duties. Presumably the turntable saw occasional use in emergencies, when tender engines arrived with long distance e.c.s. workings, or when turn-round engines were used on stock duties. Also, it may have been used by Holloway's 'resident' pilot; in LNER times, until 1939, Hornsey allocated the job to J3 No.4039, complete with domeless boiler and Stirling cab. The table was removed, on a date as yet unknown, but certainly prior to 1947, while the engine pits remained in use until the end of steam working on the King's Cross e.c.s. duties.

ILKESTON

Ilkeston became a servicing/stabling point in a somewhat fragmented manner. The GN arrived in the town in January 1878, when the company's Derbyshire & Staffordshire Extension opened. After eight years, Ilkeston became a junction, when the first section of the branch line to Heanor was completed, as far as Nutbrook, on 7th June 1886. Traffic over the Derby-Nottingham line increased in a very satisfactory manner, with the yards at Ilkeston being very busy and the station becoming a terminal point for suburban passenger workings from Nottingham. The resulting need for locomotive turning facilities was further enhanced by completion of the Heanor line in 1891, so a 44ft 7in. turntable was installed on the north side of Ilkeston station, coming into use on 25th September that year; construction had not been straightforward, as an embankment had to be cut into and supported with a retaining wall. A dead-end siding, on the Up side, was available for standing locomotives, from which access could be gained to the water crane situated on the Up station platform; no engine pit was provided, however.

There matters rested for almost a quarter of a century, until 1st February 1915, on which date the GN completed provision of a coal stage at Ilkeston, at a cost of £93. Use of Class L1 0-8-2T (known locally as the "Baltics") on the district's coal trains was the popularly quoted reason behind the addition, no doubt aggravated by expanding traffic and the added demands of World War One carryings. Certainly, these would have stretched the shed facilities at Colwick and Derby, so Ilkeston, situated almost exactly half-way between those points, was a logical place to site a coaling facility.

Thus did the servicing point remain, with the turntable later being enlarged in capacity by the use of 2ft extension rails, and lasting until the end of steam. Ex-GC Class O4 2-8-0 arrived at Colwick about 1924 and their increasing use, particularly from the early 1930's, saw the inevitable displacement of the ex-GN 0-8-2T. With their disappearance, use of the coal stage dwindled and over a span of some years, it slowly fell to pieces.

LEEDS (HUNSLET GOODS)

For such a short line (4½ miles), the GN branch from Beeston, to a goods depot at Hunslet, had a complex beginning. Originally promoted by affluent private interests at Beeston, it was soon complicated by the East & West Yorkshire Union Railway's proposal for a similar line, via the Midland Railway. Because of this rival scheme the GN agreed, after the private promoter's Bill had passed through Parliament on 27th July 1893, to build the Beeston line and absorb it. Absorption was at first objected to by the MR and North Eastern Railway, but later withdrawn, enabling the GN to take over the £360,000 financed concern, by a Bill passed on 3rd July 1894. The GN then promptly postponed construction because of other commitments!

About mid-1896, the NER announced its intention of building a goods branch from Neville Hill to a goods depot at Hunslet. This caused the GN to react and quickly come to an agreement with the NER for parallel establishments at Hunslet, but with separate facilities and approaches. This reduced the GN's siding requirements and thereby costs, to £280,000. In October 1896, the GN produced plans for its line, which included, at the Hunslet Goods Depot, a three road engine shed, scaling 150ft x 50ft, complete with 52ft turntable and a coal stage with water tank over. Contracts were let in the same month, but progress was slow, with opening not finally occurring until 3rd July 1899. Presumably as a further cost-cutting exercise, the engine shed was not built, but a servicing point was provided, comprising the 52ft turntable, two engine roads with pits and a water column. This equipment supported the goods engines and shunting tanks until the passing of steam, at which time it was removed.

NEWSTEAD

The 1882 working timetable shows the commencement of a passenger service where the first and last trains of the day started and finished at Newstead. Contemporary maps show a turntable and two sidings at the terminus so it may be inferred that the branch engine was stabled there overnight.

This procedure lasted some 20 years as, according to the relevant WTTs, the passenger workings were re-arranged between the years 1898 and 1902, with no apparent further need for an engine to be present at Newstead through the night. The turntable, however, remained in use until the end of steam on the GN's Leen Valley line.

SKEGNESS

The 5½ mile extension of the GN-worked Wainfleet & Firsby Railway, from Wainfleet to Skegness, opened on 28th July 1873, one year and ten days after the granting of its Act. Because there was already an engine shed at Wainfleet - without a turntable - Skegness terminus was provided with only a 44ft 7in. turntable, some engine sidings and a water standpipe. Originally single track, such was the growth in traffic that the line had to be doubled, with enlargement of Skegness station. This operation ended about mid-1900 and included in the works was provision of a coal stage at the terminus.

Traffic continued to increase though (for example, 177,194 passengers at Skegness in 1921, had risen to 646,026 by 1934), with consequent demands on the servicing point. The water supply was an obvious weakness so, on 29th April 1912, an estimate of £580 was approved for installation of a 20,000 gallon water tank, on a tankhouse which would contain a locomen's mess room. The contract for the tankhouse/mess room was let on 6th June 1912, to Messrs. I.T.Turner & Son, for £242-19-6d; the tank, pipes and cranes came of course, from the GN's own sources. even this improvement was not the end as the LNER spent £10,000 in 1936 on the installation of nine 850ft. stock sidings, a triangle for turning locomotives (the turntable was retained though), a 120ft. engine pit, new coaling stage and a water crane.

Thus augmented, Skegness servicing point remained in use until steam locomotives disappeared from Lincolnshire. But, in its time, its basic facilities had coped even with the huge volumes of traffic prevalent before, and especially in the decade following the Second World War, when many engines a day would be dealt with in the holiday period. An example of the weight of traffic handled at Skegness can be appreciated from the WTT for the summer of 1937. That shows the following Saturday extras complementing the normal schedule of about a dozen Up and Down trains, plus the nine or ten round trips made by the Firsby 'shuttle' and a couple of return goods workings:

1141 arrival from	Derby.
1209 arrival from	Leicester.
1221 arrival from	Barnsley.
1229 arrival from	Birmingham.
1237 departure to	King's Cross.
1246 arrival from	Manchester.
1312 departure to	Derby.
1351 arrival from	Leeds and Bradford.
1406 departure to	Barnsley.
1411 arrival from	Leicester.
1500 departure to	Leicester.
1506 departure to	Birmingham.
1515 arrival from	King's Cross.
1533 departure to	Leeds and Bradford.
1540 departure to	Leicester.
1546 departure to	Manchester.

On summer Saturdays there could be up to thirty holiday extras arriving at Skegness - stock disposal saw rakes of coaches stabled all along the line - even as far away as Boston! Therefore, it will be no surprise to learn that for many years it was the practice to have a Running Foreman, fitter, and several enginemen outstationed from Boston, during summer weekends. They were accommodated in the tankhouse room and also in a room on the north side of the station.

On the demise of steam the various locomotive facilities were taken away but Skegness remained an interesting place to watch trains, especially on summer Saturdays.

ADDENDUM TO VOLUME 1.

HORNSEY:

(1) Further research into the history of Hornsey engine shed revealed that in fact, there had been an earlier shed at the original station. That two road building, which goes totally unremarked in the GNR archives examined by the authors, is seen here to the north east of the station in an extract from the first edition map of the Ordnance Survey. The assumption is made that the shed opened in August 1850, with the first London section of the GNR and was closed for station enlargement around 1866, to be replaced by Wood Green engine shed. Whatever was its actual history, the engines stabled at the first Hornsey shed were probably engaged in local shunting and most likely, a few suburban passenger duties.

(2) As a final note in the section on Hornsey engine shed it was believed that the last steam locomotive to use the depot, in 1967, was ex-GWR 4-6-0, CLUN CASTLE. However, thanks to information supplied by our correspondent, Mark Bailey, we now know that in May 1968, Gresley Pacific 4472 FLYING SCOTSMAN stabled overnight at the shed. Thus were East Coast sensibilities and pride amply restored!

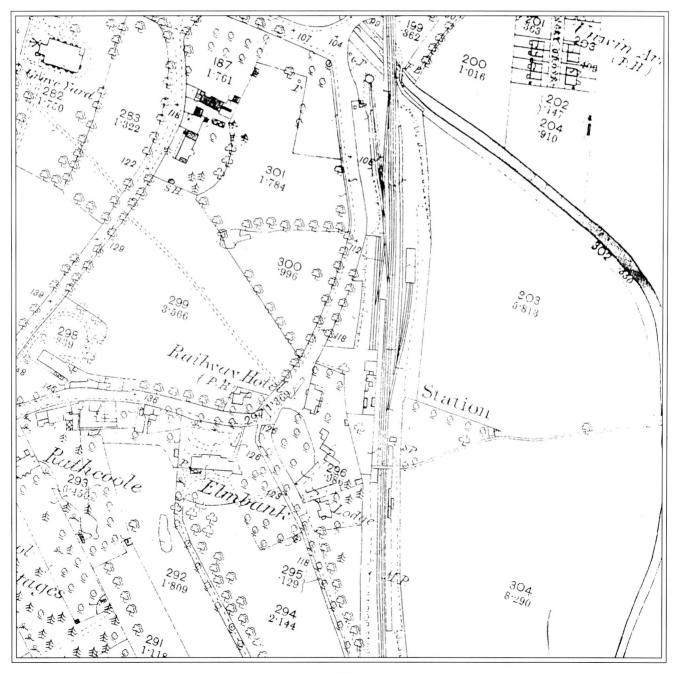

ADDENDUM TO VOLUME 2.

OTHER COMPANIES' ENGINE SHEDS: This seemingly secondary chapter really opened up a can of worms! Our thanks go to the inimitable Dick Riley and his encyclopaedic knowledge, for the information that locomotives from GN sheds used to rest between duties at two depots not previously mentioned. What is more, Dick supplied photographs as evidence:

Cross-London workings took LNER engines to the Southern Railway's depot at Hither Green. Such duties almost certainly did not occur before the 1923 Grouping - the more so because Hither Green shed opened only in 1933. However, we make mention here on the slightly flimsy premise that engines from a former GNR shed at Hornsey were involved. Here we see 68972 from 34B - together with Statford's 64664 - resting on shed at Hither Green in 1960. 73C resident 31916 seems almost to be guarding the visitors from Norf Lunden! *R.C.Riley.*

Stewarts Lane Workings from north to south London in early years, took GNR engines to the former LCDR depot at Stewarts Lane, a practice which continued through LNER days, into BR times. Seen here in September 1958, Hornsey's J50 No.68989 rests inside ex-LBSCR 0-6-2T No.32413 in the familiar surroundings of "The Lane". *R.C.Riley.*